Christopher Marlowe

Christopher Marlowe

A Renaissance Life

CONSTANCE BROWN KURIYAMA

CORNELL
UNIVERSITY PRESS

ITHACA AND
LONDON

First published 2002 by Cornell University Press

Printed in the United States of America

Library of Congress Cataloging-in-Publication Data

Kuriyama, Constance Brown, 1942–
   Christopher Marlowe : a Renaissance life / Constance Brown Kuriyama.
      p. cm.
Includes bibliographical references and index.
   ISBN 0-8014-3978-7 (cloth : alk. paper)
   1. Marlowe, Christopher, 1564–1593. 2. Dramatists, English—Early
modern, 1500–1700—Biography. I. Title.
   PR2673 .K87 2002
   822'.3—dc21
                                        2001007519

Cornell University Press strives to use environmentally responsible suppliers and materials to the fullest extent possible in the publishing of its books. Such materials include vegetable-based, low-VOC inks and acid-free papers that are recycled, totally chlorine-free, or partly composed of non-wood fibers. For further information, visit our website at www.cornellpress.cornell.edu.

Cloth printing   10 9 8 7 6 5 4 3 2 1

To Kurt and David

Contents

Illustrations

Acknowledgments

BIOGRAPHIES, BECAUSE THEY are inherently open-ended projects, are notoriously recalcitrant and slow to evolve. This one was no exception, and while it gradually took shape its author inevitably incurred a large number of obligations.

I owe special thanks to Kate Urry, both for granting me access to the unpublished work and library of her late husband, William Urry, and for extending extraordinary hospitality to me and my family while I was conducting research in Canterbury. She is the true patroness of this book. I also wish to thank Anne Oakley, archivist of the Canterbury Cathedral Archives and Library during the two summers I worked there, who quickly grasped my aims and made an extraordinary effort on several occasions to provide material I needed. Catherine Hall of the Corpus Christi College Library at Cambridge was also exceptionally helpful, guiding me expertly through the records held by this college and supplying useful information about them.

I am indebted to the officers and members of the Marlowe Society of America, past and present, for providing opportunities to present and publish some of the material I gathered during the early stages of my research. I thank Roma Gill in particular for her friendly encouragement of this project, and Sara Deats for her longstanding and enthusiastic support of my work.

My research was facilitated by funds from a variety of sources. The National Endowment for the Humanities provided a Travel to Collections Grant, and a stipend for study at the Newberry Library Summer Institute in the English Archival Sciences, whose instructors, Diana Greenway and Jane Sayers of the University of London, were remarkably tolerant of their overstressed, purblind, and somewhat unruly charges. A grant-in-aid from the American Council of Learned Societies, and a Folger Shakespeare Library Short-Term Fellowship, made part of my work with the Marlowe documents possible, as did a grant from Texas Tech University's Institute for University Research—Arts and Sciences. Texas Tech also provided a one-semester Faculty Development Leave. Ed George helped me identify some of the authors and works in Mr. Gresshop's library. I thank Kelley Lynch for permission to use a quotation from an interview with Leonard Cohen as an epigraph to chapter 4.

However, my husband, Kurt Kuriyama, and my son, David, who were obliged to live with this book on a day-to-day and year-to-year basis, often to their inconvenience, have contributed the most to its successful completion. It is therefore dedicated to them, with deepest affection and gratitude.

Chronology

ca. 1536   Marlowe's father, John Marlowe, is born in Ospringe beside Faversham.

1559–60   John Marlowe is enrolled as an apprentice of a Canterbury shoemaker, Gerard Richardson.

22 May 1561   John Marlowe marries Katherine Arthur, a native of Dover, in the church of St. George the Martyr, Canterbury.

21 May 1562   Mary Marlowe is christened at St. George's.

26 February 1564   Christopher Marlowe is christened at St. George's.

April 1564   John Marlowe is admitted as a freeman of Canterbury, paying a reduced fee of 4s 1d.

18 December 1566   Margaret Marlowe is christened at St. George's.

28 August 1568   Mary Marlowe is buried in St. George's churchyard.

31 October 1568   Unnamed son of John Marlowe is christened at St. George's.

5 November 1568   Unnamed son of John Marlowe is buried in St. George's churchyard.

20 August 1569   Jane Marlowe is christened at St. George's.

26 July 1570   Thomas Marlowe I is christened at St. George's.

7 August 1570   Thomas Marlowe I is buried in St. George's churchyard.

14 July 1571   Anne Marlowe is christened at St. George's.

Spring 1573   Richard Baines, possible informer on Marlowe, petitions for permission to advance to his B.A. at Cambridge.

August 1573	Queen Elizabeth holds court in Canterbury.
18 October 1573	Dorothy Marlowe is christened at St. George's.
Spring 1576	Richard Baines proceeds to his M.A. at Cambridge.
8 April 1576	Thomas Marlowe II is christened in St. Andrew's parish.
4 July 1579	Richard Baines arrives at the English seminary at Rheims to begin study for the priesthood.
14 January 1579–ca. December 1580	Christopher Marlowe is a scholar at the King's School, Canterbury.
Early December 1580	First entry of Marlowe's name in the Buttery Book of Corpus Christi College, Cambridge.
Early 1581	Marlowe pays entry fee of 3s 4d as a "pensioner," or scholarship student, at Corpus Christi.
17 March 1581	Marlowe matriculates at Cambridge.
7 May 1581	Marlowe is formally granted his scholarship.
21 September 1581	Richard Baines is ordained as a priest.
22 April 1582	Jane Marlowe and John Moore marry at St. Andrew's.
18 April 1582	James Benchkin, father of John Benchkin and husband of Katherine Benchkin, is buried in St. Mildred's churchyard.
Summer 1582	Richard Baines is exposed as a traitor to the Catholic cause and forced to confess; he is eventually released and returns to England, probably in 1583.
July–August 1582	Marlowe's first absence from Cambridge.
January 1583	Jane Marlowe dies, apparently in childbirth.
April–June 1583	Marlowe is absent from Cambridge; his roommates also miss part of this term.
Spring 1584	Marlowe completes requirements for the B.A.
July–December 1584	Marlowe is absent from Cambridge; other students are apparently absent as well.
May–mid-June 1585	Marlowe is absent from Cambridge, along with most other students; there are extensive absences also in the first and second terms, from September 1584 to February 1585.

30 June 1585 (or after)	John Benchkin registers as a pensioner at Corpus Christi; Marlowe is in residence.
ca. 15 July 1585	Marlowe leaves Cambridge for the remainder of the summer (with John Benchkin?).
19 August 1585	Marlowe, his father, his uncle Thomas Arthur, and his brother-in-law John Moore sign Katherine Benchkin's will in Canterbury, in which she leaves the bulk of her estate to John Benchkin.
ca. 15 September 1585	Marlowe returns to Cambridge with John Benchkin, who stays for several weeks.
Early November 1585	Marlowe is absent from Cambridge for two weeks.
December 1585	John Benchkin returns to Cambridge during Christmas week.
ca. 25 February 1586	Marlowe leaves Cambridge for two weeks. He returns with John Benchkin, who stays for one week.
25 July 1586	Katherine Benchkin is buried.
1586–87	John Benchkin reenters Corpus Christi as a fellow commoner.
1587	Richard Baines, M.A., becomes rector of Waltham, Lincolnshire.
31 March 1587	Marlowe is admitted to candidacy for the M.A.
29 June 1587	Privy Council intervenes with a letter to the Cambridge authorities, praising Marlowe's "good service" to the queen and urging that rumors about him be quashed and that his degree be granted on schedule.
1587–88	Marlowe's *Tamburlaine, Parts 1 and 2* is performed with great success in London; Marlowe's association with the Admiral's Men, their leading actor Edward Alleyn, and the theatrical manager Philip Henslowe begins.
1587	Robert Green obliquely accuses Marlowe of atheism in his Epistle to *Perimedes the Blacksmith*.

1587	John Benchkin matriculates at Cambridge.
1588–92	Marlowe writes *Doctor Faustus, The Massacre at Paris, The Jew of Malta,* and *Edward II*; the exact order of composition is uncertain, although *Edward II* is usually assigned to 1592. *Dido, Queen of Carthage,* the translation of Ovid's *Amores,* and the translation of *The First Book of Lucan* may (or may not) belong to the university period. The famous lyric "The Passionate Shepherd to His Love" also cannot be dated precisely.
18 September 1589	Marlowe is involved in a swordfight in London in which William Bradley, an innkeeper's son, is killed by Thomas Watson, Marlowe's fellow playwright and poet, and his probable mentor; Watson and Marlowe are jailed on suspicion of murder.
19 September 1589	Coroner's jury finds that Marlowe withdrew from combat and that Watson killed Bradley in self-defense.
1 October 1589	Marlowe is released on bail of £20; he agrees to appear at the next Newgate Sessions.
3 December 1589	Marlowe and Watson appear at the Newgate Sessions and are exonerated; Marlowe is released; Watson's pardon is issued on 10 February 1590.
1590	*Tamburlaine the Great* is published, without the author's name on the title page.
6 April 1590	Sir Francis Walsingham, often supposed to be Marlowe's employer in government service, dies in London.
1591	Marlowe and Thomas Kyd share the same workroom, as well as the patronage of Ferdinando Stanley, Lord Strange, whose players, Lord Strange's Men, perform their plays.
1592–93	Outbreak of plague seriously disrupts theatrical activity in London.
26 January 1592	Marlowe, in Flushing, is accused by Richard Baines of counterfeiting and of intent to go over to the enemy (Spain and Catholicism). He is sent back to London by Sir Robert Sidney, the governor of

	Flushing, to be examined by Lord Treasurer Burghley, but is apparently released.
9 May 1592	Marlowe is bound to keep the peace by the constable and subconstable of Holywell Street. At some point in 1592, Marlowe loses the patronage of Lord Strange, perhaps because he mentioned Strange's name to Sir Robert Sidney while being questioned in Flushing.
19 June 1592	John Benchkin is identified in a plea roll in Canterbury civil court as a student of Cambridge; he becomes an admitted freeman of Canterbury in November.
3 September 1592	Robert Greene dies. Shortly thereafter, stronger, more explicit allegations of Marlowe's atheism appear in Greene's *Groatsworth of Wit*, possibly authored or co-authored by Henry Chettle. This pamphlet also attacks Shakespeare, whose work as a playwright is just beginning to be recognized.
15 September 1592	Marlowe fights William Corkine in Canterbury. A suit by Corkine and countercharges by Marlowe are filed. The case is dismissed on 9 October.
26 September 1592	Thomas Watson is buried at St. Bartholomew the Less in London, possibly a victim of plague.
December 1592	Henry Chettle, in his preface to *Kind-Hartes Dream*, reports that Marlowe and Shakespeare took offense at the allegations in Greene's *Groatsworth of Wit*.
Early 1593	Marlowe writes *Hero and Leander*. His current patron is Thomas Walsingham, the nephew of Sir Francis Walsingham. Marlowe is known to frequent Scadbury, Walsingham's estate in Kent, probably as a refuge from the plague in London.
12 May 1593	Thomas Kyd is arrested on suspicion of libel and imprisoned; some papers containing heretical arguments, which he later claims were Marlowe's, are found in his possession.
18 May 1593	The Privy Council issues a warrant for Marlowe's arrest.

20 May 1593 Marlowe appears before the Privy Council and is instructed to give his "daily attendance"; he is not imprisoned.

26 May 1593 Possible date of the delivery of the Baines Note alleging Marlowe's "damnable judgment of religion and scorn of God's word." A second copy of the note claims that the note was delivered on 2 June, but this may be a mistake, since Marlowe was already dead on 2 June.

30 May 1593 Marlowe is killed by Ingram Frizer at the house of Widow Bull in Deptford. According to witnesses, Marlowe attacked Frizer after a heated "public" dispute over the "reckoning" or bill in which "divers malicious words" were exchanged.

1 June 1593 The coroner's jury finds Frizer acted in self-defense; Marlowe is buried in the churchyard of St. Nicholas's Church, Deptford.

10 June 1593 Ann Marlowe marries John Cranford at St. Mary Bredman in Canterbury.

28 June 1593 Ingram Frizer is pardoned; Richard Cholmeley is arrested on suspicion of seditious activities. Cholmeley was the subject of two reports by an anonymous spy, one of which alleges that Cholmeley claimed he had been persuaded by Marlowe to become an atheist. Two warrants for Cholmeley's arrest had been issued in March 1593 and on 13 May 1593.

1594 Publication of *Dido, Queen of Carthage* and *Edward II*, both bearing Marlowe's name as author.

29 May 1594 John Benchkin takes out a license to marry Katherine Grant of Kingston.

30 June 1594 Dorothy Marlowe marries Thomas Graddell at St. Mary Bredman in Canterbury.

16 July 1596 Thomasin Benchkin, daughter of John, is christened at St. Mildred's, Canterbury; other children, Thomas (1598) and Katherine (1605), follow.

1597 Thomas Beard cites Marlowe's death as an instance of divine retribution in *Theatre of God's Judgments*.

Thomas Walsingham is knighted.

1598 *Hero and Leander* is published, with a dedication to Sir Thomas Walsingham by Edward Blunt; Marlowe is identified as author.

1599 The Bishop of London and the Archbishop of Canterbury order Marlowe's translation of *Ovid's Elegies* burned.

1600 *Lucan's First Book* is published; Marlowe is identified as author.

1602 Philip Henslowe pays William Birde and Samuel Rowley £4 for additions to *Doctor Faustus*.

1604 The A-text of *Doctor Faustus* is published; Marlowe is identified as author.

23 January 1605 John Marlowe makes his will.

25 January 1605 John Marlowe is buried.

17 March 1605 Katherine Marlowe makes her will.

19 March 1605 Katherine Marlowe is buried.

1616 The B-text of *Doctor Faustus* is published; Marlowe is identified as author.

2 December 1616 John Benchkin, aged fifty, deposes that he wrote a will for Thomas Harflete, knight.

1633 *The Jew of Malta* is published, with a dedication by Thomas Heywood; Marlowe is identified as author, and praised in the prologue as "the best of Poets in that age."

Abbreviations

BAC   Canterbury city court records

BL   British Library (Harleian, Lansdowne, and additional MS)

CCA   Canterbury Cathedral archives

CKS   Centre for Kentish Studies, Maidstone

DAC   Canterbury diocese records

GLRO   Greater London Record Office (Middlesex Records)

PRC   Records of the Prerogative Court (currently held at CKS; also available on microfilm at CCA)

PRO   Public Record Office, London

Christopher Marlowe

Introduction

With cheerful hope thus he accosted her.

Hero and Leander, 198

ALTHOUGH BIOGRAPHY IS technically nonfiction, all life-writing is an amalgam of fact and interpretation, logical inference and speculation, truth and myth. Biographers, like all writers, inevitably bring cultural and personal biases to their work, and, consequently, what they write often reveals more about the author than about the subject. When the subject is a sixteenth-century playwright such as Marlowe, whose life is sparsely documented at best, the biographer's task becomes doubly problematic, for generally speaking biographical speculation is inversely proportional to biographical information. Particularly when the biographical record is deeply tinged with actual or potential sensationalism, as it happens to be in Marlowe's case, the temptation to weave hypothetical scenarios, and to mistake one's conjectures for fact, becomes all the more powerful.

Various strategies for minimizing this temptation exist, all of which have pitfalls amply demonstrated in existing Marlowe biographies. Perhaps the most obvious method is to emphasize the documents that make up Marlowe's life record, a tactic widely employed by early biographers and biographical researchers such as Leslie Hotson, F. S. Boas, Mark Eccles, C. F. Tucker Brooke, and John Bakeless. Old documents seem to offer safe ground because they are concrete objects and, as a rule, indisputably factual. No one doubts that Christopher Marlowe was christened on 26 February 1564 in St. George's Church, Canterbury, as the parish records indicate.

Unfortunately, not all documents are as straightforward as parish records, and even parish records can be problematic—as they are in the case of the christening record of Margaret Marlowe, the sibling who immediately followed Christopher. Three completely different dates for Margaret's christening exist in the surviving parish register of St. George (which is a copy of the original records) and in the archdeacon's transcript. Since Margaret's arrival was a significant event in Marlowe's early childhood, this is no trifling matter, but records, like the people who keep them, are subject to error and corruption.

Records are particularly problematic when they are isolated and fragmentary. Marlowe's incomplete school records, for example, while they are strictly factual, often raise more questions than they answer. We know that Marlowe held a scholarship at the King's School, Canterbury, in 1579–80, and that he also won a scholarship to Cambridge. Unfortunately, we do not know how he achieved either distinction, or if there was some connection between the two, or where he was educated before he entered the King's School. Similarly, we know (mostly) what Marlowe's scholarship payments were during each term at Cambridge and also (mostly) what he spent in the buttery for items over and above what he ate and drank in commons. Information from the Corpus Christi Audits and Buttery Book, which are both incomplete, can be combined to provide some information about Marlowe's entire period of residence at Cambridge. These records tell us a great deal about Marlowe's patterns of attendance, but they do not tell us where he was or what he was doing when he was absent—much biographical speculation to the contrary. Documents often mean both more and less than they seem to mean, instilling a false sense of security that may deter and often has deterred scholars from examining them more closely and critically.

The tantalizing partial information that these documents contain can also lead to the second pitfall of a document-based approach: rather than simply fostering the complacent belief that we know enough by taking them at face value, they may also encourage premature inferences. Isolated scraps of information, like the pieces of an incomplete jigsaw puzzle, may seem to fit together when actually they do not, and a chronic shortage of information makes the urge to leap to conclusions hard to resist. For example, given that the Privy Council wrote a letter to the Cambridge authorities commending Marlowe for his "good service" to the queen and urging that his M.A. degree be granted on schedule, and also that one of Marlowe's patrons was Thomas Walsingham, Marlowe biographers have concluded that his long absences from Cambridge were spent in government service. Similarly, his biographers often assume that because Marlowe, according to the council, was rumored to have gone to Rheims, he actually went there, and so on. But if Marlowe's records are compared to those of other students at Cambridge, his patterns of attendance do not appear to be exceptional, and one of his long absences was demonstrably spent visiting his family in Canterbury. In this case, consideration of a broader range of evidence points to a less exciting but far more likely conclusion: Marlowe spent most of his absences from Cambridge doing the same things that other students were doing.

Yet another pitfall of relying heavily on documents, as the example of the Privy Council's letter also illustrates, is that they tend to record exceptional rather than routine events. This can lead to a highly distorted, sensationalized view of the subject. Legal and government documents in particular can be quite misleading, especially when there are so few markers on the trail. Two undisputed facts, that Marlowe was summoned by the Privy Council to appear before them and that he was killed ten days later, are regularly construed by Marlowe biographers as ominous, sinister, and interconnected events. Yet there may be no causal connection whatsoever between them. The fact that Marlowe was merely summoned rather than being imprisoned like his fellow playwright Thomas Kyd could be viewed as a positive rather than a negative sign—and this argument has of course been made by Tucker Brooke, William Urry, and others. But conspiracy theories had a powerful emotional appeal in the jaded anti-authoritarian climate of the later twentieth century, and the sensational or potentially sensational content of some of the Marlowe documents also seems to encourage suspicion.

Legal documents also have a strong tendency to encourage negative rather than positive conclusions. Marlowe's virtually iconic status as the designated outlaw or bad boy of Elizabethan drama rests mainly on the records of his clashes with William Bradley, William Corkine, the constable and subconstable of Holywell Street, and finally Ingram Frizer. Yet the first twenty-five of Marlowe's twenty-nine years passed without incident. Instead of judging Marlowe's character solely on the basis of the last few years of his life, perhaps we should ask what he was like during the first twenty-five, when he had already begun to produce his most important work. We could then ask, as we should, what caused the apparent shift in his behavior, particularly during his last sixteen months.

The last and perhaps the most pernicious drawback of a document-based approach to Marlowe biography is that it encourages piecemeal analysis, digression, and rambling. The tendency of Marlowe biographers to organize their books around locations—Canterbury, Cambridge, and London—does reflect the geographical progression of Marlowe's life, but it also seems to be influenced by the locations of key documents on which Marlowe biographies are based, and by the availability of other material evidence that may help fill the gaps in documents, such as maps, drawings, and photographs. This geographical scheme has its merits, but relying too heavily on such a loosely defined framework tends to result in a wayward, almost arbitrary presentation of material.

Perhaps the most egregious illustration of this vice is Bakeless's massive two-volume life-and-works compendium, *The Tragicall History of Christopher Marlowe*.[1] Any discussion of this book should begin with an acknowledgment of its strengths, for Bakeless was a formidable archival scholar who was able to work directly with the Marlowe documents, a skill that became increasingly rare after New Criticism began to discourage interest in authors' lives. His book, though it is now seriously dated in many ways, will probably continue to be mined by students of Marlowe because of its sheer comprehensiveness. Indeed, I have made considerable use of it myself. Nevertheless, even with the aid of a detailed index (located in the ponderous volume 2, of course, while Marlowe's life is surveyed in the equally ponderous volume 1), it is an extremely cumbersome book to use. Finding a given fact and separating fact from conjecture can be maddening. To establish the precise sequence of events culminating in Marlowe's birth and infancy, for example, the reader must thrash through a lengthy discussion of Canterbury Marlowes who, we now know, were not directly related to Marlowe; sort out a confusing argument regarding the date John Marlowe became an apprentice in Canterbury; dismiss an incorrect theory of Katherine Arthur's origins; skim a discussion of the regulations of Canterbury shoemakers regarding marriage; finally arrive at the date of Marlowe's christening, followed by a discussion of the baptismal font in St. George's Church and the probable actual date of his birth, followed by a lengthy survey of records of christenings, marriages, and burials of Marlowe's siblings, followed by a detailed discussion of documents relating to their spouses.[2] Much of Bakeless's account of Marlowe's life consists of a jumble of irrelevant, erroneous, or tangential material intermingled with important information, and this indiscriminate clutter seems a direct result of Bakeless's immersion in documents. Once a documentary biographer finds a new document, which is never done without considerable effort, he becomes deeply attached to his foundling and has a strong tendency to quote from and comment on it, whether it is important or not.

And if a biographer deals with too many tangential or irrelevant documents, there is an even stronger tendency to examine the important ones cursorily, overlooking critical details and important connections to other documents. Such was the case in Bakeless's handling of the will of Katherine

[1] John Bakeless, *The Tragicall History of Christopher Marlowe*, 2 vols. (Cambridge, Mass., 1942).
[2] Ibid., 1:1–19.

Benchkin, which preserves the only undisputed sample of Marlowe's handwriting, his signature as a witness. Bakeless saw the will, saw the depositions of Marlowe's relatives concerning its signing, and noticed that Marlowe was absent from Cambridge for two weeks in November 1585. He therefore concluded that the will was signed in November.[3] However, the will is plainly dated 19 August 1585, and must have been signed during Marlowe's absence from Cambridge in mid-July through mid-September 1585. Bakeless also overlooked the fact that the chief beneficiary of the will, John Benchkin, made his first appearance at Marlowe's college shortly before Marlowe left for Canterbury in July. Bakeless's biography was so influential that every subsequent biographer of Marlowe has misdated the will, even William Urry, who transcribed it quite accurately and published the entire text, including the date, in his book.[4]

Yet in spite of my exasperation with the biographies of Bakeless and others who had adopted a document-based approach, it seemed obvious that I could not write a biography of Marlowe worth reading without returning to the documents and studying them carefully. What I needed was a fresh approach, and a strategy that would help me avoid some of the weaknesses I had observed in other Marlowe biographies. Both the approach and the strategy evolved gradually and sometimes painfully as the project advanced, first as I conducted the basic research and then as I attempted to shape the results into a readable narrative, but the strategy eventually resolved itself into four basic principles.

To avoid being lulled into complacency by the sometimes deceptive appearance of documents when they are scanned superficially or taken at face value, I decided at an early stage that I would scrutinize the Marlowe documents firsthand, rigorously and critically, rather than accepting previous scholars' interpretations of them. As part of this scrutiny, I would look for clues that might lead to other, supplemental information, either in other documents or in printed sources. In most cases this procedure simply confirmed what we already knew or suspected, for Marlowe's scholarly biographers had carefully transcribed, translated, and interpreted the documents they studied, and many of their conjectures were correct. But other documents, such as Katherine Benchkin's will and the Corpus Christi Buttery Books, yielded surprising discoveries on close inspection. Once these two sources were linked to one another and combined with other sources, they offered our first strong evidence that Marlowe had a close personal relationship with someone other than members of his immediate family.

---

[3] Ibid., 1:74–75. However, earlier, 1:25, Bakeless states that Mrs. Benchkin made her will in April.
[4] William Urry, *Christopher Marlowe and Canterbury* (London, 1988), 123.

The tendency to leap to conclusions on the basis of limited evidence was much harder to resist, but apart from simply staying alert and trying to curb the impulse, the best approach seemed to be an extension of one that worked well for individual documents—namely, seeking more information. The issue of Marlowe's attendance at Cambridge, for example, becomes far more complex if one does more than simply note that some of Marlowe's absences were lengthy, and leap to the conclusion that he was active as a spy during those absences. If we compare Marlowe's attendance to that of other students, it becomes clear that in some instances many other students were absent at the same time Marlowe was absent, suggesting that some disruptive event, such as an epidemic, led to a temporary suspension of instruction. Some of Marlowe's absences occurred during vacation term, such as the one in 1585, when we know he was at home in Canterbury. Just a casual glance at the attendance of other students reveals that it was routine for students to leave Cambridge for part or all of the summer, unless they were using the time to catch up on work they had missed or trying to accelerate their progress toward a degree.

But some speculation is inevitable in Renaissance biography, and at times it is even desirable, because informed guesses can lead to further discovery. F. S. Boas and other scholars suspected that Marlowe's antagonist Richard Baines had returned to England to work for Walsingham after leaving the English College in Rheims, and, partly thanks to this suggestion, I was later able to find a document that appears to confirm this. Perhaps the best way to keep reasonable speculation from galloping out of control is simply to label it clearly. With this in mind, I have made liberal use of words and phrases such as *could have, might have, perhaps, possibly, seems,* and *appears.* As Shakespeare's Touchstone concludes, there is much virtue in that "if."

Counterbalancing the tendency toward disproportionate sensationalism in Marlowe biography is more difficult than curbing speculation, although the two are closely related. One method I chose to adopt was devoting more attention to documents that illuminated the less turbulent and potentially sensational moments of Marlowe's life (that is to say, most of his life). Another was to follow the lead of Tucker Brooke and deliberately take a cooler, more dispassionate view of certain events than most Marlowe biographers have taken. There is wisdom in Montaigne's argument that the essence of personality is just as clearly, if not more clearly, expressed in ordinary actions than in extraordinary ones: "Every moment reveals us. That same mind of Caesar's which shows itself in ordering and directing the battle of Pharsalia, shows itself also in arranging idle and amorous affairs. We judge a horse not only by seeing him handled on a racecourse, but also by seeing him walk, and even by seeing him resting in the stable."[5]

Accordingly, rather than devising yet another conspiracy theory, I have tried to convey a sense of Marlowe's life as he normally experienced it, basing the portrayal on previously known documents, new documents, a number of secondary sources, and long walks through locations Marlowe frequented in Canterbury, Cambridge, and London. This last activity was often disappointing, since much of Marlowe's world has vanished completely, but it was still revealing to visit Marlowe's old neighborhood in Norton Folgate and Holywell Street; to stroll down Bishopsgate Street past St. Paul's; to see the newly discovered foundation of Henslowe's Rose Theater; to amble through the Old Court of Corpus Christi College and watch students from Canterbury's King's School perform *Dido, Queen of Carthage* in its great hall; or to gaze up at massive Westgate Towers, the old city gate that Marlowe passed through on his journey from Canterbury to London and Cambridge. Visiting the actual locations where Marlowe lived and died gives Marlowe's life a sensual immediacy that a biographer cannot grasp or convey to a reader in any other way.

To prevent my discussion of Marlowe from wandering off onto tangents, as documentary biographies tend to do, I gave considerable thought to its construction. After several false starts, I decided to subdivide Marlowe's life according to what I saw as successive stages of his personal development, followed by a discussion of how others perceived him. Whether the reader would be thrilled with this approach or not, it would at least make any given part of my argument easy to locate. This method was also consistent with my desire to present Marlowe's life to some extent from his own point of view, insofar as that could be reasonably inferred from the available evidence, while at the same time developing my own interpretations. I decided to devote one chapter to Marlowe's family background and childhood, two to his undergraduate and graduate education at Cambridge and the problem of financing his career as a poet, one to his phenomenal early success as a playwright in London, one to his patrons, one to the reversals he encountered in 1592–93, one to his death, and two to his afterlife in the minds of others. To make all the essential information about Marlowe available in a convenient and easily accessible form, I decided to add a detailed chronology, as well as an appendix consisting of fresh transcriptions and translations of all the

[5] Michel de Montaigne, "Of Democritus and Heraclitus," in *The Complete Works of Montaigne: Essays, Travel Journal, Letters*, trans. Donald M. Frame (Stanford, 1967), 219.

major Marlowe documents, with commentary, for the benefit of readers who may want to examine the evidence for themselves. All this material has never been gathered together in one book before, and consequently such a measure seemed long overdue.

While I often correct the facts or question the conclusions of earlier Marlowe biographers, I want to stress that I have the greatest respect for everyone who has done basic research on Marlowe. The work of these scholars has been invaluable to me, as my numerous footnotes indicate, and my respect for them is only increased because I know from experience what complex skills and patience are required to conduct archival research, and how time-consuming and expensive it can be. I also know very well that my own interpretations may be just as liable to revision by future biographers as many of my predecessors' have been. What looks virtually certain in light of limited evidence can prove to be completely wrong as more information becomes available. Sooner or later, someone will find one or more new documents, notice an overlooked connection between seemingly unrelated facts, recognize the significance of a neglected piece of information, or simply think of a better argument. That is the inevitable risk one takes in writing Renaissance lives, and I will be content if I have merely succeeded in making it easier for my successors to challenge my conclusions.

1

A Canterbury Tale

Now is he born, his parents base of stock.

Doctor Faustus, Chorus, 11

MOST BIOGRAPHERS ASSUME that family history and early experience played a critical role in shaping the elusive self they hope to portray. Therefore a chapter devoted to the subject's parents, place of birth, and childhood, or at least a brief glance at the subject's origins, is indispensable. Yet this seemingly routine business of documenting the early years of a life is never purely empirical and straightforward, because individual and cultural biases and personal experience inevitably color the biographer's perceptions and interpretations. In the case of Christopher Marlowe, the genteel post-Victorian notions of his early-twentieth-century biographers powerfully influenced their depiction of Marlowe's childhood, beginning with their eagerness to provide Marlowe with a respectable family background.

Even cautious scholarly biographers such as F. S. Boas, C. F. Tucker Brooke, and John Bakeless wanted to believe that Marlowe's father John Marlowe (or Marley, as the family spelled and pronounced their name) was the posthumous son of a wealthy tanner of Canterbury. This tanner, named Christopher Marley, dictated a will on his deathbed in 1540 in which he made detailed provision for an unborn child. Since the tanner's name was the same as the playwright's, and since his trade was closely allied to shoe-making, the trade John Marlowe later entered, it was tempting to conclude that this respectable tradesman who showed such admirable concern for his potential offspring was Christopher's grandfather. The theory of John Marlowe's posthumous birth had obvious dramatic appeal, and furthermore, it cast Christopher Marlowe in a favorable light twenty-four years before his birth by presenting him with an industrious and conscientious ancestor. Any facts that seemed to contradict this attractive theory were therefore ignored or rationalized.

Some compelling evidence had to be ignored, for in several surviving depositions, John Marlowe plainly stated that he was born not in Canterbury but in Ospringe beside Faversham, a village ten miles west of Canterbury. Bakeless tried to remove this difficulty by suggesting that the tanner's widow, whose family lived in Canterbury, had chosen to "withdraw to a neighboring town" during her pregnancy.[1] However, Bakeless did not explain why a pregnant widow would withdraw from Canterbury and her family to a place where she had no relatives or property, far from the female friends who would gather around and support her at her time of delivery, in order to bear her child.[2] Nor did he explain why her son did not return to Canterbury for sixteen years, for in these same depositions, John indicated that he had arrived in Canterbury in about 1556, at which time he showed no sign of owning the considerable property the unborn male child of Christopher Marley would have inherited. In his earliest deposition John declared that he was about thirty years old, which would place his birth in 1536 rather than 1540, and it is unlikely that such a young man would be greatly mistaken about his age. Furthermore, when he became a freeman of Canterbury in 1564, John had to pay a fee of four shillings, one penny, a fee that sons of freemen were exempted from paying. The obvious conclusion is that John was not the posthumous son of Christopher Marley, and this conclusion is further borne out by William Urry's discovery of evidence of a Marley family in Ospringe.[3] If John was related to the wealthy tanner, he was at most a poor country cousin.

The numerous documents recording the activities of John Marlowe, to which Urry added many more, allow us to trace the adult life of Marlowe's father in considerable detail. He came to Canterbury in 1556 at about the age of twenty. In 1559 or 1560 he was formally enrolled as the apprentice of Gerard Richardson, an immigrant shoemaker. Within a few years John was already married and in business for himself, and in 1564 he was admitted as a freeman of the city. Since twenty-three was an advanced age for apprenticeship and three or four years was a very brief term of service, John had probably learned something about shoemaking before he was apprenticed to Richardson. Nevertheless, he actually worked with Richardson for a time,

---

[1] John Bakeless, *The Tragicall History of Christopher Marlowe* (Cambridge, Mass., 1942), 1:10.

[2] David Cressy, *Birth, Marriage, and Death: Ritual, Religion and the Life Cycle in Tudor and Stuart England* (Oxford, 1997), 54–55.

[3] William Urry, *Christopher Marlowe and Canterbury* (London, 1988), 150 n. 2. Unless otherwise indicated, details about the Marlowe family in Canterbury are based on Urry's work.

because the men who administered Richardson's estate suspected John of appropriating some of his late master's property.[4] This semi-fictitious apprenticeship benefited both John and his master. Richardson collected a premium without having to take responsibility for a raw youth and train him completely, while John found it easier to establish his own business in Canterbury because of his association with Richardson. Certainly his enrollment as Richardson's apprentice entitled him to acquire the status of freeman at the reduced fee he later paid.[5]

Even these earliest records hint at John Marlowe's character. He was not the privileged firstborn son and heir of an established Canterbury tradesman, but an energetic, shrewd, resourceful upstart—the Renaissance new man on a humble scale. Like many other young people who flocked to England's cities and towns during the sixteenth century seeking greater opportunity, John saw no harm in using the system to his advantage. Indeed, to a practical, ambitious man who lived by his wits, this might have seemed the only reasonable course. John's opportunism was perhaps as much a reflection of class as of character; certainly his son Christopher would show a similar pragmatism by using his scholarship to Cambridge for his own purposes.

John's ambition was apparently furthered by a rudimentary education. The numerous samples of his writing which survive indicate that he was literate, though just barely. Like most petty school graduates, he could probably read better than he could write, but he was not schooled long enough to develop a smooth, confident copybook hand. His signatures, representing his best efforts at orthography and penmanship, exhibit the tentativeness and poorly formed letters of an inexperienced writer, and also betray some indecision about the spelling of his first name. Presumably he had attended one of the rapidly growing number of schools where boys, and sometimes girls, were taught to read and write English, cipher, and cast accounts. This level of education was considered appropriate and sufficient for a boy who hoped to enter a trade. During John's childhood, many free petty schools had sprung up in England to accommodate the children of the poor, and even the lowest-paid laborers could often afford the small fees required by those schools that were not completely free.

Soon after his arrival in Canterbury, John met his future wife, Katherine Arthur, a native of Dover. The same biographers who wanted to believe that John was the posthumous son of a wealthy tanner were naturally hopeful of finding an equally solid middle-class background for Katherine. They con-

[4] Ibid., 21.
[5] Bakeless, *Tragicall History*, 1:21; Urry, *Christopher Marlowe and Canterbury*, 13.

cluded that she must have been the daughter of a clergyman, the Reverend Christopher "Arthur," rector of St. Peter's, Canterbury. According to this fanciful genealogy the future playwright had two grandfather Christophers, one of whom had modest pretensions to gentility. Unfortunately for this highly symmetrical and socially elevating theory, the rector's name was Archer, not Arthur.[6] Marlowe fetched all of his gentry from the university, through his own talent and effort, and both of his parents were recent immigrants to Canterbury, not members of established families. What little we know about Katherine Arthur suggests that her origins were as humble as her husband's, if not humbler. Her father, William Arthur, was not a freeman of Dover, and made his living by unknown means.[7] Katherine, who signed her will with a mark, was probably illiterate, although her brother Thomas, who also moved to Canterbury and eventually served as a joint bailiff, could certainly read and write.

John and Katherine were married on 22 May 1561 in the church of St. George, and settled immediately in that parish. St. George's parish was located in the southeastern sector of Canterbury, adjacent to Newingate (or St. George's Gate) on Canterbury's main thoroughfare, the London-Dover Road. Entries in the old parish register of St. George and other surviving evidence suggests that St. George's parish was a relatively poor neighborhood. It was generally true of pre-industrial English cities that wealthier families tended to live in the commercial centers, poorer families on the periphery.[8] Although this residential pattern never existed anywhere with complete uniformity, the general trend seems to have fit the parish where Marlowe spent his early childhood. A few notable citizens and professionals, such as Alderman Rose, Alderman Nutt, and the lawyer John Smith, lived in the neighborhood, but the majority of communicants at St. George's were artisans and craftsmen like John Marlowe. Among the Marlowes' neighbors were Harman Verson, a glazier of German origin, Thomas Atkinson, a barber, William Man, a pewterer, and Lawrence Applegate, a tailor.

Of these, only Verson was middle-aged. Man and his wife, Joan, had married about five years before the Marlowes and were probably slightly older. Atkinson and his wife, Lora, were about the same age as the Marlowes, while Applegate was a randy bachelor who boasted to several of his neighbors that he had "occupied" Goodwife Chapman's daughter Godelif four times, describing his exploits in lascivious detail. Godelif, who had married Robert

---

[6] William Urry, "Marlowe and Canterbury," *Times Literary Supplement*, 13 February 1964, 136.
[7] Urry, *Christopher Marlowe and Canterbury*, 14.
[8] John Patten, *English Towns, 1500–1700: Studies in Historical Geography* (Folkestone, 1978), 37.

Hurte on 15 October 1564 in St. George's, sued Applegate for slander in early 1565, when Christopher was about a year old.[9] John Marlowe, Harmon Verson, and Lora Atkinson all gave damaging testimony against Applegate, whose evasive responses to questioning in the Archdeacon's court provoked the presiding officer to exclaim, "Belike ye have done it indeed!"[10] Applegate was sentenced to do penance, and shortly afterward, on 13 October 1565, put an end to his wayward bachelorhood by marrying Tomsyn Dyne.[11]

The exact location of the first Marlowe household has never been established, though Urry combed diligently through all the available evidence. The old house that local residents once identified as Marlowe's birthplace—No. 57 St. George's Street, at the corner of St. George's Lane—was demolished during a German air raid on 1 June 1942, along with most of its surroundings.[12] This was perhaps not as great a loss as it might seem, since No. 57 had already been stripped of much of its period character. The façade had been remodeled, and, as Bakeless noted in the late 1930s, "its carved paneling was so beautiful that the wood from two of its rooms has been removed wholesale to provide a 'Marlowe bedroom' for one of the modern Kentish gentry and a paneled drawing-room for another."[13] Through one of time's devious little ironies, this mindless plundering of the old house's historic riches became an inadvertent act of preservation.

Urry concluded that the designation of No. 57 as Marlowe's birthplace was "an unfounded invention of the later nineteenth century at a time when a scheme for a Marlowe memorial was being promoted, and the need for a 'birthplace' became insistent."[14] Bakeless also doubted the credentials of No. 57, citing "a vague story that the Marlowes did not live in this particular house but in another, since destroyed, a few yards eastward, nearer to the city wall."[15] However, No. 57 did offer clues to the probable general appearance of Marlowe's childhood surroundings, and Bakeless accordingly included a picture of it as a frontispiece to his first biography of Marlowe, *Christopher Marlowe: The Man in His Time*. Although the old house had obviously undergone several remodelings, it was originally a typical three-story half-tim-

[9] Urry, *Christopher Marlowe and Canterbury*, 30.

[10] Urry, "Christopher Marlowe and Canterbury," quoted by permission of Mrs. Katherine Urry. This unpublished manuscript contains a few details not included in the published version edited by Andrew Butcher. It is impossible to cite it conventionally by page numbers because chapters are paginated separately and extensive portions of the manuscript are cut and pasted together.

[11] CCA Parish Register of St. George.

[12] The Michael Powell–Emric Pressburger film *A Canterbury Tale* (1948) contains footage of the ruins of this area.

[13] John Bakeless, *Christopher Marlowe: The Man in His Time* (New York, 1937), 18.

[14] Urry, "Christopher Marlowe and Canterbury."

[15] Bakeless, *Christopher Marlowe*, 17.

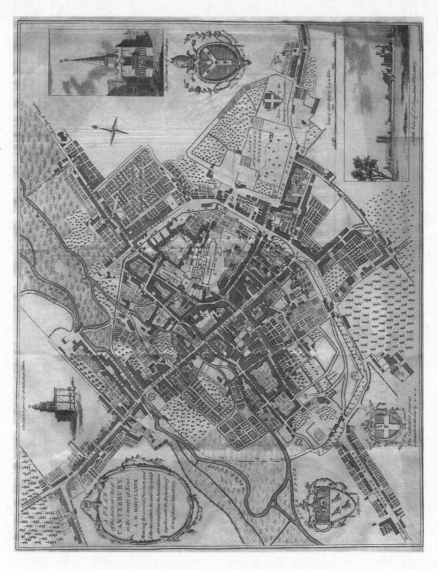

This detailed eighteenth-century map of Canterbury identifies many locations familiar to Marlowe. From William Gostling, *A Walk in and about the City of Canterbury*, 1777.

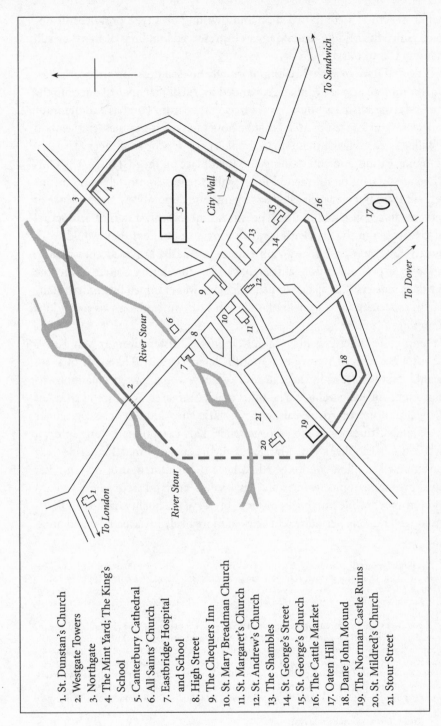

From William Gostling, *A Walk in and about the City of Canterbury*, 1777.

1. St. Dunstan's Church
2. Westgate Towers
3. Northgate
4. The Mint Yard; The King's School
5. Canterbury Cathedral
6. All Saints' Church
7. Eastbridge Hospital and School
8. High Street
9. The Chequers Inn
10. St. Mary Breadman Church
11. St. Margaret's Church
12. St. Andrew's Church
13. The Shambles
14. St. George's Street
15. St. George's Church
16. The Cattle Market
17. Oaten Hill
18. Dane John Mound
19. The Norman Castle Ruins
20. St. Mildred's Church
21. Stour Street

bered structure, a combined shop and dwelling of a type prevalent in England since the Middle Ages. Many well-preserved buildings of this type still stand in Canterbury.

The first floor of such dwellings normally housed the shop and work area. This commercial space could be expanded by a stall that opened out onto the street during business hours. As we may gather from Barabas's contemptuous remark in *The Jew of Malta* that he hopes to see his enemies "starve upon a stall," the earnings of these small shopkeepers were often meager (2.3.26).[16] Cooking, eating, and entertaining also took place on the first floor. The family generally slept on the second floor, while the less comfortable and inconvenient third floor was relegated to servants and apprentices. The presence of servants in a household of this type was not necessarily a sign of prosperity. Many people in the sixteenth century were so poor that they would work merely for room and board. Apprentices, similarly, provided cheap labor, while their premiums were a desirable and even essential source of income for their masters. The space in such dwellings was cramped by modern standards, especially for a growing family. And of course there was no indoor plumbing.

John and Katherine's first child, Mary, was christened on 23 May 1562.[17] Christopher arrived twenty-one months later. His birth, like that of most healthy firstborn sons in the sixteenth century, would have been a momentous event for his parents.[18] The third child, Margaret, as a careful study of the Canterbury records reveals, was not christened until 18 or 28 December 1566, almost three years after Christopher. This exceptionally long interval between Christopher's and Margaret's births suggests that Katherine may have nursed her first son longer than her other children, thus delaying her third pregnancy. Since women in Renaissance England were advised to abstain from sex while nursing in order to preserve the quality of their milk,[19] a prolonged nursing period would be even more likely to have prevented preg-

---

[16] All quotations of Marlowe's plays and poems are from *Christopher Marlowe: The Complete Plays*, ed. Mark Thornton Burnett (London, 1999), and *Christopher Marlowe: The Complete Poems*, ed. Mark Thornton Burnett (London, 2000).

[17] See the appendix for a transcription of the records of christenings, marriages, and burials in the Marlowe family.

[18] For discussions of the culturally ingrained preference for males, and the especially intense relationship between fathers and firstborn males in Renaissance England, see Miriam Slater, *Family Life in the Seventeenth Century: The Verneys of Claydon House* (London, 1984), 27, 29, 31–34, 82–83, 110. See also Cressy, *Birth, Marriage, and Death*, 31–33. This preference also prevailed in continental Europe, as Benvenuto Cellini's depiction of his relationship with his father in his *Life* clearly reveals. Cellini was named Benvenuto (welcome) because he was his father's long-awaited firstborn son. See *The Life of Benvenuto Cellini: Written by Himself*, trans. John Addington Symonds (New York, 1936), 1:77–78.

[19] Cressy, *Birth, Marriage, and Death*, 90.

nancy than would merely the biological effects of nursing. The average interval between the other surviving Marlowe children and the siblings who followed them was twenty-one months, implying an average nursing period of about twelve months, the amount of time usually recommended for nursing.[20] The interval between the births of Christopher and Margaret was even longer than the interval before the birth of Katherine's last child, the second Thomas, at a time when her fertility was declining. But whether or not Christopher was nursed longer than his siblings, which seems probable, his privileged status as the first male child was assured from the moment of his birth. All he had to do to maintain this status was to stay alive, which was hardly a guaranteed outcome.

Christopher remained the only surviving male child for twelve years, reigning unchallenged until the birth of the second Thomas in 1576. Furthermore, his older sister, Mary, died when he was two and a half, making him not only the firstborn male but also the eldest surviving child. These favorable circumstances of his birth and early childhood gave Christopher all the psychological and intellectual advantages of firstborn or only children, facts that correlate well with his later academic and professional success.

However, Christopher's childhood could scarcely have been free of anxiety. Like other children in Renaissance England, he had ample opportunity to contemplate the precariousness of life, a point often underlined in his works.[21] As the weakling Mycetes casually comments in *Tamburlaine the Great, Part 1*, "Our life is frail, and we may die today" (1.1.68). During Christopher's early childhood, both his older sister and two of his younger brothers died. John Marlowe lost his second, unnamed son in July 1568, a few days after his christening, and in 1570 a third son, Thomas, probably a premature infant, was buried two weeks after his birth. In contrast, Marlowe's younger sisters Margaret (1566), Joan (1569), Ann (1572), and Dorothy (1573) all thrived. The fact that the boys in his immediate family seemed somewhat more likely to die than the girls could hardly have been reassuring.

Marlowe's biographers have often evoked the casual violence in Canterbury, including bull baiting and frequent executions on Oaten Hill, as possible formative influences. Even the grotesquely carved telamones on the cantilevered buildings have been seen as prototypes for the demons in *Doctor Faustus*.[22] But other events that occurred during Marlowe's childhood probably had far more impact. During his childhood Christopher survived

---

[20] Ibid., 88.
[21] Slater, *Family Life in the Seventeenth Century*, 138.
[22] John H. Ingram, *Christopher Marlowe and His Associates* (London, 1904), 37–38.

uncontrollable epidemics such as the one that swept through St. George's parish in 1565, probably a provincial outbreak of the London plague of 1564. The parish register of St. George reveals the appalling toll of this epidemic: deaths in the parish more than tripled. Entire families were wiped out, including the family of John Marlowe's friend Harman Verson. Although the epidemic subsided in a few months, it was so devastating that Marlowe's parents must have recalled it for years afterward. And it was followed by another wave of plague in 1575, when Marlowe was eleven; this time deaths in the parish doubled.[23]

Even without such outbreaks, deaths of Marlowe's playmates and schoolfellows were commonplace. In the sixteenth century, the mortality rate of children under fifteen was high—about fifty percent overall, and highest among the urban poor. John Marlowe's family fared slightly better than average, as only four of their nine children died before reaching their teens, but parents could never be confident of seeing their children live to adulthood. Canterbury was a small city compared to Bristol or London, but it was subject to the same crowded and unsanitary conditions that made urban areas generally more disease-prone than rural areas,[24] and since St. George's parish was located between the cattle market and Butchery Lane, close to the shambles, it can hardly have been the most salubrious district of Canterbury. Death and danger were routine presences in the young Marlowe's life. Under such circumstances, even a privileged firstborn male might be unceremoniously snatched away, his fate attracting little more attention than those of the cattle driven past his family's door to the shambles, some of their hides destined for his father's shop.

Still, the Marlowe family seems to have been quite stable. By all indications John Marlowe was happily married, self-confident, and continually busy with his own affairs and those of others. At times he was too ambitious, since he often undertook obligations he was unable to meet. Urry aptly characterizes him as "a noisy, self-assertive, improvident fellow."[25] He was repeatedly sued for debt and nonpayment of rent. His arithmetic may have been no better than his handwriting; conceivably it was worse. After being elected warden and treasurer of his company of leathermen, John was predictably found "deficient in his accounts."[26] He seems to have made many attempts to increase his income, first by moving to Canterbury, then by relocating his shoe shop to a more central site in St. Andrew's parish when Christopher was

[23] Urry, *Christopher Marlowe and Canterbury*, 4.
[24] Patten, *English Towns, 1500–1700*, 32.
[25] Urry, "Marlowe and Canterbury," 136.
[26] Ibid.

about ten, possibly in hope of attracting a wealthier clientele or expanding his trade. A few years later, he began to supplement his income by serving occasionally as a bondsman for couples applying for marriage licenses, a practice in which he was later joined by two of his sons-in-law, John Jorden and Thomas Gradell. In later years he secured the post of parish clerk of St. Mary's, and not long before his death he took up victualing instead of shoemaking, a venture in which his wife, Katherine, undoubtedly assisted him. In addition to these activities, he served as a sideman and churchwarden, joined a company of volunteers to defend the English coast from the Armada, and was always ready to sign a will, give a deposition, serve on a jury, or testify for or against his neighbors. Yet in spite of this constant activity, John never prospered, and his hold on respectability was tenuous. His approach to life was vigorous and expansive, but he seems to have lacked the crucial ability to focus on attainable goals.

John's enormous energy, of course, may not have been entirely reassuring to his children. A man of such manifest self-assertiveness would probably have been a powerful presence in his own household, where his patriarchal authority was traditionally sanctioned to the point of petty tyranny. Indeed, when Christopher was thirteen John came to blows with his apprentice Lactantius Presson, injuring Presson severely enough that he was subsequently fined a shilling for drawing blood. While the beating of children and apprentices was tolerated in England until well into the nineteenth century, John evidently exceeded what were considered acceptable bounds in sixteenth-century Canterbury. A later attack on John Marlowe by his former apprentice William Hewes suggests that John may have done Hewes a similar disservice, for which Hewes nursed his resentment until the chance came to repay the favor.[27] Still, John was not an exceptionally violent man; by the standards of the time he might even be considered mild-mannered. Unlike many of his contemporaries, John never killed anyone, nor was he a habitual brawler, nor was he even peripherally involved in anyone's death. His very short will suggests that he was devoted to his wife, but this softer side of his nature may not have been apparent to his sons and daughters, who would have been taught to defer to and obey him from earliest childhood. The available records, including those concerning his interaction with his apprentices, do not support any definite conclusions about John's relationship to his own children, although his temperament seems better suited to an authoritative parent than to an indulgent and tolerant one.

Katherine Marlowe, like most women of the sixteenth and seventeenth

[27] Urry, *Christopher Marlowe and Canterbury*, 24.

centuries, is much less fully represented than her husband in legal records and other documents. To some extent this lack of evidence is reassuring. Unlike many of her neighbors and her two youngest daughters, Katherine escaped scandal and notoriety. She and John show strong mutual affection for one another in their wills, and the survival rate of her children suggests that she was a conscientious mother. There are hints, both in the representation of maternal figures in Christopher's plays and in the birth intervals of the Marlowe children, that Katherine especially favored her firstborn son, which the paternalistic bias of the culture would only have encouraged. Her energetic efforts in 1597 to secure the estate of her niece, Dorothy Arthur, are understandable given the Marlowes' perpetually strained finances. The fact that John made Katherine the sole executrix of his will indicates that he trusted her to manage her affairs, while in her own will, Katherine justifies his confidence by showing an impressive command of the details of her household. Her scrupulous attempt to deal fairly and reasonably with her three surviving daughters and her grandchildren when her health was failing rapidly (like John, she died almost immediately after making her will) seems particularly commendable.

It is perhaps not surprising that Katherine's two youngest daughters cut a less admirable figure in the Canterbury records than their mother. The Marlowe family was large, and Katherine's responsibilities increased with each child. Like all craftsmen's wives she had to care for her husband, bear and raise her children, shop, cook, sew, keep house, wash, supervise servants when she had them, and occasionally mind her husband's shop. She was pregnant for six and a half of her forty-three years of marriage, and nursing infants for an additional six years. Her older children, for whom she had more time, turned out rather well. Christopher behaved demurely enough until well after he left Cambridge; Margaret, the eldest surviving daughter, was far better behaved than her youngest sisters Ann and Dorothy; and Jane (or Joan), although she married young and apparently died in childbirth, chose a husband much to her parents' liking. John Moore, Joan's husband, was the younger brother of Ursula, her uncle Thomas Arthur's wife, as well as being her father's apprentice. He remained close to the Marlowe family long after his young wife's death, and in Katherine's will, he is bequeathed "fortye shillinges, and the joyne presse that standeth in the greate chamber where I lye"—no small token of her esteem for him.[28]

As he grew older, Christopher would have become increasingly aware of

[28] See the appendix for the full text of Katherine Marlowe's will.

his family's precarious hold on its already marginal social niche,[29] and of the dangers this posed to his own future. Part of the problem, aside from the fact that the Marlowes were not an established Canterbury family, was his father's limited education. John's example, both positive and negative, may well have reinforced Christopher's own powerful ambition, strengthening his determination to pursue his education as far as his ability and opportunities would take him. Fortunately, circumstances favored that ambition, for Christopher's generation was to be proportionally better educated than any previous and many subsequent generations.[30] Although craftsmen and freeholders were generally the lowest classes whose children attended the universities, their sons began to take degrees in unprecedented numbers in the later sixteenth century, thus escaping the cycle of drudgery and poverty in which their families had been trapped for generations.

Precisely when and where Christopher began his studies we do not know. Since John Marlowe was no doubt satisfied with the modest benefits he had gained from his own limited schooling, he must have encouraged his son's early education, although he obviously could not afford to pay high fees for this privilege. Christopher might have acquired basic literacy at any one of a number of small schools in Canterbury, some of which were free. He would have begun attending whenever his parents felt he was ready, or whenever they could afford to send him. Children commonly started school at six or seven in the sixteenth century,[31] but sometimes they began earlier or, not infrequently, much later. As Lawrence Stone has shown, students from poorer families generally entered the universities later than students from wealthy or aristocratic families,[32] which would suggest that their education typically started later, and progressed more slowly or sporadically, than that of children of the upper classes, whose families could afford private tutors.

Certainly one of the best free schools in Canterbury was the new school at Eastbridge (St. Thomas's) Hospital, founded in 1569 by Archbishop Matthew Parker.[33] This school opened its doors to twenty poor children at about the time Christopher was ready to begin his education, offering instruction in reading, writing, and singing. The school provided all books, paper, and writing implements. The only restriction was that study there was limited to

[29] Andrew Butcher, introduction to Urry, *Christopher Marlowe and Canterbury*, xxiii–xxiv.

[30] Lawrence Stone, "The Educational Revolution in England, 1560–1640," *Past and Present* 28 (July 1964): 69.

[31] Kenneth Charlton, *Education in Renaissance England* (London, 1965), 98.

[32] Lawrence Stone, "Size and Composition of the Oxford Student Body 1580–1909," in *The University and Society*, vol. 1, *Oxford and Cambridge from the 14th to the Early 19th Century*, ed. Lawrence Stone (Princeton, 1974), 30–31.

[33] William Townsend, *British Cities: Canterbury* (London, 1950), 60; Joan Simon, *Education and Society in Tudor England* (Cambridge, Eng., 1966), 313.

four years, so that a larger number of poor children could benefit.[34] Because of this limitation, it was impossible to complete grammar school there, since grammar school normally required six years of study beyond the initial two or three years of petty school. Christopher received his scholarship to Canterbury's King's (or, during Elizabeth's reign, Queen's) School in December of 1578, not long before his fifteenth birthday, and presumably finished his work there in late 1580. His scholarship therefore supported only his last two years of grammar school. His petty schooling and his first four years of grammar school were completed without this scholarship support, and at least part of the work was done elsewhere, because students were not admitted to the King's School until they had learned to read and write English and had mastered the essentials of Latin grammar.

The fact that Eastbridge School included music in its curriculum would also tend to make it a likely provider of Marlowe's early schooling. According to the statutes of the King's School, scholars were expected to assist the choristers of the cathedral,[35] although the King's School itself did not teach music. At some point Marlowe must have been trained in vocal music, for his scholarship to Cambridge, one of several founded by Archbishop Parker, specified that "said scholars shall and must at the time of their election be so entred into the skill of song as that they shall at the first sight solf and sing plaine song."[36] Moreover, some formal cooperation existed between Eastbridge Hospital and the King's School. Funds from Eastbridge Hospital were used to support two of Parker's Canterbury Scholars at Cambridge, who were chosen from among King's School scholars, and the master of Eastbridge Hospital participated in the selection of these two scholars.[37]

Although we cannot document Marlowe's early education in detail, we can form an approximate idea of his schooling from what we know about Renaissance education in general. In petty school, at the very least, he would have learned to read and write English. His studies would probably have included basic arithmetic, and, depending on the interest and ability of his instructor, he might have learned to sing and read music. He would then have proceeded to grammar school, where the first three years were devoted to mastering Latin grammar, with much emphasis on rote learning and memorization; his instruction would have included reading and translation of simple Latin texts, as well as the writing of grammatically correct Latin sen-

[34] Simon, *Education and Society in Tudor England*, 313.
[35] D. L. Edwards, *A History of the King's School, Canterbury* (London, 1957), 65.
[36] Bakeless, *Tragicall History* 1:64.
[37] William Gostling, *A Walk in and around the City of Canterbury* (Canterbury, 1777), 380–81.

tences. In many schools, more advanced reading and writing of English, and casting accounts, were also taught in the first two forms. The last three years of grammar school were devoted to more specialized tasks, such as reading and translating selections from the "chastest" classical authors and historians, writing rhetorically effective prose modeled on the work of Latin masters, especially Cicero, learning the elements of Latin poetry, writing Latin verse, and composing and delivering declamations.[38]

The ideal was for the scholar to progress from reading and study of rhetorical principles to paraphrasing model authors, and finally to producing original compositions. In the words of the schoolmaster William Kempe, "First the scholar shall learn the precepts; secondly he shall learn to note the examples of the precepts in unfolding other men's works; thirdly to imitate the examples in some work of his own; fourthly and lastly to make somewhat alone without an example."[39] At the King's School, where Marlowe became a Queen's scholar at the age of fourteen, a student seeking admission was expected to be able to read English freely, to recite the Lord's Prayer, the Angelic Salutation, the Apostle's Creed, and the Ten Commandments in English, and to know the "accidents" (declensions and conjugations) of Latin grammar.[40] As these requirements suggest, religious and moral instruction was an integral part of Renaissance education.

What we know about the King's School conforms closely to general educational practice in the sixteenth century, although the quality of education there was exceptionally high. In the upper three forms, which Marlowe was completing during the period of his scholarship, the headmaster himself conducted studies rather than merely directing them. During most of Marlowe's tenure as a scholar the headmaster would have been John Gresshop, an M.A. of Christ Church, Oxford, who had occupied the post since 1566. According to the school statutes, no boy was allowed to enter the fourth form until he had thoroughly mastered Latin grammar, " 'so that no noun or verb may be found which they do not know how to inflect in every detail.' "[41] In the fifth form the boys studied and memorized figures of classical oratory and the rules of Latin verse, and put this knowledge into practice by writing verses and composing speeches. They also translated " 'the most chaste Poets and the best Historians.' "[42] In the sixth form they were taught the formulae of Erasmus's *De Verborum Copia ac Rerum* (Concerning abundance of words

[38] Charlton, *Education in Renaissance England*, 106; A. D. Wraight, *In Search of Christopher Marlowe; A Pictorial Biography*, photography by Virginia F. Stern (New York, 1965), 40.
[39] Charlton, *Education in Renaissance England*, 106.
[40] Ibid., 98.
[41] Edwards, *A History of the King's School, Canterbury*, 66.
[42] Ibid.

A rare engraving of the King's School, Canterbury, now demolished. The structure on the roof near the center chimney appears to be the belfry. According to Urry, the building had other amenities besides a school bell, including a notice board and a lavatory. From William Gostling, *A Walk in and about the City of Canterbury*, 1777.

and matter), learned "'to vary speech in every mood, so that they may acquire the faculty of speaking Latin, so far as is possible in boys.'"[43] They also studied Horace, Cicero, and other suitable authors, and competed with one another in declamations, "'that the competition may encourage them in their studies.'"[44]

It is probable that the boys also performed in school plays at Christmas. Records of expenses for such plays performed by King's School students have survived from 1562, 1563, and from the early seventeenth century, and Urry found other evidence suggesting a continuous tradition of dramatic activity by King's School scholars,[45] even though the records are incomplete. Furthermore, as we know from the inventory of his books, Mr. Gresshop had a keen interest in drama. This is indicated not only by his copies of the universally taught Plautus and Terence (with commentary), but also, more surprisingly, by his editions of Sophocles in both Latin and Greek, and by several volumes of Aristophanes in Greek, including an edition of *Peace*.[46]

[43] Ibid.
[44] Ibid.
[45] Urry, *Christopher Marlowe and Canterbury*, 6. Further details regarding theatrical activity in Canterbury during Marlowe's childhood are included in the unpublished manuscript.
[46] Ibid., 47, 112, 117, 120.

While Marlowe certainly read selections from Ovid in grammar school, the racy *Amores,* which he translated later, would not have found a place on Mr. Gresshop's approved reading list. As the repeated emphasis on "chaste" material in the literature of Renaissance education indicates, Renaissance pedagogues saw Venus as inimical to education, and tried to avoid exposing their highly distractible charges to temptation.[47] Marlowe probably did not see the more contentious parts of Lucian, whom Greene later accused him of emulating, until he went to Cambridge; however, two volumes of Lucian, one of them possibly Erasmus's translation and selection for schoolboys, were included in Mr. Gresshop's library. Marlowe would of course have studied the *Aeneid,* the major source of *Dido, Queen of Carthage,* in grammar school. Presumably his early exposure to this work led him to conceive his play of Dido as a quasi-didactic work suitable for performance by boys. Indeed, the thematic immaturity of *Dido,* its decidedly adolescent portrayal of love and destiny, and its direct appropriation of passages from Virgil, suggest that it may have originated as a truly juvenile work, an adaptation of Virgil for a school production. If so, it would have been natural enough for Marlowe to expand and revise it later, making it into a slightly more sophisticated work intellectually and a considerably more sophisticated work dramatically, while still retaining the original concept of a play intended for performance by schoolboys. Given Mr. Gresshop's interest in drama—and the fact that another of his students, Stephen Gosson, also went on to write plays—it is possible that he encouraged the young Marlowe in such a project, and that Marlowe's facility in writing dramatic verse had more than a little to do with his winning a scholarship to Cambridge. Gosson, of course, later repudiated his dramatic career in *The School of Abuse* (1579), but a copy of another book by Gosson, the euphuistic *Ephemerides of Phialo,* found its way into Mr. Gresshop's library.

Marlowe's intellectual development was necessarily impacted by the King's School headmasters with whom he studied, and probably also by a former headmaster about whom he heard diabolical rumors. The least significant of these figures was Nicholas Goldsborough, an M.A. of Queen's College, Cambridge, who succeeded Mr. Gresshop as headmaster in 1580. Goldsborough began teaching at the King's School in March 1580 at the earliest, and since Marlowe presumably completed his studies later that year, Goldsborough had little time to work with him. Indeed, Goldsborough seems to have had minimal interest in teaching. He left the King's School in

---

[47] Gerald Strauss, "The State of Pedagogical Theory c. 1530: What Protestant Reformers Knew about Education," in *Schooling and Society: Studies in the History of Education,* ed. Lawrence Stone (Baltimore, 1976), 75–76.

1584 to become Vicar of Linsted, Kent, where he remained until 1589. He was then succeeded as Vicar by Christopher Pashley, the first holder of the Cambridge scholarship awarded to Marlowe.

Probably far more influential than Goldsborough, at least by dint of his scandalous reputation, was John Twyne, the first headmaster of the King's School under the new foundation of Henry VIII. Twyne remained headmaster until 1561, when he was replaced by Anthony Rushe. He nevertheless continued to live in Canterbury, possibly teaching boys privately, until 1581, the year after Marlowe went up to Cambridge.[48] Twyne seems to have lost his post as headmaster through drunken and disorderly conduct, and possibly through his indiscreet attentions to a woman who later made some rather dangerous allegations about him. According to his accuser, Mrs. Basden, Twyne had used "filthy and unseemly talk" in the Precincts of the cathedral, and had once battered her house and frightened her so thoroughly that she took three months to recover. On another occasion, when he invited her into his house, Twyne advised her to recite "God save all" before crossing the threshold. Mrs. Basden believed this was a charm to ward off evil spirits, since she had seen "'a black thing, like a great dog'" dancing around the headmaster's house when the scholars came down at five in the morning to warm themselves at his fire. This apparition, she believed, was Twyne's familiar spirit.[49] It hardly matters whether Marlowe actually knew Twyne, since such people are often more impressive in report than they are in person. Marlowe could not have grown up in a small town like Canterbury and attended the King's School without hearing gossip about its wicked former headmaster, who still lived and walked the streets to keep rumors of his sorcery alive. Such delicious schoolboy gossip may well have kindled Marlowe's later interest in another reputed scholar-necromancer, Dr. Johan Faust.

John Gresshop, who supervised most of Marlowe's studies at the King's school, died in early 1580, just a little over a year after Marlowe was elected to his scholarship. Fortunately we know a great deal about Gresshop, mainly through the extensive inventory of his possessions—particularly his large library—made shortly after his death.[50] Gresshop was obviously devoted to learning, and probably contributed significantly to Marlowe's lifelong respect for scholars and scholarship. As an index of Gresshop's devotion to learning, we might observe that he spent a great deal more on books than on his clothes. His most expensive item of clothing was his best gown, valued at 54s 4d. In comparison, the twenty-three folio volumes he kept in his lower

---

[48] Edwards, *A History of the King's School, Canterbury*, 71.
[49] Ibid.
[50] See the appendix for the complete text of the inventory.

study, which composed the most expensive portion of a library of well over three hundred volumes, were valued at 73s 10d. When we add up the sums at which his books and clothes were valued, we discover that Gresshop spent approximately twice as much on books as on clothes, at a time when clothes were quite expensive.

Through the inventory of his belongings, we can visualize Gresshop as he must have appeared to Marlowe. He was a bachelor of about fifty when Marlowe knew him. In addition to his best gown, he had two other old cloth gowns faced with budge (lambskin fur) which he presumably used for everyday classroom wear. For the frequent attendance of church services required by the school statutes, he had an "olde mockadowe cassok," a surplice, and a hood. His wardrobe included two pair of "olde carsey hose," a best pair of hose of "rashe" (silk or silky fabric), a best doublet of rash, two old doublets of rash and mockado, "an olde spanishe lether Jerkin," a cap and a hat, "an olde crowne of a velvet hat," two girdles, one of changeable silk, with a silver boss to adorn them, a jacket of old damask, two good shirts, five old shirts, two "peeses of shirts," a dagger, an old wallet, and a dozen handkerchiefs. In cold weather he might wear his good round cloak with silver clasps, valued at thirty shillings, or a less elegant cloak with sleeves, or a simple black cloth coat. Overall he presented the respectable and dignified figure of a scholar who lived frugally but comfortably among his beloved books. In addition to his many other possessions, some of them of moderate value, Mr. Gresshop had a silver whistle. This was probably used to direct or summon his students at recess, for according to the recommendation of the school statutes, "when leave is given they shall play together and sport together."[51] Even in the academically intense Elizabethan grammar schools, schoolmasters knew that children needed physical activity and equipped themselves accordingly.

From his library, we can infer a great deal about Mr. Gresshop's interests. Most educated men of the Renaissance devoted a fair amount of attention to religious controversy, but the vast majority of Gresshop's books were on religious topics, suggesting that theological issues particularly fascinated him. His collection included books by Calvin, Luther, Beza, Melancthon, Bucher, Fisher, Cranmer, and Knox, among others, as well as numerous biblical commentaries, a sizable portion of them by Peter Martyr, who was resident at Oxford while Gresshop studied there. He owned several versions of the Bible and a number of Nowell's catechisms, the latter presumably intended for instruction. His classical holdings naturally included works that formed the core of the grammar school curriculum—Virgil, Ovid, Cicero's *Offices* and *Familiar Letters*, Caesar's

---

[51] Edwards, *A History of the King's School, Canterbury*, 66.

Commentaries, Plutarch, Plautus, and Terence. Among these classics were works of a more skeptical tenor—Lucian, Cicero's *Tusculian Questions* in English, and a modern companion piece, Cornelius Agrippa's *Vanity of the Sciences*.

As we might expect of the master of one of the best grammar schools in Renaissance England, Gresshop was proficient in Greek. His library included Greek grammars and lexicons, a book of Greek pronunciation, and many works in Greek editions, including Homer, Demosthenes, and Aristotle, as well as Sophocles and Aristophanes. He was also familiar with the latest humanist pedagogical theories, as evidenced by his possession of books by Vives, Sturm, Ascham, Elyot, and Sadoletus. He fancied modern as well as ancient literature, for copies of Chaucer, More, Petrarch, Erasmus's *Praise of Folly*, *The Mirror for Magistrates*, and *Songs and Sonnets* were among his holdings. Rounding out his library were histories, medical books, and volumes on civil and canon law. It was an enviable collection, which appears to have aroused the acquisitive instincts of one of the valuers of the estate. A number of the titles in the inventory of Gresshop's books have a large *H* entered beside them in the margin. Presumably Canon John Hill, who supervised the inventory,[52] wished to reserve some of these choice items for himself.

The grammar school education Marlowe completed at the King's School, which was typical of Renaissance education in its general outlines, might fairly be characterized as an intense bilingual program of training in language and its expressive possibilities. This type of education was likely to produce individuals of refined taste who had great respect, even reverence, for literature, and who had acquired all the skills they needed to develop into skilled and confident writers themselves. It is therefore not surprising that out of a very small population base of approximately 5.2 million, sixteenth- and seventeenth-century England and Wales produced a remarkable number of talented poets and playwrights, and legions of versifiers. In the drama in particular, between 1560 and 1640 Gascoigne, Lyly, Greene, Peele, Kyd, Marlowe, Shakespeare, Jonson, Dekker, Heywood, Webster, Ford, Middleton, Beaumont, Fletcher, Massinger, and Shirley all flourished, a concentration of dramatic talent unequaled in literary history. Since Kyd, Shakespeare, Jonson, and Dekker had only grammar school educations, the contribution of English grammar schools to this efflorescence was very considerable.

The rapid increase in educational opportunity from which these writers benefited also created a large literate and semiliterate audience for their works. While contemporary writers on the theater sneered at the ground-

---

[52] Urry, *Christopher Marlowe and Canterbury*, 47.

lings, not a few of these enthusiastic playgoers were apprentices who had acquired basic literacy in the petty schools. Some of them could read English well, they valued and respected education, they had tasted just enough knowledge to develop an appetite for it, and they were attentive and appreciative auditors of plays, which extended their knowledge and experience in a condensed, entertaining, verbally sophisticated, inexpensive, and relatively effortless manner. This new audience, as much as the playwrights, created a climate favorable not only to the resurgence of great drama but to the development of a new genre, the English history play, to which Marlowe would contribute significantly.

It seems safe to assume that Marlowe found school highly gratifying, if only because the demands of the curriculum perfectly matched his talents. Recognition of his aptitude by his schoolmasters, as evidenced by his scholarships to the King's School and Cambridge, would have reinforced his already considerable self-esteem. Since Mr. Gresshop owned a number of humanist pedagogical writings, among them Ascham's *The Schoolmaster*, it is reasonable to assume that he adopted at least some of their methodology. Ascham, like most Renaissance pedagogues, recommended positive incentives, such as an appeal to ambition, competitiveness, and the craving for praise, to motivate students. The best students in humanist schools were often given conspicuous preferential treatment, such as being seated in the front of the class, to reward their achievement, fire their ambition, and spur their envious classmates to greater efforts. Corporal punishment, on the other hand, was almost universally condemned in the pedagogical literature of the period; many schools had rules prohibiting or restricting it, which suggests both that it was sometimes used and that it was not encouraged. Humanists considered it demeaning to beings of higher intellect, accepting Plutarch's view that it was a punishment unfit for freeborn children. Mr. Gresshop probably resorted to this distasteful method seldom, if ever, although he may have reserved it as a threat, which Vives felt was its only effective use. Verbal criticism or shaming was the recommended form of punishment.[53]

An unintended but important side effect of Renaissance humanism and its approach to education was that it tended to encourage narcissism in its most talented and ambitious youth, a character trait or psychological tendency already conspicuous throughout sixteenth-and seventeenth-century Europe. This result was especially likely if the able young person—as often happened—was a firstborn male already conditioned to expect special treatment. The humanist insistence on the dignity and potential of each individ-

[53] Strauss, "The State of Pedagogical Theory c. 1530," 78–81.

ual encouraged everyone to consider himself somewhat special, and the spread of literacy and learning gave more men than ever before a reason to regard themselves as accomplished persons whose achievements commanded respect. Even John Marlowe, we may assume, took pride in his modest attainments and would tolerate no slight to his honor. Dogberry's comic outrage in *Much Ado about Nothing* at being disrespectfully called an ass by Conrade, and the litany of self-praise with which he tries to nullify this insult, were, I believe, responses completely recognizable to Shakespeare's audience. The Renaissance was an age in which every apprentice might fight to defend his honor, an attitude pointedly burlesqued in Beaumont's *The Knight of the Burning Pestle*.

This intense desire for respect and honor was further encouraged by a society which increasingly based rewards on achievement rather than birth. Although family name and title still dominated the social hierarchy, wealth and education—particularly education—were more respected than ever before. A man with a special gift or talent, *virtù*, could hope to gain recognition and advancement through his individual effort, a hope fanned by expanding educational and economic opportunity. Yet competition for rewards was keen, even among the upper classes, and a good education was considered vital for a young gentleman or nobleman who wished to maintain or extend his power and influence. Praise and recognition, honor and fame, good name or reputation were equated with success, while shame, ridicule, or loss of reputation or honor eroded self-esteem and, from the subjective perspective of the victim of such treatment, annihilated the self. Humanist educational theory both tapped into and reinforced these broader social attitudes.

While the Renaissance encouraged ambition and achievement, it was less effective in rewarding them once a young man moved beyond the grammar school or university. The favor and patronage of the great or established, which were virtually the only means for a talented individual to advance himself, were capricious and unreliable, a fact reflected in frequent complaints about the scorn and empty promises of patrons. Furthermore, the system imposed contradictory demands. Individuals were encouraged to excel, but only in ways consistent with the paternalistic interests of the powerful. To survive, an individual needed not only talent and ambition, but also a flair for self-promotion and at least a moderate capacity for diplomacy, tact, and duplicity.

Such a society might be expected to produce the positive results that the Renaissance often did produce—ambitious striving, planning on a grand (or grandiose) scale, an enormous upsurge of creative energy, and brilliant individual achievement. Unfortunately, it might also experience some less agreeable side effects. Men who were conditioned to expect constant praise and recognition, and who therefore became psychologically dependent on these marks of respect, might show a definite propensity to depression, rage, and destructive or self-destructive violence when honor, praise, and personal advancement were denied. On the other hand, to gain recognition they might adopt an extreme style of self-promotion that might be called aggressive auto-inflation, a relatively distasteful but exceedingly common variant of Renaissance individualism and the artful self-culture Stephen Greenblatt calls "self-fashioning." Shakespeare's Benedick acknowledges these social realities in *Much Ado about Nothing* when he justifies his self-praise to Beatrice: "In this age ... it is most expedient for the wise ... to be the trumpet of his own virtues, as I am to myself" (5.2.78, 83–86).[54] In the Renaissance these high expectations of personal glory, and violent reactions to real or perceived slights by others, might have been attributed to pride, the swelling of self-conceit. However, we may find narcissism a more convenient term, since it highlights the social causes of these actions and their prominence in certain historical periods, rather than ascribing them solely to universal human nature.[55]

Christopher had not yet experienced such threats to his equanimity. He must have been encouraged and liberally praised in school, and his parents, at the very least, did not discourage him from pursuing an education. If John Marlowe was a typical Renaissance father, he may have hoped his son would succeed him and have sent Christopher to petty school to prime him for apprenticeship. However, his ambition for his son was more than satisfied by Christopher's exceptional academic performance, and, unlike Ben Jonson's stepfather, John chose not to quarrel with success. The birth in 1576 of John's second healthy son (named Thomas, like the child who had died six years previously) would have lessened any temptation John might have felt to appropriate Christopher's life.

Although Renaissance education was not necessarily painful or onerous, it was rigorous. Christopher spent long weekdays, from 6 A.M. until 5 P.M., in school. He also attended school on Saturdays, although often not for a full day. On weekdays he devoted an additional hour to study in the evening, from 6 to 7 P.M. During these evening sessions students first recited their les-

[54] All quotations of Shakespeare are from *The Riverside Shakespeare*, 2d ed., ed. G. Blakemore Evans et al. (Boston, 1997).
[55] Narcissism has received considerable attention in psychology during the last few decades. Heinz Kohut's *The Analysis of the Self* (New York, 1971) and *The Restoration of the Self* (New York, 1977) are two of the more important theoretical studies, while Christopher Lasch, in *The Culture of Narcissism: American Life in an Age of Diminishing Expectations* (New York, 1978), suggests connections between particular cultural traits and the prevalence of narcissism.

sons to more advanced students and assistant schoolmasters, then listened to younger students recite lessons they had mastered, a system of peer tutoring traditionally used in the King's School. However, Marlowe's schooldays were not so grueling as this bare description might suggest, for instruction was not continuous. School began with prayers at six and continued until eight. After a break of an hour, which may have included breakfast or a snack, studies resumed at nine and continued until eleven. School was then recessed for lunch until one, resumed until three, recessed again until four, and concluded at five.[56] This meant a total of seven hours of instruction, comparable to modern practice, with the addition of an hour in the evening. Renaissance pedagogues were more realistic about children's attention spans than early Marlowe biographies might lead us to believe. Mr. Gresshop's whistle was as essential a tool of his profession as his books.

The rest of Christopher's early education was supplied by his daily experiences in Canterbury, which were necessarily far richer than the early experiences of many children in sixteenth-century England. Marlowe's early-twentieth-century biographers often emphasized the violence of life in Elizabethan Canterbury—its bull stake, street brawls, and public executions—to adduce a rather simplistic explanation for the violence of Marlowe's plays. In fact Marlowe's Canterbury was not much more violent than Shakespeare's Stratford, and considerably less violent than Ben Jonson's London. For that matter, it was less violent than the world of his twentieth-century biographers—who managed to witness trench warfare, widespread terrorist bombing of civilian populations, and genocide without losing confidence in their moral superiority to the Elizabethans. Marlowe's personality was primarily a product of his innate temperament and specific family and interpersonal dynamics rather than of his physical surroundings, and his plays suggest far more about these interpersonal relationships than does the biographical record. Canterbury influenced Marlowe intellectually and aesthetically more than it affected him psychologically, helping to shape his interests and tastes, and directing his attention to problems that fascinated him for the rest of his life.

Like other large towns or small cities in sixteenth-century England, Canterbury was neither precisely urban nor precisely rural. It was a walled city of approximately six thousand inhabitants, an oval enclosure roughly half a mile in diameter, strategically located among the lush green hills of Kent, which it had served since pre-Christian times as a commercial, administra-

---

[56] T. W. Baldwin, *Shakespeare's Small Latine and Lesse Greeke*, (Urbana, 1944), 1:168.

tive, and religious center. While the citizens of Canterbury remained in touch with the surrounding countryside, where they hunted, enjoyed other outdoor sports, or engaged in part-time farming, the area within its walls, and the suburbs that had begun to sprawl around them, were recognizably urban. The streets were crowded, narrow, and channeled; space in general was highly compressed, so that all the city's business could be conducted within walking distance. Parts of Canterbury hummed with commercial activity, especially the houses where the Huguenot and Walloon weavers lived and worked, and the marketing center around the cathedral, near which John Marlowe relocated his business. Canterbury also had long traditions of trade in wool and leather. The cattle market just outside St. George's gate had been a mainstay of the town's economy for centuries.

Adding to this urbanity was Canterbury's location on the London-Dover road. During Christopher's boyhood Canterbury was no longer a shrine attracting thousands of pilgrims from England and abroad, but it was still a convenient stop for foreign travelers and Englishmen on their way to and from continental Europe. Because of its favorable location and its active trade in wool and cloth, Canterbury drew settlers both from other parts of England and from the Continent. By simply looking around him and listening to the babble of French, Dutch, Welsh, German, and assorted dialects of English, Christopher could develop a vivid awareness of exotic places with strange names far removed from St. George's parish. When his family traveled the sixteen miles to Dover to visit his grandfather William Arthur in St. James's parish, he could see great ships riding the waves of the English Channel on their way to and from foreign ports. One of them, the *Flying Dragon*, had an especially appealing name that he later gave to del Bosco's ship in *The Jew of Malta*.[57]

Canterbury was (and still is) a school in its own right, reaching out to distant places and back to distant times. Marlowe's sense of history originated there, along with his sense of place. The city was indeed, as Marlowe's fellow Canterburian John Lyly described it, "an old city somewhat decayed yet beautiful to behold," containing buildings so ancient, some still in use and good repair and some in ruins, that the boy Christopher could scarcely comprehend how long they had existed.[58] The great tower in the center of the cathedral, Bell Harry, had been built over sixty years before, and was therefore older than Christopher's grandfather. Other parts of the cathedral were

[57] Urry, "Christopher Marlowe and Canterbury."
[58] Quoted in Urry, *Christopher Marlowe and Canterbury*, 1.

four hundred years old. St. Martin's Church, located outside the city walls southeast of John Marlowe's first shop, was in use before St. Augustine came to Britain. Parts of the city wall had stood for more than a thousand years. In Canterbury, the past was everywhere—on all sides, underfoot, constantly present to stir the imagination.

While growing up in Canterbury, Marlowe often had opportunities to contemplate Caesar, St. Augustine, Becket, and Henry VIII, all of them prominent figures in local history. He would also have been prompted to contemplate another group of historical figures, which arguably included Becket—Christian martyrs. While reverence for martyrs was part of every medieval and Renaissance Christian's religious heritage, the tradition was especially strong in Canterbury, which had been the cradle and center of English Christianity long before it became associated with Becket's shrine. An impressive array of alleged saints' relics had once occupied virtually every corner of the cathedral, including bodies, limbs, heads, pieces of the true cross, a spine from the crown of thorns, a tooth and a finger of St. Steven, as well as some of the stones that killed him, St. Lawrence's bones and a piece of his gridiron, and, of more immediate local interest, Becket's blood, clothing, and the severed crown of his head.[59] This last prize, however, had been exposed as a fraud when the actual fragment of Becket's skull was discovered in his tomb during his exhumation.[60]

Canterbury's local martyrs included St. Alphege and St. Edmund, the ancient king of East Anglia, both killed by marauding Danes, but Becket had much more than local importance. He had come to represent the primacy of religious authority over secular authority, and it was precisely for this reason that Henry VIII was determined to eradicate his cult by desecrating and looting his shrine, burning his bones and scattering his ashes. However, Mary revived the cult, and Becket's martyrdom was commemorated only six or seven years before Christopher's birth. Indeed, it was impossible to erase all traces of this cult, for much of Canterbury's splendor and beauty, including most of its great cathedral and the noble Christ Church Gate, had been financed by the veneration of Becket. Paintings of Becket's martyrdom survived in the cathedral and in Eastbridge Hospital, in spite of the iconoclastic housecleaning that followed the desecration of his shrine. Catholics and Catholic sympathizers still lived quietly in Canterbury,[61] and Catholic pilgrims still came

---

[59] A. L. Rowse, *Christopher Marlowe, His Life and Work* (New York, 1964), 4–5.
[60] Gostling, *A Walk in and about the City of Canterbury*, 124n.
[61] Butcher, introduction to Urry, *Christopher Marlowe and Canterbury*, xix–xxi.

to Canterbury to pay furtive devotion to St. Thomas. Like Catholicism itself, the cult had not been destroyed but had merely gone underground.

However, the Reformation had lent the concept of martyrdom a new ambiguity, as Becket's case prominently illustrated. A martyr was no longer a person who died for a unified Christian faith, but a person who died for the beliefs of a specific sect. Anyone who gave his life for principles other than, or opposed to, those of the faction in power risked being condemned as a fool or a traitor, or both. In this altered and more contentious sense of the word, Canterbury had seen numerous recent martyrdoms, both Catholic and Protestant. Catholics who died for resisting the Reformation included Elizabeth Barton, the nun of Kent, hanged with her followers at Tyburn in 1534, and John Stone, an Austin friar. Friar Stone had perhaps the better claim to martyrdom, since he was indisputably sane and a victim of massive overkill. Stone was hanged, drawn, quartered, and parboiled at Dane John mound in Canterbury in 1540, and his quarters set up on Westgate to preach a mute sermon on royal supremacy.

Sometime after 1535, Canterbury became the clandestine resting place of the head of another Catholic martyr, Thomas More. After his execution, More's body had been buried at the Tower, but his head was exposed with those of other traitors on Tower Bridge. However, More's favorite daughter, Margaret, who lived with her husband William Roper in the suburb of Canterbury just outside Westgate, managed to obtain the head and place it in the Roper family vault at St. Dunstan's Church. These odd doings evidently caused gossip in the small community, for according to rumors still current in Canterbury in the eighteenth century, Margaret had asked to be buried with her father's head in her arms.[62] Margaret's husband, who revered More and wrote a life of his sainted father-in-law, lived well into Marlowe's lifetime, dying when Christopher was fourteen.

Canterbury's Protestant martyrs were more numerous, and often anonymous. The most prominent of Canterbury's victims of Marian persecution, Archbishop Thomas Cranmer, was tried and executed in Oxford, but many Protestants died in Canterbury. After her accession, Mary established commissions to root out heresy, and in order to placate the queen without seriously inconveniencing their neighbors, the Canterbury commission chose to direct their inquisitional zeal at foreign scapegoats. Forty-one Protestants, mostly immigrant weavers who had fled to Kent from the continent to escape Catholic persecution, were imprisoned, tried, and burned in Canter-

[62] Gostling, *A Walk in and about the City of Canterbury*, 55n.

bury in what was later called Martyr's Field, the greatest holocaust in the city's history.[63]

In the context of the Reformation, these tales of tragic heroes—or pathetic victims—were puzzling and paradoxical. Marlowe found himself in the troubling position of trying to define his values and ideals in a culture that perversely cast what it deemed the noblest human acts into the deepest ethical and metaphysical doubt. Christianity taught that self-sacrifice and a steadfast commitment to belief and principle in the face of danger and death were among the greatest human virtues. This idea was deeply impressed on Marlowe from his earliest childhood. Yet what if a man sacrificed himself for a worthless or evil cause? What if his convictions were false? Was his action still noble and admirable, or was he a fool and a traitor, an enemy to himself and to all mankind? And how could one tell whose beliefs were correct, whose sacrifice was worthy of reverence? Was Becket a saint or a traitor, a self-sacrificing imitator of Christ or a man who sought power greater than a king's, perhaps even through his own destruction? To the Puritan William Lambarde, writing in 1570, the answer was obvious; still, Lambarde could only marvel at the outcome: "Yet the death of this one man not martyred (as they feigne, for the cause onely, and not the death, maketh a martyr) but murdered in his Churche, brought thereunto more accesse of estimation and reverence than all that ever was done before, or since."[64] Certainly Becket acquired more power in death than he had ever enjoyed in his lifetime. Henry II humbled himself by walking barefoot into Canterbury and subjecting himself to a savage, nearly fatal penitential whipping. In the following centuries, countless thousands revered Becket until Henry VIII ended his triumph overnight, subjecting his ashes to a second and more ignominious martyrdom.

Musing on these ironies and contradictions of history might well lead the sharp intellect of a confident and daring youth to more radical conclusions. Viewed from a purely historical and secular perspective, Becket was only a merchant's son with an exaggerated sense of his own importance who had provoked and defied secular authority, been destroyed by it, and gained enormous power and influence through his death, partly because of his followers' zealous advocacy of his sainthood. Was this so different from the history of Jesus of Nazareth? This logical leap would hardly have been encouraged in the churches and schools, yet the Reformation made it possible, even invited it, and more than a few Renaissance freethinkers pushed the parallel

[63] William Urry, undated lecture notes.
[64] William Lambarde, *Perambulation of Kent* (Bath 1970), 272.

to its logical conclusion. The thought almost certainly occurred to Marlowe, if not during his adolescence then not long afterward, for in 1593 Richard Baines and others attributed to Marlowe opinions consistent with this view, among them "that he [Christ] was the sonne of a carpenter, and that if the Jewes among whome he was borne did crucify him theie best knew him and wence he came."[65] If Becket, so idealized in the paintings of his martyrdom, was only a humbug, as current official doctrine insisted, then so perhaps were all the others. Perhaps religion was just another highly effective means of getting one's way. If so, Marlowe would use it to his advantage. If he could not change the course of history, he could at least gain more control over his own life.

Canterbury shaped Marlowe's taste and thought in more ways than we know, but some of its influences are obvious. The man-made splendor of the city, its "infinite riches in a little room" (*The Jew of Malta*, 1.1.37), fostered his preference for curious and intricate artifice. In Canterbury he also had ample opportunity to see plays—school productions, morality plays, and performances by strolling players from London, among others. Although surviving evidence is spotty, it suggests a vigorous and continuous tradition of stage performance in Canterbury, including a saint's play of Becket's martyrdom that could no longer be acted—publicly at least—in Marlowe's lifetime.[66] It is likely that Canterbury's Huguenot population occasionally staged plays in their own language as well, drawing on traditions that ranged from religious plays to robust farces. Civic and religious pageantry were also part of the fabric of daily life in Canterbury. Indeed, Christ Church, where the Queen's scholars were required to spend hours attending services, was a ceremonial showcase. When Christopher was nine, he had a chance to see the queen ride in triumph through Canterbury during a two-week visit, resplendent in her silk and jewels. Such spectacles heightened the stark contrast in Renaissance England between extravagant, almost unimaginable wealth and abject poverty. While they hinted at tantalizing possibilities, they also served to remind Marlowe of his family's tenuous claim to status and material comfort. Knowledge, wealth, and power were the surest means of escaping this precarious condition, if one could only get them. In Renaissance England a shoemaker's son might hope to attain one or more of these benefits if he had a marketable talent—a quick wit, which Ascham deemed suitable for poets, and, as Spencer cynically jokes in *Edward II*, "a special gift to form a verb" (2.1.55).

[65] See the appendix for the full text of the Baines note.
[66] Bakeless, *Tragicall History*, 1:31–33.

In 1580, Christopher's special gifts won him a scholarship to Cambridge—one of several such scholarships created by the late Archbishop Matthew Parker. The Parker scholarships specifically supported students from the King's School who wished to attend Corpus Christi College, Cambridge, where Parker had been master from 1544 to 1553. In addition to having a thorough mastery of Latin grammar, the recipients were expected to sight read and sing plain song, and, if possible, should be "such as can make a verse."[67] Parker probably created these scholarships to encourage academically talented youths to pursue ecclesiastical careers. A serious drive was underway in England in the late sixteenth century to upgrade the clergy, and one way to create an educated clergy was to offer scholarships to capable boys from poorer families, many of whom had no better prospects. Some of the Corpus Christi scholarships specified that the recipients were to be "such as were likely to proceed in the Arts and afterwards to make Divinity their study."[68] Initially, they could be held for three years, and if the recipient was inclined to take holy orders, they could be held for six. However, we do not know whether these conditions applied to all the scholarships or how stringently they were enforced. Most of the holders of these scholarships did enter the church, but since a religious vocation cannot be compulsory, the possibility of other outcomes, even for students who held the scholarships for six years, must have been assumed. Indeed, the use of the word "likely" to describe the prospects of scholarship recipients suggests that nothing was taken for granted. Marlowe was by no means the only student to exploit this inevitable ambiguity and flexibility in the terms of his scholarship.

For these and other reasons, we cannot conclude that Marlowe was seriously contemplating an ecclesiastical career as he prepared to leave for Cambridge. On the contrary, he may already have resolved, like Faustus, to "be a divine in show, / Yet level at the end of every art" (1.1.3–4). Biographers who believed Katherine Marlowe was a clergyman's daughter imagined Christopher growing up in "the odour of conventional piety and domestic tranquility,"[69] but Urry's research suggests that quite a different atmosphere prevailed in the Marlowe household. In later life John Marlowe seems to have become moderately religious. He served as clerk of St. Mary Breadman—probably for economic rather than religious reasons; he and Katherine piously bequeathed their souls to God in their wills according to the conventional formula; and the only book found among John's possessions was a Bible. Still,

[67] Frederick S. Boas, *Christopher Marlowe: A Biographical and Critical Study* (Oxford, 1940), 12.
[68] Bakeless, *Tragicall History*, 1:47.
[69] C. F. Tucker Brooke, *The Life of Marlowe and The Tragedy of Dido, Queen of Carthage*, in *The Works and Life of Christopher Marlowe*, ed. R. H. Case (New York, 1966), 15.

the young John Marlowe that Christopher knew was sometimes lax in church attendance,[70] and neither he nor Katherine made any pious bequests in their wills. Judging from the reports of casual irreverence on the part of Christopher and his two youngest sisters, Ann and Dorothy,[71] it seems likely that religion was a routine, rather automatic part of the Marlowe family's lives rather than a central preoccupation.

Christopher probably saw a career in the church as a last resort, a bare means of livelihood that offered highly dubious rewards. He must have known that the minister who baptized him, the Reverend William Sweeting, died in miserable poverty in 1574, even though he had incomes from two churches,[72] and this was hardly an isolated instance. Rather than craving the obscure, penurious life of a clergyman, Christopher probably found the prospect of wealth, fame, and the secular immortality promised to great poets far more alluring. Since he had just distinguished himself by winning a scholarship, partly on the basis of his ability to "make a verse," he had good reason to hope that a more glamorous, brilliant future lay before him.

[70] Urry, in "Christopher Marlowe and Canterbury," writes, "In these early days when he was building up a business, John Marlowe no doubt had a very busy time, leading to a disinclination to attend church on Sundays. On 10 July 1569 the churchwardens of St. George . . . were obliged to report as follows, at the diocesan visitation . . . : 'We present John Marly for that he commeth not to church as he ought to doe.' A church official said he had summoned John to appear, but as he was absent, he was 'declared contumacious.' "

[71] Urry, "Marlowe and Canterbury," 136.

[72] Urry, *Christopher Marlowe and Canterbury*, 8–9.

2

Fetching Gentry from the University

\# ❦

At last, like to a bold sharp sophister.

Hero and Leander, 197

TOWARD THE END of Michaelmas term 1580, in late November or early December, Christopher Marlowe knelt for his father's blessing, said goodbye to his family, and set off on the long journey northwest to Cambridge. His studies at the King's School were complete, and rather than wait until his scholarship became available, he decided to proceed immediately to the university. This early departure suggests that he was eager to begin a new phase of his life, but it was also a practical decision given the terms of the scholarship. Parker scholarships could be held for a maximum of six years, if they were extended beyond the first three; however, seven years were normally required to take both B.A. and M.A. degrees. Even if Marlowe had planned to take only the B.A., which was generally regarded as preparation for the more prestigious degree, the M.A., this normally took four years to accomplish, whereas the scholarship was subject to termination after only three. Whether he hoped to take one degree or two, Marlowe would have to complete his work quickly or find some other means of support. Even when fortune favored him, he could not entirely escape economic constraints.

We have no records to document Marlowe's journey north, although we can visualize it in terms of probabilities. Certainly the weather was cold, and Marlowe had to travel more than a hundred miles, at least partly on roads that were apt to be muddy and foul when they were not frozen and icy. He would have taken a small store of possessions with him in a chest, as students customarily did, so he presumably did not travel on horseback, as Ingram imagined him doing.[1] His nights were probably spent in inns whose accom-

---

[1] John H. Ingram, *Christopher Marlowe and His Associates* (London, 1904), 46, 49.

modations were spartan at best, sharing rooms, beds, chamber pots, and quite possibly vermin with other travelers. In all probability he passed through London, but he had neither the time nor the money for leisurely sightseeing. Like many students traveling to Cambridge from or through London, he may well have taken advantage of the services of Thomas Hobson, who regularly transported goods and passengers between London and Cambridge.

Marlowe arrived in Cambridge in early December 1580 and spent a penny at the Corpus Christi College buttery for refreshment. This first record of his presence in Cambridge also marks the first of the many mutations his name would undergo in written records as he moved to new locations, for the debtor is identified as "Marlen." Nevertheless, it is clear from later records that this is a corruption or variant of Marley. Marlowe soon discovered that his new surroundings offered a number of amenities besides instant credit. The small quadrangle of Corpus Christi was not so grand as nearby King's College, but it provided more than adequate shelter from the raw December weather. Once a poor hostel, the college had gradually improved its buildings and grounds in the decades before his arrival, partly through the generosity of Archbishop Parker. Windows had been glazed, walls plastered and paneled, and the paths in the courtyard paved for easier crossing in wet weather. Marlowe's room had recently been converted from a storeroom to a residence for holders of three Parker scholarships, and was "repaired and finished for that purpose."[2] It would therefore have been more freshly outfitted than many of the other rooms in the college. A chimney and two flues had been installed in the room much earlier, in 1542.[3] Unlike students in earlier decades, Marlowe would not have been obliged to run up and down the halls to warm his feet.[4] To insure an atmosphere conducive to learning, Archbishop Parker provided firewood for the college in his will, as well as enriching its library with his books. Marlowe would have to share his new room with two strangers from Norfolk, but since he had once lived in a small house occupied by himself, his parents, numerous siblings, apprentices, and servants, he would hardly have felt cramped. His college may have been less imposing than some of its sister colleges, but it supported a vigorous intellectual life in a reasonably gracious style. To the shoemaker's son it must have seemed luxurious.

An inventory of furniture to be left in the rooms of "certaine Norwich

---

[2] John Bakeless, *Tragicall History of Christopher Marlowe* (Cambridge, Mass., 1942), 1:65.
[3] Ibid.
[4] Ibid., 1:58.

Corpus Christi College, Cambridge, ca. 1688. The college, known today as the Old Court, is still easily recognizable. Marlowe's room was located somewhere beneath the roof in the lower-right-hand corner of this view. Author's collection.

scholars" at Corpus Christi College gives us some idea of the interior of Marlowe's room:

ffirst ii several bedstedes corded	vs	
item ii matresses for the same	xiiis iiiid	
ii bolsters of Fethers	xiiis iiiid	
ii coverlets of Tapistry	vis viiid	ffor the
ii chaires of iii feete	xxd	first 2
a Table & iii Tressels	iis	Chambers
ii formes to the same	viiid[5]	

Like the student of 1541 whose meager possessions were catalogued by Bakeless,[6] Marlowe would have kept his clothing and personal belongings locked in the chest he brought with him from home. Whatever else he kept in that chest, his possessions must surely have included a second pair of shoes.

Before long, Marlowe would have begun to feel at home in Cambridge. After passing through the mass of humanity packed in the great metropolis of London, he was now back in a small community of about 5,000 (approxi-

---

[5] A. D. Wraight, *In Search of Christopher Marlowe; A Pictorial Biography*, photography by Virginia F. Stern (New York, 1965), 55.

[6] Bakeless, *Tragicall History*, 1:54.

mately 1,900 in the university itself) where people either knew or soon would know who he was. Here he had a face and a name, however often the name might be mispronounced and misspelled, and he had already achieved some small recognition by winning a scholarship, although many of his fellow students could say the same. His new surroundings were not as familiar and homey as the Marlowe household was, but he could look forward to support and encouragement in his studies. His young tutor Thomas Harris was an M.A. from Kent who had just taken his degree that year. Probably the new Canterbury scholar was assigned to Harris because they came from the same region; local ties were strong in the sixteenth century, and this shared background would help promote a cordial, productive working relationship between the tutor and his new charge.[7]

Since Marlowe's scholarship had not yet been vacated, the college came to his aid, paying his first weekly stipend of one shilling during the last week of December. On 17 March 1581 his name, still spelled "Marlen," was entered in the university matriculation book, and on 7 May "Marlin" was at last formally elected to his scholarship, as recorded in the Registrum Parvum of his college. Altogether, the college supported him for more than a full term beyond the twenty-four terms allowed by his scholarship. However, the amount paid him during this period, 17s, seems more or less counterbalanced by the payments he did not receive because of absences during his undergraduate years. As a graduate, of course, he was often absent, almost never collecting his full stipend for a term. The early payments were probably regarded as an advance against payments to be forfeited later, since students as a rule never collected the full amount of their scholarships. As long as a scholarship holder's payments did not exceed the full value of his scholarship, the college seems to have been flexible about when he received them.

Contrary to a common misconception, Marlowe was no older than most students matriculating at Cambridge.[8] According to a quantitative study of the age of matriculants at Oxford by Lawrence Stone, the average age of matriculation at the universities for students of plebeian background was slightly over eighteen, not fourteen as Wraight suggests.[9] Marlowe arrived in

[7] See Victor Morgan, "Cambridge University and 'The Country,' 1560–1640," in *The University and Society*, vol. 1, *Oxford and Cambridge from the 14th to the Early 19th Century*, ed. Lawrence Stone (Princeton, 1974), for a detailed discussion of the importance of local ties in the university. Morgan specifically mentions the connection of Corpus Christi College to Norwich, 196–205, but its ties to Kent and particularly to Canterbury were strong also.

[8] See Ingram, *Christopher Marlowe and His Associates*, 55, and Bakeless, *Tragicall History*, 1:66, for the origins of this idea.

[9] Lawrence Stone, "Size and Composition of the Oxford Student Body, 1580–1909," in *The University and Society*, 30–31; Wraight, *In Search of Christopher Marlowe*, 53, 64. As Stone notes in "The Educational Revolution in England," *Past and Present*, no. 28 (July 1964): 57, the most common ages for

Cambridge at sixteen and had only just turned seventeen when he matriculated, so he was actually younger than the average entering student of comparable socioeconomic background. Some of the very young students at the universities were precocious, but many of them were sons of gentlemen, noblemen, or wealthier families who could afford individual tutors or other private instruction; some, of course, were Catholics whose youth conveniently excused them from taking the oath of supremacy. Marlowe was not a hulking youth surrounded by striplings during his years at Cambridge. Many of the university students were far younger than students today, but a full 13 percent of the students entering the universities in the early 1590s were twenty-one or older.

Marlowe must have begun his studies almost immediately on his arrival. As in Canterbury, his education would not have been limited to the material formally assigned, but the general requirements for Cambridge degrees provide a useful starting point for determining what kind of knowledge he acquired during his university years.

As M. H. Curtis notes, the B.A. degree in the sixteenth century was often considered a preparatory degree for the M.A. rather than an end in itself; the B.A. program therefore stressed the basic skills needed to obtain the more prestigious and substantive M.A.[10] Students studied rhetoric during their first year, concentrated on dialectic in the second and third years, and began to read philosophy in their fourth year. Training in logic was based on Aristotle's dialectical works and Cicero's *Topics*, while philosophy had to include " 'The problems, ethics, or politics of Aristotle, Pliny, or Plato.' "[11] Since Marlowe spent three full terms and part of another at Cambridge in 1580–81, remaining there for the entire summer term, he began his second year in the first (Michaelmas) term of 1581–82, when he is listed as attending "Mr. Johnes" lectures in dialectic. He also seems to have maintained his progress toward the B.A. by attending the entire fourth or summer term for a second of his four undergraduate years, in 1583. Students often took breaks of at least two weeks, and often much longer, during the summer term, in spite of the university's strict attendance requirements. This informal policy apparently evolved because the marshy land surrounding the university bred epidemics that led to general dismissals more often during the summer months, rendering the university's official attendance policy unenforceable. When a stu-

students entering Caius and St. John's Colleges in the 1630s were sixteen and seventeen. Marlowe's age was therefore about average for all students.

[10] Mark H. Curtis, *Oxford and Cambridge in Transition, 1558–1642* (Oxford, 1959), 91.

[11] Ibid., 87.

dent attended the full summer term, he usually did it to make up for time lost during another term, or to accelerate his progress toward a degree.

As Curtis indicates, by the time Marlowe came to Cambridge, the respective colleges and individual tutors were assuming a larger role than ever before in the education of students. Partly because books and other printed material were more readily available to students, university requirements were less strictly observed than they had been in the past.[12] The college provided its own lectures and activities, which implemented and in some cases supplemented university requirements. A student might get better instruction in some subjects by attending lectures within his college or by working with his tutor than by attending the public lectures offered by the university, depending on the expertise of the fellows in his college.

A schedule prepared by Robert Norgate in the 1570s gives us at least an approximate idea of the daily routine within Marlowe's college, whether or not this schedule was ever actually implemented or still in effect when Marlowe studied there. According to Norgate's schedule, the scholars rose before five in the morning and spent the hour between five and six at morning prayer, which was a general practice throughout the university. On Wednesdays and Fridays, the chapel concluded with a "proof" by a fellow of a scriptural passage or commonplace, the evidence to be drawn from "Scripture and Doctors," which was also a common practice.[13] This was followed by a one-hour lecture on Aristotle's natural philosophy, while at noon, two Greek lectures, one "of construction, as Homer or Demosthenes or Hesiod or Isocrates; the other of the grammar," were scheduled. These lectures on philosophy and Greek were intended primarily for bachelors working on their second degree. At three in the afternoon, Norgate scheduled a lecture on rhetoric, with Cicero as the text, an offering Marlowe might have taken advantage of during his first three terms. The remaining hours of the day would have been spent attending university lectures, working with one's tutor, observing and eventually participating in the formal exercises or debates that made up part of the requirements for the degree, or studying privately.

The activities of Cambridge undergraduates were, in theory at least, extensively regulated, owing partly to the extreme youth of some of the students and partly to the monastic traditions of the university. Within their own rooms, students were not allowed to read irreligious books, or to play

---

[12] Ibid., 100–101.

[13] H. C. Porter, *Reformation and Reaction in Tudor Cambridge* (Cambridge, 1958), 50–51. For a fuller discussion of Norgate's schedule, see Richard Hardin, "Marlowe and the Fruits of Scholarism," *Philological Quarterly* 3 (1984): 387–400.

cards or dice immoderately during the Christmas holidays (indulgence in these pastimes moderately, or at other times, seems to have been acceptable), or to keep dogs or "fierce birds."[14] Rules forbade them to go beyond the walls of their colleges except to attend lectures in the public schools, or to walk into town unaccompanied by their tutors, or to leave the university for more than one month in a year.[15] While in town, they were not allowed to loiter, to go into taverns, to attend court sessions, or to witness boxing matches, dancing, cock fights, or bearbaitings.[16] Dress was restricted to a properly cut gown of "sad color." Swimming in the Cam or any other water in the county of Cambridge was forbidden, and in 1580 student football games were permitted only within "the precincts of their several colleges."[17]

This last restriction was imposed for good reason. A report dated May 1581,[18] written by the Chancellor Andrew Perne, alleges that some two years earlier Thomas Parish, head constable of the town of Chesterton, had sanctioned and encouraged an assault on Cambridge scholars during a football match at Chesterton between these scholars and the townsmen. According to Dr. Perne, the students had gone to the match peaceably and without weapons, but the townsmen had "layd divers staves secretly in the church-porch of Chesterton, and in playing did pike quarrels agenst the schollers, & did bringe owte there staves, wherewth they did so beat the schollers that divers had there heades broken, divers being otherwise greatly beaten, wear driven to runne through the river." The football game was apparently being played in the churchyard, a common practice. This same iniquitous Parish and his brother Richard were charged in another document with trying to protect a bearward (bear keeper) who had held a bearbaiting on a Sunday during sermon time.[19] The university's restriction of football playing was obviously intended to prevent further incidents like the one incited at Chesterton, and possibly clashes between students from different colleges as well.

Most of these rules were difficult to enforce, and, as the flagrant trespass of the bearward suggests, it is not likely that they were much more effective than present attempts to regulate student conduct. Ingram claims that bathing in the Cam was "a daily practice,"[20] although presumably not in the winter. The Duke of Stettin-Pomerania noted in his diary that the students

[14] Ingram, *Christopher Marlowe and His Associates*, 70.
[15] Ibid., 69; Bakeless, *Tragicall History*, 1:64.
[16] Ingram, *Christopher Marlowe and His Associates*, 70.
[17] Bakeless, *Tragicall History*, 1:52–54.
[18] BL Lansdowne 33, ff. 67–68.
[19] Ibid., f. 56.
[20] Ingram, *Christopher Marlowe and His Associates*, 75.

"perhaps keep more dogs . . . than they do books";[21] however, keeping dogs and "fierce birds" was presumably a luxury enjoyed by gentlemen scholars who could afford spacious lodgings rather than a common indulgence of students billeted three or four to a room. Chancellor Burghley's repeated attempts to enforce the dress code suggest that the level of compliance was alarmingly low.[22] The Buttery Books of Corpus Christi College reveal that students were often absent for much longer than their allowed month, and students were known to visit the Dolphin, Rose, and Mitre, which they proclaimed "the best tutors in the University."[23] Probably the tutors, who were supposed to oversee their charges' conduct but had only two eyes, devoted most of their attention to shepherding the very young students, and tacitly let the older students exercise their discretion. As a result, most of the rules governing student conduct suffered the same fate as the required attendance at university lectures. The extracurricular education of students was therefore less circumscribed than it might appear on paper.

Of course students were allowed other forms of recreation besides intramural football. Card playing and other pastimes were acceptable within reasonable limits, and the open meadow across the Cam, now known as "the Backs," was available for pleasurable strolls. Of more specific interest to Marlowe, plays were frequently performed, especially during the Christmas holidays, because of their potential educational value. Classical Latin comedies and Latin plays in general were favored, although plays in English were also performed. Some of these plays were composed by members of the university, such as the Latin *Richardus Tertius* by Thomas Legge, Master of Caius College. Thomas Nashe, who attended Cambridge at about the same time as Marlowe, later recalled three satirical plays written by students, *Pedantius*, *Duns Furens*, and *Tarrarantara*, which ridiculed the three Harvey brothers: Gabriel (a professor of rhetoric at Trinity College), Richard, and John. Plays by students also lampooned the mayor of Cambridge and other local citizens.[24] Farcical burlesque and satire seem to have been particularly popular forms.

Partly because of their close association with festivity, these performances were often occasions for disorder. Since the plays were staged in the halls of individual colleges, space for the audience was limited. Would-be spectators who could not (or would not) be seated frequently amused themselves by

[21] Bakeless, *Tragicall History*, 1:56.
[22] Ibid., 1:51–53.
[23] Ingram, *Christopher Marlowe and His Associates*, 75, citing Masson's *Life of Milton*.
[24] Bakeless, *Tragicall History*, 1:52–63; Ingram, *Christopher Marlowe and His Associates*, 76.

breaking the glass windows of the college. According to Nashe, when *Duns Furens* was acted at Peterhouse College, Richard Harvey avenged himself in the customary way: "*Dick* came and broke the Colledge glasse windowes," Nashe reports, and as a result was "set in the Stockes till the Shew was ended, and a great part of the night after."[25] Plays frequently gave rise to other types of violence as well, mainly personal assaults, and stage keepers armed with visors, steel caps, and sometimes weapons were posted to keep order. Even these measures were not always sufficient. Violence broke out at Marlowe's own college during at least two dramatic performances. The year before Marlowe arrived, a student named Punter, who had already disrupted performances at Caius and Trinity Colleges, dressed like one of the stage keepers at Corpus and assaulted a student of Trinity College.[26] In 1583, during Marlowe's residence, a scholar named Evance of Pembroke Hall was beaten with rods in Public School Street " 'because he had propounded scandalous, foolish, and opprobrious questions at the disputations of the questionists, and because he had made an assault with a club and had thrown stones when a play was exhibited in the College of Corpus Christi.' " In addition to his beating, Evance was sentenced to three days in prison " 'because he lay hid when sought for by the Bedel and had neglected to appear.' "[27]

If we may judge by his later taste for danger and conflict, Marlowe probably found the intellectual ferment and clash of personalities associated with performances of plays at Cambridge irresistible, and he must have involved himself in the staging of plays whenever he could. If he sampled the other, officially forbidden pleasures, which most students indulged in occasionally, he did so discreetly. The university records suggest that during his first three years at Cambridge, Marlowe devoted himself rather intently to his studies. Like other students, he spent the first year on rhetoric, reading Cicero and other works of classical literature chosen by his tutor to enhance his rhetorical skill.

At this time he would also have been introduced to the ideas of Ramus and Talaeus, for the Protestant Ramus had gained a wide following at Cambridge, especially among reformers. Gabriel Harvey was one of his most ardent proponents, and his tenets and methodology were frequently and hotly debated.[28] Marlowe would hear more about Ramus when he studied logic. His later depiction of Ramus in *The Massacre at Paris* suggests that he was fa-

[25] Quoted in Bakeless, *Tragicall History*, 1:63.
[26] Ibid., 1:63–64.
[27] Ingram, *Christopher Marlowe and His Associates*, 76.
[28] Wilbur Samuel Howell, *Logic and Rhetoric in England, 1500–1700* (Princeton, 1956), 178–79, 194–200.

miliar with the main criticisms of Ramus as well as with Ramus's answers to those objections, but he gives no sign of partiality in the dispute. Ramus apparently interested Marlowe more as a man than as a thinker, for he was the son of poor parents who had become a brilliantly successful scholar, an intellectual rebel who had challenged Aristotle's authority and converted to Protestantism. He was also, Marlowe believed, a sexual nonconformist to whom Talaeus was both a physical and intellectual "bedfellow" (*Massacre at Paris*, 9.12), as well as a martyr of sorts who paid for his unorthodoxy with his life. Marlowe's ambivalent fascination with this kind of figure, which was rooted in his early exposure to the ethical and political paradoxes of post-Reformation martyrdom, was one of the most characteristic and persistent features of his adult life.

Once Marlowe became an auditor of Mr. Jones's lectures on dialectic, he also began to attend and observe the disputations of other students. At the end of his first year of logic, he was required to debate twice himself, once as a respondent who defended three propositions, and once as an opponent who refuted the respondent. These debates were presided over by a master who acted as a moderator or "determiner"; the determiner summed up the students' arguments, evaluated their performances, handed down a final decision on the question, and occasionally intervened if the students had difficulty with their arguments.[29] Such exercises served many of the same instructional purposes as the student essay does today;[30] however, because they were composed in Latin and delivered orally, they also involved advanced language instruction and demanded at least modest declamatory skill.

Upon successful completion of these exercises, Marlowe was proclaimed a "general sophister" who had mastered the rudiments of dialectic. The "bold sharp sophister" then continued his studies and exercises in debate for a third year, performing once each term, after which he began his study of philosophy and completed the requirements for his degree.[31] During his last term he was required to debate four times, twice as a respondent and twice as an opponent. The final exercises of the "determining bachelors" were public occasions. Since they were the climactic demonstrations of the scholar's skill and knowledge, considerable effort was typically put into them.[32]

Marlowe also had to satisfy other requirements in order to proceed to his degree. To understand one of these, the residence requirement, we need to

[29] Curtis, *Oxford and Cambridge in Transition*, 88.

[30] Kenneth Charlton, *Education in Renaissance England* (London, 1965), 143.

[31] *Hero and Leander*, 197; Curtis, *Oxford and Cambridge in Transition*, 88–89.

[32] Curtis, *Oxford and Cambridge in Transition*, 90; Charlton, *Education in Renaissance England*, 143.

recall that the university year consisted of four terms: Michaelmas (October 10–December 16); Lent (January 13 until the tenth day before Easter); Easter (the second Wednesday after Easter until the Friday after commencement, which was held the first Tuesday in July); and vacation (from the end of the third term until October 10). During the fourth or vacation term, no public lectures or examinations were held because of the heat and the frequent epidemics, and students were unlikely to remain in residence for the entire fourth term unless they had some special reason for doing so. The university statutes required four years of residence for the B.A., and many students did take four years to complete their work. However, the *supplicat*, or formal request for advancement to the degree, specifies that the student has completed twelve terms (three full years of four terms each). The fact that many students did not attend the entire fourth or vacation term, and therefore would have needed more than three years to complete twelve terms, probably accounts for this discrepancy.

In 1579, the university tried to clarify the residence requirement by issuing a decree stating that any student enrolled in the university on or before the day of the sermon *ad clerum* at the beginning of Easter term would be considered a resident for that full academic year, and could therefore claim a *quadrennium completum*, or four years of residence, in the third Lent term after the sermon. (The decree, however, actually says "the fourth Lent next following the said sermon," which, if taken literally, would hardly have permitted Marlowe to proceed to his degree in 1584. Apparently, the Lent term immediately preceding the sermon was meant to count as one of the four.)

In addition to the completion of twelve full terms of residence, a condition that Marlowe had satisfied at the end of Michaelmas term 1583, the candidate for a degree had to appear in the arts school for questioning by the proctors and the regent masters of arts.[33] If he successfully passed this examination, his college then forwarded his *supplicat* to the Senate, which, when approved, would be followed by another examination. The second examination, however, was a mere ritual. The candidate appeared once more in the schools to answer a question posed by an officer of his college called "the father," the director of undergraduate studies. The "children," or scholars, would then proceed to answer his question in turn, proceeding from the eldest to the youngest. If "the father" tried to dispute any of their answers, the beadle drowned out his objections by beating his staff on the door.[34] We can therefore understand why this potentially fearsome enforcer, the beadle,

[33] Curtis, *Oxford and Cambridge in Transition*, 90.
[34] Ibid., n. 23.

whose custody Evance "lay hid" to evade, was feted annually by those students planning to graduate. Marlowe, as recorded in his college's Buttery Book, prudently contributed the customary shilling to the beadle's feast in the Easter term of 1583, the year before he would proceed to his degree.

We do not know what propositions Marlowe chose to defend in his final exercises, but unlike Evance, whom he may have seen beaten with rods in Public School Street, we can be sure that he wisely avoided any "scandalous, foolish, and opprobrious questions," however much he might have been tempted to offer one. While he had technically managed to take his B.A. in three years and could choose to end his education at this point without violating the terms of his scholarship, he had apparently already decided to proceed to his M.A. He therefore had more reasons than one not to risk offending his benefactors. The M.A. degree carried more weight than the B.A., and the continuation of his studies would give him time and opportunity to seek some suitable employment for himself outside the church. He had now seen more of the world, and he understood even more clearly than before that the vast majority of churchmen were wretchedly underpaid and overworked. Although educated clergymen enjoyed higher social status than a shoemaker such as his father, they might earn even less money.[35] Furthermore, positions in the church were not abundant. They required some expense and considerable effort to obtain. A young man like Marlowe, who still indulged in occasional daydreams of world conquest and incalculable wealth, could surely command more than a paltry £10 a year. He had earned almost half that much as a mere boy, a King's Scholar, and his present scholarship was worth more than some ecclesiastical livings.

Further study would also give him time for writing. He had probably not done a great deal of this while working on his B.A. beyond what was required for his exercises. Now that he had finished the first degree in just over three years, three additional years to take the M.A. would have seemed more than sufficient, affording him time to do what he liked best. If he could make money at it besides, so much the better.

Marlowe was listed at the bottom of the second group of Corpus Christi College graduates in the *Ordo Senioritatis,* or Order of Seniority. The precise meaning of this list is unclear. Since the graduates are grouped by their respective colleges but numbered consecutively throughout, the number assigned to each student (in Marlowe's case, 199) does not appear to indicate academic rank. The Corpus Christi graduates were divided into three groups separated by listings of scholars from other colleges, and these groups may

[35] Charlton, *Education in Renaissance England,* 161–62.

have indicated high, middle, and low rankings. If so, Marlowe was ranked in the middle of his graduating class of eleven. The numerical order assigned him is less significant than the fact that he took his degree, which many students did not, and did so in less than the normal time. This suggests that his performance as an undergraduate was not merely satisfactory, but creditable, and that he was well prepared to continue his studies.

Commencing M.A.

ACQUAINTANCES, FRIENDS, AND CONNECTIONS

These are my friends, in whom I more rejoice
Than doth the King of Persia in his crown.

Tamburlaine the Great, Part 1, 1.2.240–41

AS SOON AS MARLOWE met the requirements for his bachelor's degree in mid-February 1584, he acquired the new title of Dominus or Sir Marlowe— or, rather, Sir Marley, because Cambridge record keepers began spelling his name correctly more often around the time he took his first degree. Perhaps the new B.A., feeling that he had achieved some eminence and was therefore entitled to more respect, began to insist that his name be spelled and pronounced properly. If so, he must have been persistent, for it took more than a year for him to appear regularly in the Buttery Books as "Ds. Marly" rather than as "Ds. Marlin."

Marlowe's growing self-confidence, bolstered by the white furred hood his new rank entitled him to wear, may also be reflected in the fact that his attendance now became more erratic.[1] As an undergraduate he had taken

---

[1] John Bakeless reproduces the Corpus Christi Buttery Book entries regarding Marlowe in Appendix A of *Christopher Marlowe: The Man in His Time* (New York, 1937), 333–47. His printed version purports to be complete, but it is not entirely. Bakeless does not accurately quote the entry regarding "Sr Grenewood," for example, nor gloss the entry regarding the beadle, nor compare Marlowe's entries to those of other students in much detail, though he makes a few comparative comments. But since the Buttery Books are not entirely understood even today and cannot be adequately transcribed unless one undertakes the entire text, I have made no attempt to improve on Bakeless's printed version. It is adequate for most purposes. However, anyone undertaking a detailed comparison of Marlowe's expenses to those of other students will have to return to the original document.

Records of Marlowe's scholarship payments in the Corpus Christi Audit Books are discussed in a number of sources, but these records are most conveniently summarized in Bakeless, *Tragicall History of Christopher Marlowe* (Cambridge, Mass., 1942), 1:72–75.

only two significant breaks, the first for seven weeks during July and August of 1582, after nearly seven terms of almost continuous residence. Since many other students were absent at the same time, including Marlowe's fellow Parker scholar Thomas Lewgar, this absence might be attributed to one of the frequent epidemics that made a visit home seem opportune during the Cambridge summers. Or perhaps Marlowe was simply enjoying a long-delayed reunion with his family. His second extended absence as an undergraduate occurred in 1583, when he missed seven weeks at the end of Easter term. This time he left for unknown reasons, but the timing of the absence is closely mirrored by another absence in 1585, when virtually all the Corpus Christi scholars were absent.

After commencement in July of 1584, Sir Marley took his longest vacation yet, beginning in September and continuing until December. He returned for three weeks during the Christmas holidays, quite possibly to participate in the dramatic activities during that period, then disappeared again until late January 1585, at which point he seems to have resumed his studies in earnest. His new tutor, Henry Ruse, evidently regarded his twenty-one-year-old charge as an adult. This informal recognition of the maturity of older students led in 1608 to the dropping of all residence requirements for graduates on the premise that " 'A man once grounded so far in learning as to deserve a Batchelorship in Arts is sufficiently furnished to proceed in study himself.' "[2]

As a graduate student Marlowe continued his study of ethics and political philosophy. Natural philosophy and metaphysics were added to his reading list, along with astronomy, perspective, mathematics, and Greek.[3] Cosmography, astronomy, arithmetic, geometry, and perspective were treated as an academic cluster. Study of these subjects included the reading of Euclid, Ptolemy, Tunstall or Cardan in arithmetic, and Mela, Pliny, Strabo, or Plato in cosmography. Candidates for the master's degree were also required to attend disputations of regent masters of arts. They disputed three times with a master as an opponent, offered two responses, which were opposed by other candidates for the master's degree, and delivered a declamation.[4]

Such training might well make a man with settled beliefs into a subtle orthodox theologian, which was its primary intent. On the other hand, it might lead a person without firm religious convictions, someone perhaps like the young Christopher Marlowe, to entertain more profound doubts and to consider more dangerously original lines of thought than he had ever imag-

---

[2] Quoted in Mark H. Curtis, *Oxford and Cambridge in Transition, 1558–1642* (Oxford, 1959), 97.
[3] Ibid., 92.
[4] Ibid.

ined before. The range of ideas to which students were exposed was often greatly expanded by these formal debates. While they were reading Ptolemy, they might also be debating whether the earth was in fact in the center of the cosmos, or whether there was a plurality of worlds, to cite two topics disputed at Oxford in the 1570s and 1580s.[5] A student subjected to this regimen could reinforce his convictions by choosing to defend or oppose positions that suited his biases, although he could not escape being exposed, in the process of defense or opposition, to competing points of view. A student without strong beliefs, on the other hand, might well conclude, after witnessing and participating in a number of these formal exercises, that conviction was arbitrary and subjective, that individuals had a strong inclination to believe what they wanted to believe, and that truth, if it existed at all, had a protean capacity to elude the firmest intellectual grasp and the most sophisticated verbal nets. The shrewd and worldly wise man would therefore accept the limits of his knowledge, and, like a true Sophist and a sound Machiavel, learn to exploit the arbitrary beliefs of others for his own benefit.

Many of the intellectual activities at the universities that might foster a skeptical and pragmatic point of view in some students were of course extracurricular. By the time Marlowe went up to Cambridge, the intellectual ferment of his century was being felt in full force at both universities, including the intense and sometimes deadly religious controversies. Even before he left Canterbury, Marlowe was well acquainted with the crises of belief created by the Reformation, although his general awareness of these religious differences would have had little impact on his daily life. At Cambridge he was routinely exposed to religious conflict and debate, as well as to other intellectual disputes. Puritanism was strong at both Oxford and Cambridge, and crypto-Catholicism persisted at both in spite of vigorous efforts to suppress it. Cambridge, however, offered a climate somewhat more hospitable to religious nonconformity. In 1581, Oxford had adopted a Matriculation Statute requiring all matriculants of sixteen or older to subscribe to the Thirty-nine Articles. Cambridge, on the other hand, did not impose such a requirement until 1616, and then only on candidates for a degree.[6]

In this highly volatile atmosphere, debates involving large segments of the university community often arose spontaneously. In 1581, for example, a dispute at Cambridge between the Puritan Laurence Chaderton and the French-born theologian Peter Baro on the issue of free will and predestination caused a temporary stir within the university.[7] Marlowe would certainly

[5] Ibid., 233.
[6] Ibid., 194.
[7] Ibid., 213.

have heard about this through conversation with his fellow students if not through direct exposure to the arguments of Baro and Chaderton. This inconclusive debate, which was resumed with more significant consequences in 1595, may well have influenced Marlowe's ambiguous treatment of the problem of free will in *Doctor Faustus*.[8] Certainly arguments over predestination, which Whitgift's Lambeth Articles of 1595 tried unsuccessfully to resolve, persisted throughout Marlowe's youth and adulthood as well as after his death, and would certainly have been a familiar feature of intellectual life at Cambridge.

While he was deeply engaged in the intellectual ferment at Cambridge and working to complete the requirements for his degrees, Marlowe would inevitably have formed associations with other students. However, only one of these associations seems to have resulted in a lasting friendship, and that relationship probably began in Canterbury rather than Cambridge. During his years at Cambridge, Marlowe was in daily contact with his tutors, roommates, and students from his own and other colleges, and yet none of these individuals, as far as we know, exerted a critical influence on him. After he left the university, we have no evidence that he maintained close contact with anyone he met there.

Francis Kett, an eccentric fellow of Corpus Christi College whose residence overlapped Marlowe's by a few months, is sometimes suspected of influencing Marlowe's unorthodox beliefs. Such influence, while possible, does not seem highly probable. Kett was a fervently religious man who held or later developed anti-trinitarian views. About eight years after leaving Cambridge, he was burnt at Norwich for heresy. Marlowe's fellow playwright Thomas Kyd later alleged that a manuscript fragment of an anti-trinitarian argument found in his lodgings belonged to Marlowe, and anti-trinitarianism may have interested Marlowe because of its demystifying tendencies. Kett, however, was himself a possibly psychotic mystic who believed that Christ, although a man, would be "made God after his second resurration."[9] It is hard to imagine such a person leaving a deep impression on the pragmatic, ambitious Marlowe. Perhaps Marlowe met and conversed with Kett, who would have been quite noticeable in a small college like Corpus Christi. If Kett carried some aura of his impending martyrdom about him, he may well have piqued the curiosity of a new student who felt a powerful ambiva-

<hr>

[8] Gerald M. Pinciss, *Christopher Marlowe* (New York, 1975), 74. Pinciss develops this point in greater detail in *Forbidden Matters: Religion in the Drama of Shakespeare and His Contemporaries* (Newark, Del., 2000), 22–38.

[9] Bakeless, *Tragicall History*, 1:108.

lent attraction to such figures. Curiosity, however, is not the same as admiration or affection, and knowledge is not the same as influence.

Some evidence from Marlowe's first year at Cambridge suggests that he did take an interest in fellow students who harbored unusual and possibly dangerous ideas. The Corpus Christi Buttery Books, which record the amounts students paid for food and drink in addition to their regular commons, contain two unusual notations by Marlowe's name during the vacation term of 1581. The first accompanies a charge of 16 pence: "he left peetrs in commons being absent." On rare occasions, students might yield their places in commons to needy fellow students as a favor, and this first entry records one of these acts of accommodation by Marlowe. (The student receiving the favor, of course, would be expected to pay the 16 pence.) However, Marlowe yielded his place a second time only two weeks later, when another charge of 16 pence was added to his account with the notation "for putting Sr Grenewood in commons."[10] Although the first notation indicates that Marlowe was absent, the second does not, and in fact during both of these weeks Marlowe spent substantial sums on himself in the Buttery, more than he spent during any week of the Easter term. Apparently he was not absent for long, if at all, and while his yielding to Peters may have been merely a courtesy, his accommodation of "Sr Grenewood" is more intriguing, for this Greenwood was no ordinary student.

"Sr Grenewood" was apparently John Greenwood, later to be executed, like Kett, for his religious beliefs.[11] The title "Sr" or "Sir," the English equivalent of the Latin "Ds." or "Dominus," was reserved for students who had fulfilled the requirements for the bachelor's degree, and in July of 1581 Greenwood was scheduled to take his bachelor's degree at commencement. He did not plan to proceed to the M.A., but was not ordained until 1582. This presumably put some strain on his finances, and he must have welcomed the help of friendly fellow students until he could formally claim his degree and secure a living. Greenwood later became a radical Puritan activist and separatist who was jailed along with Henry Barrow for his outspoken views. During the height of the Marprelate controversy, he and Barrow authored and disseminated a number of tracts while in prison. Barrow was suspected by some of being Martin Marprelate, although this is far from certain. Later, after being freed, Greenwood and Barrow joined forces with John Penry, another suspected author of the Marprelate tracts. All three were apprehended

---

[10] Bakeless very inaccurately reprints this in *Christopher Marlowe*, 336.

[11] This identification is also made by William Urry, *Christopher Marlowe and Canterbury* (London, 1988), 59–60.

and subsequently executed in 1593, Greenwood and Barrow in late April and Penry on 29 May, the day before Marlowe himself died. Although Greenwood, like Kett, was destined for an ambiguous martyrdom, his sanity is indisputable, for his few surviving writings are cogent and incisively argued.

Perhaps Marlowe was struck by the forceful, confident manner that rings so distinctly in Greenwood's prose, and offered this impressive person access to the inexpensive fare of his old college as a means of learning more about him. Marlowe was hardly a Puritan, but unorthodox religious views of all kinds intrigued him as an adult, and this interest was apparently already active during his first year at Cambridge. It is possible that Greenwood, Penry, and Marlowe all knew each other as students. Penry was Marlowe's and Greenwood's contemporary at Cambridge, taking his bachelor's degree from Peterhouse in 1584, the same year Marlowe took his first degree from Corpus Christi, and then moving on to Oxford for his M.A. The execution of Greenwood, Barrow, and Penry shortly before Marlowe's death is one of those tantalizing conjunctions in Marlowe's life that lead nowhere in particular given our present knowledge, but seem well worth keeping in mind.

Thomas Nashe, whose vigorous, eccentric prose has earned him a secure niche in English literature, was certainly one of Marlowe's university acquaintances. Nashe arrived at Cambridge not long after Marlowe, where he studied at St. John's College between 1582 and 1588. He refers to Marlowe several times in his writings by his familiar nickname "Kit," and recalls their mutual distaste for the two elder Harvey brothers, Gabriel and Richard, who were fellows at Cambridge during Marlowe's and Nashe's tenure as students. Nashe is credited with co-authorship of *Dido, Queen of Carthage* on the title page of the 1594 edition, and there may be some basis for the attribution. Marlowe and Nashe shared an interest in poetry and drama, and both aspired to be professional writers, although Nashe's personality was in many respects quite different from Marlowe's. Nashe was a poor clergyman's son who largely depended on the good will of patrons to survive. He was therefore critical, even scornful, of extreme religious opinions, but his flair for the grotesque, outrageous, and absurd gave him a temperamental affinity with Marlowe that might well have overridden their religious differences. Still, Nashe's passing references to Marlowe do not suggest that they were in close contact after leaving the university. Nashe seems to have been more closely associated with Robert Greene, to whom he makes detailed, affectionate references. If Nashe and Marlowe did collaborate on *Dido*, this probably occurred while they were students.

The one firm, lasting friendship that Marlowe apparently formed or strengthened at Cambridge has passed almost entirely unnoticed. The omis-

sion is not surprising, because the other party in this friendship is obscure, and to recognize the relationship we have to piece together information from several documents. Urry, who first noted some indications of this association, cautiously called it a "possible connection."[12] This friend was a young man from Canterbury named John Benchkin, whose arrival at Cambridge was recorded in the Registrum Parvum or admission book of Corpus Christi College on 30 June 1585.[13] The admission records describe Benchkin as a fellow commoner who ate with the scholars. Since a fellow commoner paid for his own education, most fellow commoners were wealthy gentlemen who ate at the master's table. Perhaps Benchkin was not yet able to afford this luxury, or perhaps he chose to eat with the scholars because he wanted to associate with one of the students in that group, Christopher Marlowe. Judging from what we know of Benchkin's background and his later history at Corpus Christi, the latter possibility seems highly likely.

Benchkin was born in 1567 and was therefore about three years younger than Marlowe.[14] He was the son of the late James Benchkin, who had been lay clerk in the Canterbury cathedral choir and had also held the office of beadle, or general agent, of the dean and chapter of the cathedral, collecting rents and other monies due from the manor of Monkton on the Isle of Thanet. The elder Benchkin had held other posts, including constable, and was once involved in illegal trade in grain,[15] but at the time of his death in 1582, judging from the inventory of his property, he was primarily a dealer in wool and woolen cloth.[16] His second wife, Katherine, was a kinswoman of the wife of Thomas Greenleaf, a shoemaker well known to the Marlowes. It was Greenleaf who, as master of the shoemaker's company, would resort to legal action against John Marlowe in 1591 over his deficient treasurer's accounts.[17]

In mid-July, a few weeks after John Benchkin's admission to the college, Marlowe's name disappears from the Buttery Books of Corpus Christi and does not reappear until mid-September. During this two-month absence, far from being engaged in spying, which some of his biographers have suggested he might have been doing during his longer absences from Cambridge, he

[12] Ibid., 57.
[13] Portions of the following discussion of Marlowe's friendship with John Benchkyn, and of the discussion of his relationships to Thomas Watson and Nicholas Faunt in chapter 4, first appeared in "Second Selves: Marlowe's Cambridge and London Friendships," *Medieval and Renaissance Drama in England* 14 (2001), ed. John Pitcher. They are included here by permission of the publisher, Fairleigh Dickinson University Press.
[14] Benchkin's year of birth can be determined by a deposition dated 2 December 1617 (CCA DAC X.11.15, 245b–247b) in which he gives his age as fifty.
[15] William Urry, "Christopher Marlowe and Canterbury" (unpublished manuscript).
[16] The inventory of James Benchkin's goods, CKS PRC 10/10, ff. 740–50, which provides this information about his profession, is transcribed in the appendix.
[17] Urry, "Christopher Marlowe and Canterbury."

was evidently visiting his family, as students tend to do during long vacations. During this stay in Canterbury, which may well be connected to John Benchkin's earlier arrival at Corpus Christi College, Marlowe read aloud and signed the will of John's mother, Katherine Benchkin, thus helping his friend secure his inheritance. This will, when combined with the depositions later given by the three other witnesses and the inventory of the property of John Benchkin's father, James, allows us to re-create this afternoon of Marlowe's life in extraordinary detail. Indeed, these records document a few hours of Marlowe's life far more minutely than the coroner's report of 1593 records the day of his death.

Mrs. Benchkin lived in a large house near the southeast end of Stour Street in Canterbury, a long street running parallel to the western branch of the Stour River.[18] The house was a short walk from St. Mildred's churchyard, where Mrs. Benchkin wished to be buried near her husband, James, and from the ruins of Canterbury's old Norman castle. According to the inventory of James Benchkin's property dated 30 November 1582, the house contained seven large rooms and a wool loft. The parlor where Marlowe read and signed Mrs. Benchkin's will was elaborately furnished when the inventory was taken, and probably looked the same in August of 1585. James Benchkin the chorister, not surprisingly, had owned several musical instruments, one of which, a "pair of virginals," stood in the parlor. The room also contained a joined press and two small cupboards, a round table with nine stools that would have been convenient for signing the will, two matted chairs, cushions, a table with the queen's arms on it, and a fireplace furnished with tongs, andirons, bellows, and a pot hanger. In that fireplace, according to the witnesses' later depositions, Mrs. Benchkin burned her old will in their presence. The walls of the parlor were decorated with painted cloths and a map. Two calivers, a cuirass, and two helmets were on display. Other items in the room included a Bible, a testament, a Book of Common Prayer, three dozen trenchers, and a little casket of bone. Stored in other rooms of the house were weapons that a young man like John Benchkin might have enjoyed showing off to his friends—especially a friend like Marlowe who was interested in the art of war and was perhaps already writing a play about Tamburlaine's conquests. These included a dag (pistol) with a case, four swords, two daggers, a halberd, a poleax, two bills, and three javelins.

We can reconstruct the sequence of events at the signing of the will in detail because three of the four witnesses—John Marlowe, his brother-in-

---

[18] The location and dimensions of Mrs. Benchkin's house are discussed in detail in ibid.

The Norman castle, Canterbury. Marlowe read and signed Katherine Benchkin's will a short distance from these ruins, part of which still stand. From William Gostling, *A Walk in and about the City of Canterbury*, 1777.

law Thomas Arthur, and his son-in-law John Moore—described the signing in depositions taken in late September and early October of the following year. Christopher, who had returned to Cambridge, was not available to depose. The three depositions differ slightly, but John Marlowe's account is detailed and probably quite accurate. According to his deposition, the signing of the will took place on a Sunday "abowte a twelmonethes agon or moe." The will is dated 19 August 1585, which was indeed a Sunday a little more than a year before the deposition. John Marlowe recalled that John Benchkin asked him to go to Mrs. Benchkin's house, and when he arrived with his apprentice Thomas Arthur he found that his son Christopher and his son-in-law John Moore were already there. If this detail is correct, it suggests that at first only the two younger men were asked to witness the will, since two witnesses were normally sufficient. However, someone decided to summon the two older men as well, perhaps because Christopher might not be available to testify if the will were contested. Since John Benchkin was indeed later obliged to prove the validity of the will and the witnesses were asked to give depositions, we might ask why John and Katherine Benchkin anticipated this problem.

At least two explanations are possible. One is that John Benchkin was not Katherine's biological son, although he was James Benchkin's natural son, which might well cause Katherine's relatives to object to her making him the executor and chief beneficiary of her will. Since she sometimes refers to John in her will as "the sonne of my late husband James Benchkin," this is at least a possibility. The will might also have been contested because of the circumstances of its preparation. Unlike James Bissel and Thomas Hudson, who wrote the wills of John and Katherine Marlowe, the preparer of Katherine Benchkin's will does not identify himself or represent himself as an additional witness. One possible explanation for this is that John Benchkin himself wrote out Katherine's will. John was certainly competent to perform this task; probably he was a former paying scholar at the King's School. Furthermore, in a document in the Canterbury archives dated 2 December 1617, John Benchkin, then fifty years old, deposed that at the request of Sir Thomas Harflete, Knight, who was sick in bed on the eighteenth of September, he had written out his will, returned with it the next day, and read it aloud to him, whereupon Sir Thomas had signed it, declaring it to be his last will and testament.[19] But since in the case of Katherine's will the writer was also the executor and chief beneficiary, this might arouse suspicion and make it necessary to prove the validity of the will. John therefore recruited more witnesses among his friend Christopher's relatives.

The depositions of John Marlowe, John Moore, and Thomas Arthur provide further details about this day. According to Moore and Arthur, Mrs. Benchkin appeared to be in "very good health." Upon their arrival, she went immediately up into a chamber of her house, probably the richly furnished bedroom situated over the parlor whose contents are described in the inventory of James Benchkin's property, and returned with two wills. She threw her old will into the fire and burned it in the presence of the witnesses, then took her new will to Christopher Marlowe and asked him to read it aloud. This request appears to have been an intentional compliment to Christopher's superior scholarship, since he had just taken his B.A. the year before. Marlowe obligingly read the long and detailed will aloud; Moore, to emphasize that the witnesses fully understood the provisions of the will, declared that he read it "plainely and distinctly."[20] Mrs. Benchkin than proclaimed this to be her last will and testament, revoking and disannulling all previous wills. She sealed the document, made her mark, and asked the witnesses to sign it.

A closer look at the will reveals further details of the ceremony.[21] Someone added a notation, "This is Katherine Benchkyns mark," to Katherine's mark. The writing characteristics of this sentence closely resemble those of

[19] CCA DAC X.11.15, 245b–247b.
[20] John Marlowe's and John Moore's depositions are transcribed in full in the appendix.
[21] Katherine Benchkin's will is transcribed in full in the appendix.

Christopher Marlowe's signature. The signatures of the witnesses follow a strict hierarchy. John Marlowe—the eldest, the father of Christopher, and the master of the apprentices Arthur and Moore—signed first. Arthur—the next oldest and Christopher's uncle—signed next. Christopher signed third, probably in deference to his learning and his status as the master's eldest son. John Moore, John's son-in-law, signed last. In the presence of his family and friends, Christopher could evidently be as gracious and punctilious as the most orthodox Elizabethan, whatever subversive and rebellious thoughts he may have entertained in private.

When Marlowe returned to Cambridge in mid-September, John Benchkin apparently went back up with him, for his name first appears in the Corpus Christi Buttery Books at the same time Christopher's reappears. The two spent very similar amounts in the buttery for about a month, and then, two weeks into Michaelmas term, Benchkin left. Probably Mrs. Benchkin's failing health made it impossible for him to continue his studies at this time. He rejoined Marlowe at Cambridge during Christmas week, when no instruction was taking place, left the following week, returned the week before Lady Day, and left again. This time Christopher left also, and did not return until mid-June.

Mrs. Benchkin died the following month and was buried at St. Mildred's, as she had stipulated in her will, on 25 July 1586. By early October, John Benchkin was involved in a legal action to establish the validity of her will. John Marlowe, Thomas Arthur, and John Moore all deposed in John's behalf, and the will was allowed to stand. After observing the traditional year of mourning and putting his affairs in order, John returned to Corpus Christi College in 1587 to begin his studies. By that time his friend Christopher had taken his M.A., and since John was now enjoying the comfortable life his inheritance afforded him, he enrolled as a fellow commoner. According to the Corpus Christi Audit Books, he secured his place at the master's table by presenting half of a large silver cup weighing 14½ ounces in lieu of the normal fee of 26s 8d.

Like many gentleman students, John took no degree; however, he seems to have had a genuine passion for learning, for he is still described as a student at Cambridge in a legal document of 1592.[22] In all probability, after attaining his majority John gradually established himself as a dealer in wool and wool cloth, like his father. On Friday 29 May 1594, exactly a year after his friend Christopher's death on 30 May 1593, he applied for a license to marry Katherine Grawnte of Kingston, a village a few miles from Canterbury. Evidently he

[22] Urry, *Christopher Marlowe and Canterbury*, 59.

continued to reside in St. Mildred's parish, probably in the same house Mrs. Benchkin occupied, for several years afterward; his children Thomasyn, Thomas, and Katherine were christened at St. Mildred's in 1596, 1598, and 1605. However, by 1617, when he gave evidence concerning the preparation of Sir Thomas Harflete's will, he indicated that he lived in Woodnesborough, a small town near Sandwich.[23] Such a residence would be convenient for a merchant actively engaged in the wool trade.

These facts about John Benchkin suggest several conclusions. He seems to have been a close friend of Marlowe, probably before John went to Cambridge. The similarity of their movements in 1585–86 suggests that they made a deliberate mutual effort to spend time together. One wonders, indeed, if John went back to Cambridge during the Christmas holidays, when he certainly would not have received any instruction, for the specific purpose of enjoying the festivities and dramatic performances with his friend, and possibly even of seeing one of his friend's plays performed. His application for a marriage license exactly a year after Marlowe's death might indicate that he observed a formal period of mourning for Marlowe, a significant token of affection and respect.

One other probable acquaintance of Marlowe's may be conveniently introduced in connection with Marlowe's years at Cambridge, although it seems rather unlikely that Marlowe met him there, as Nicholl and Kendall suggest he may have.[24] This is Richard Baines, probably the same man who twice accused Marlowe of blasphemous and seditious ideas and intentions, especially in the notorious "Baines Note" of 1593. Even if Richard Baines of Cambridge is not the author of the note, as the evidence currently available suggests he was, his life has a number of curious links to Marlowe's.

Richard Baines of Cambridge was a product of the same destabilizing social and intellectual forces that fostered Marlowe's heterodoxy, although his quest for meaning took a rather different course. Baines, who was approximately ten years older than Marlowe, matriculated at Christ's College in 1568. After taking his B.A. in 1572–73, he chose to pursue his M.A. at Caius College. This move is the first hint of Baines's Catholic sympathies, for the founder of this college, Dr. John Caius, was notoriously sympathetic to Catholicism, and many Catholic activists, including John Ballard of the Babington plot, were educated there. Ballard was in fact at Caius at the same time as Baines. Baines's younger brother (or kinsman) Thomas followed him

[23] Urry found a document indicating that he was residing in Woodnesborough in 1602; see "Christopher Marlowe and Canterbury."
[24] Charles Nicholl, *The Reckoning* (London, 1992), 131; Roy Kendall, "Richard Baines and Christopher Marlowe's Milieu," *English Literary Renaissance* 24 (1994): 530–31.

to Caius in 1577, and from the record of Thomas's matriculation at Caius we learn that Baines was born and educated in Southwell, Nottinghamshire, probably the son of John Baines, yeoman.[25] Later, Baines would turn to an old acquaintance from Southwell, William Ballard, for help in procuring a benefice.

After Baines completed his M.A. in 1576, we find no further record of his movements until 1578, when he entered the English College in Rheims shortly after its removal there from Douai. The mission of this seminary and of its president, Dr. William Allen, was, of course, to reclaim England for Catholicism. In addition to publishing and disseminating tracts and other materials in English, the college trained activist Jesuit priests, "soldiers of Christ," who would bring aid and comfort to English Catholics and win back converts until Elizabeth could be deposed or assassinated and replaced by a Catholic monarch. Since the activities of these priests were regarded as seditious and treasonous by the English government, they lived in constant peril. If they succeeded in returning to England—many were intercepted when they attempted to gain entry—they were hunted down relentlessly. Many if not most of them were captured, tortured, and executed—or forced to become double agents. The English College itself led a precarious existence because of unstable religious and political conditions in continental Europe. It was forced out of Douai when the Spanish lost control of the town, and as soon as it relocated in Rheims it became a primary target of English espionage and subversion under the direction of the secretary of Queen Elizabeth's Privy Council, Sir Francis Walsingham.

We cannot be certain why Baines went to Rheims. Charles Nicholl assumes that he was an agent of Walsingham's from the beginning, as Dr. Allen and his fellow seminarians believed.[26] While this is certainly possible, it is also possible that Dr. Allen's paranoia blinded him to the facts. Much evidence suggests that Baines was initially a sincere Catholic whose desire to become a priest was completely genuine. His move to Caius College to take his M.A. while at Cambridge was probably not arbitrary, and the fact that his younger kinsman, Thomas, followed him to Caius suggests that his entire family may have been partial to the old faith. Furthermore, he made no effort to secure a living in the English church immediately upon graduation, which most holders of the M.A. did. He may have postponed going to the English College because Douai was notoriously unsafe during late 1576 and

[25] *Alumni Cantabrigienses, Part 1*, compiled by John Venn and J. A. Venn (Cambridge, 1922–27), vol. 1.

[26] Nicholl, *The Reckoning*, 122–26, 131.

1577.[27] After the college relocated at Rheims in 1578 under the protection of the Duke of Guise, he went there immediately. At first he seems to have progressed smoothly toward ordination. Among his fellow seminarians was William Clitherowe, the brother-in-law of Margaret Clitherowe, the martyr of York, who suffered "peine fort and dure" in 1586 for refusing to plead on a charge of harboring priests. Baines was ordained in 1581, Clitherowe in 1582.[28] Although Clitherowe was never implicated in a major plot against the queen, English newsgatherers were acutely suspicious of him and followed his movements closely. As we shall see, Clitherowe and Baines became close enough to carry on a correspondence a few years after Baines left Rheims.

At some point before his ordination, Baines apparently became disillusioned with Catholic orthodoxy, just as he had been dissatisfied with the English church before or during his years at Cambridge. He may have been a perpetual malcontent who was inclined to resent any form of authority; personalities of this type were common enough in the Renaissance, and Marlowe had more than a touch of this inclination himself. Or perhaps the critical faculties Baines had honed at Cambridge left him dissatisfied with any belief system. Whatever its cause, this wavering of purpose posed a serious problem for Baines, for he had ventured to the end of a very long limb: he was deeply implicated in a movement whose professed aim was to overthrow his own government. Virtually the only way to escape a charge of treason was to turn informer against the Catholics. This rather obvious strategy was evidently adopted by many discontented English priests besides Baines, as we can gather from a letter that Sir Robert Sidney, then governor of Flushing, wrote to William Cecil, Lord Burlegh on 22 March 1592/93, fourteen months after he wrote another, better-known letter to Burlegh concerning Marlowe:

> This bearer Walter Marsh having bin a certen time in the seminary at Reims (as he tels me) and finding at the last his error came hether from Cales voluntarily to yeald himself unto me and tels me that he wil discover matters which do greatly concearn her Ma:[jesty] and the State of England.[29]

A "Banes" appears on a list of "sundry Englishmen, Papists, presently abiding in Paris," dated 27 April 1580. The same list also identifies Baines's friend Clitherowe as a "Great Practiser."[30]

[27] Mark Eccles, *Christopher Marlowe in London* (Cambridge, Mass., 1934), 143–44.
[28] William Allen, *The First and Second Diaries of the English College, Douay* (Westmead, Hants., 1969), 11.
[29] PRO SP 84/144, f. 145. The full text of this letter is transcribed in the appendix.
[30] *Calendar of State Papers, Foreign Series, Elizabeth I*, 14 (1579–1580), no. 279, 250–52.

After his ordination in September 1581, Baines began to plan his escape to England and tried to persuade one of his fellow seminarians to defect with him. This unnamed friend was probably William Clitherowe, but whoever he was, Baines misjudged him seriously. To win his friend over, Baines, who later confessed to indulging in a variety of sacrilegious thoughts and practices, ridiculed what he considered erroneous or misguided Catholic beliefs and rituals. He argued that the seminary's existence was precarious and that it could not last long, and suggested that he and his friend would be handsomely rewarded if they gave the English government information about the seminary. According to his first informal confession, Baines believed that such discoveries about the seminary would earn him fame and respect, a post in a noble household, and a reward of 3,000 crowns. Somewhat ambiguously, he suggested to his friend that the entire seminary might be destroyed by poison, and that it would therefore be unsafe to remain there. Baines then tried to persuade his superiors to finance his trip back to England, professing eagerness to begin his holy work.

Unnerved by these overtures, Baines's friend betrayed him. Baines was interrogated, at which time he presumably gave his first, comparatively matter-of-fact statement. He was then imprisoned and tortured in order to extract a confession that he had plotted to murder Dr. Allen, for as Allen explains in a letter to Alphonso Abazzari, they could not keep Baines in jail under civil authority for any length of time unless they could produce evidence of criminal intent: "And unless he had added certain words about killing me, etc., it would not have been possible to punish him for heresy alone."[31] Baines seems to have resisted making this confession, for the evidence indicates that he was tortured repeatedly. As an anonymous informant wrote in May 1582, "Banes has had the strapedo and is often tormented."[32] Perhaps he resisted in an attempt to minimize his guilt, but it is also possible that he resisted because he had never seriously intended to kill anyone. Years of living in mortal peril had made Allen acutely suspicious and ruthless; he suspected the worst about Baines—that he had been a spy from the beginning—and was determined to justify his suspicions. Perhaps this theory was easier for him to accept than the thought that Baines had been alienated by life in his seminary, which is probably closer to the truth.

Finally Baines capitulated. He wrote a statement confessing his misdeeds

<hr>

[31] Kendall, "Richard Baines," 551–52. This well-researched article contains much new information about Baines. However, the tense of the verb—pluperfect subjunctive—is translated as present tense, which alters the precise shade of meaning. I have corrected this.

[32] Ibid., 518.

in the precise theological terms Allen dictated. He asked Allen and others to pardon him, but still avoided directly stating that he had intended to kill anyone, nor did he admit that he was sent to the seminary as a spy. Rather, he states, "Such were my plans and diabolic conversations. I cannot say whether they were to take effect at this time or whether the devil was leading me to reveal all this to the Queen's Council with a view to removing the president and overturning the whole seminary."[33] While this falls short of a plain declaration of murderous intent, it evidently satisfied both Allen and the civil authorities in Rheims. Eventually Baines was released and allowed to return to England.

Although Baines was denied the triumphant homecoming he had dreamed of, his dearly bought experience was still marketable, and soon he was participating actively in Walsingham's intelligence network. In September of 1586, he was corresponding with his old acquaintance, the now ordained Father William Clitherowe, using the pseudonym Gerard Bourghet.[34] In exchange for books and other information, Clitherowe reported to Baines on the activities of Catholic exiles. However, Baines seems not to have been paid well enough for this work, or perhaps he felt the need for more economic stability, for in 1587 he approached William Ballard of Southwell, an old acquaintance from his hometown. According to Ballard, Baines claimed to be "destitute of anie staye of lievinge," and asked Ballard to help him procure the benefice of Waltham, Lincolnshire, promising to reimburse Ballard for any expenses he incurred in securing this living. Ballard obligingly secured the benefice for Baines, spending twenty pounds in the process, but by 1590 Baines still owed him the twenty pounds. Ballard then tried to recover this sum by petitioning the lord chancellor, Sir Christopher Hatton, to hear his case in the Court of Chancery.[35]

Baines was not a licensed preacher, which meant that he had not taken the oath of allegiance to the doctrine of the English church required in order to obtain a license to preach.[36] Probably he remained somewhat alienated from both Catholicism and Anglo-Catholicism, but he regarded his M.A. degree, like his experience in France, as a marketable commodity. If he was the man who informed on Marlowe, he also continued to be involved, at least occasionally, in intelligence work, for in 1592 a Richard Baines was Marlowe's chamber fellow in Flushing—a nexus in the flow of information to and from

[33] Ibid., 544.
[34] Constance Brown Kuriyama, "Marlowe's Nemesis: The Identity of Richard Baines," in *"A Poet and a filthy Play-Maker": New Essays on Christopher Marlowe* (New York, 1988), 352–53.
[35] PRO C2 Eliz I, Bundle B7/8.
[36] *The State of the Church in the Reigns of Elizabeth and James I, as Illustrated by Documents Relating to the Diocese of Lincoln*, ed. C. B. Foster (Lincoln, 1926), 311; David Williams, introduction to *John Penry: Three Treatises Concerning Wales*, by John Penry (Cardiff, 1960), xiii–xiv.

the Continent—and of course in late May 1593 the same Richard Baines submitted his list of allegations about Marlowe's conversation and opinions. We shall return to Baines when we consider the last two years of Marlowe's life.

As Marlowe moved toward the completion of his M.A. in the spring of 1587, he had surely begun to give serious thought to the next stage of his life. Like the young Richard Baines, if for rather different reasons, he had no intention of entering the English church, and presumably no desire to be a schoolmaster either, although a number of graduates who did not become clergymen or could not immediately secure a benefice at least tried to teach. Since Marlowe's poetic skill had earned him some recognition even in grammar school, he must have developed a powerful desire to become a writer. We have good reason to believe, on the basis of its immature style, that he wrote *The Tragedy of Dido, Queen of Carthage* while at Cambridge, with or without Nashe's collaboration. By November 1587, judging from a reference to a scene in a letter by Philip Gawdy, *Tamburlaine the Great, Part 2* had already been staged in London, just months after Marlowe took his M.A. degree in July. It is possible that part 1 of *Tamburlaine* was performed as early as 1585, but certainly it was written while Marlowe was still a student. Quite conceivably, so was part 2, though it may well have been written in haste after he left Cambridge to capitalize on the success of part 1. If we also accept the traditional view that Marlowe's translation of *Ovid's Elegies* belongs to the university period—although the only evidence we have for this is their rather slapdash execution—Marlowe must have devoted considerable time to writing while he was at Cambridge. At least some of his absences after taking his B.A. may have been devoted to placing *Dido* and *Tamburlaine, Part 1* with acting companies in London.

Because of his family's precarious finances and his long years as a student, Marlowe was an economic realist. He knew that even the great Spenser needed patronage and additional employment to support his career as a poet, and that a novice like Christopher Marlowe had the same or greater needs. He therefore must have invested some time during his last year at Cambridge in seeking a means of support that would also allow him time to write. In this process he would no doubt have used whatever connections from his native "country," Kent and Canterbury, were available to him, just as Richard Baines had turned to William Ballard, a fellow townsman of Southwell, to help him secure his benefice.

Marlowe's efforts to find some kind of secular employment were successful, but his last long absence from Cambridge during the weeks before he was to take his M.A. degree gave rise to a rumor that he had turned Catholic, and the Cambridge authorities threatened to withhold his degree. On 29 June

1587 the Privy Council intervened on his behalf, as indicated by a notation in the Acts of the Privy Council:

> Whereas it was reported that Christopher Morley was determined to have gone beyond the seas to Reames and there to remaine their Lordships thought good to certefie that he had no such intent, but that in all his acions he had behaved him selfe orderlie and discreetelie wherebie he had done her Majestie good service, and deserved to be rewarded for his faithfull dealinge: Their Lordships request was that the rumor thereof should be allaied by all possible meanes, and that he should be furthered in the degree he was to take this next commencement: Because it was not her Majesties pleasure that anie one emploied as he had been in matters touching the benefitt of his countrie should be defamed by those that are ignorant in th'affaires he went about.[37]

This document may be much less significant than it seems. It tells us that Marlowe had performed some service for the queen. It also tells us that he was rumored to have gone to Rheims, as Baines and other Catholic sympathizers had done. It does not say that he actually went to Rheims, although many of Marlowe's biographers have assumed that he did, nor does it suggest that his services were in any way extraordinary—only that his work was beneficial to his country and faithfully performed, and therefore deserved to be rewarded. The fact that the Privy Council exerted itself to help Marlowe—presumably at his request—is not in itself unusual. The council often intervened in the most trivial affairs of individual subjects, and a threat to withhold someone's M.A. degree was not trivial. Furthermore, since Lord Treasurer Burghley was chancellor of Cambridge, he was a person to whom Marlowe might logically appeal.

While we might like to imagine that Marlowe was involved in some glamorous game of espionage, in fact this is rather unlikely. The men who worked for Walsingham, especially those he assigned to sensitive and critically important operations, were cunning, seasoned, ruthless professionals. A student just finishing his M.A. degree would be a poor choice for a major assignment: as Baines had learned to his cost, Rheims was a perilous place for an amateur to play spy. Furthermore, many of the papers of the seminary have survived, including records of arrivals and departures, and they show no trace of a Christopher Marlowe arriving there in 1587.

[37] This document is fully reproduced and discussed further in the appendix.

· 4 ·

A Poet's Life in London

❧

The sight of London . . .
Is as Elysium to a new-come soul.

Edward II, 1.1.10–11

As my friend says, "The necessary qualifications for being a poet are arrogance and inexperience." I had lots of those types of qualifications.

Leonard Cohen

WHEN MARLOWE TURNED his thoughts to London in the spring or early summer of 1587, he must have relished the prospect of choosing his own lodgings for the first time. In Canterbury and Cambridge, others had determined his living arrangements. London, in contrast, offered a dazzling array of options. Donald Lupton's description of the city gives an indication of its seemingly infinite possibilities: "She's certainly a great world, there are so many little worlds in her; She is the great beehive . . . of England; She swarms foure times in a yeare, with people of all ages, Natures, Sexes, Callings. . . . She seems to be a Glutton, for she desires always to be Full."[1] The challenge was to find a suitable nook in this omnivorous "great world" without being swallowed up by it.

By 1587, London's rapidly growing population had reached approximately 175,000. Within the city and its suburbs were a host of traditional enclaves, Lupton's "little worlds" where citizens plied their various trades and professions. The medieval custom of living near one's work, which was conducted either in one's household or within a comfortable walking distance of it, still prevailed. For writers, of course, the choice of living quarters was relatively flexible, but a playwright hoping to keep informed of the latest trends might

[1] Quoted in John L. McMullan, *The Canting Crew: London's Criminal Underworld, 1550–1700* (New Brunswick, N.J., 1984), 18.

However tempting it might be to concoct a spy scenario with Marlowe as its hero, the nature of his "service," considering his youth and inexperience, was probably far more routine. Marlowe was well qualified to be a messenger or letter carrier, and this is probably exactly what he was asked to do, for a large number of men of widely different backgrounds were employed in this capacity. Marlowe was well educated and geographically sophisticated, and he may also have acquired some knowledge of one or more foreign languages during his childhood in Canterbury—French being most likely because of Canterbury's sizable Huguenot population. Judging both from his probable use of French sources in *The Massacre at Paris* and from the garbled snatches of French conversation remaining in its highly corrupt text, Marlowe had more than a passing acquaintance with French.[38]

Furthermore, there was a strong tendency in the Renaissance to protect people who were recognized as having special talent. Queen Elizabeth's intervention in Sidney's plans to travel to the New World is only one particularly well known instance of this practice. If Marlowe was hired as a messenger partly to give him the leisure to pursue a promising literary career, it is unlikely he would have been asked to perform highly dangerous and sensitive tasks. Significantly, after decades of research we have found no evidence that Marlowe played a major role in any of the numerous intelligence operations mounted in the late 1580s and early 1590s. Unless such evidence is discovered, the only logical conclusion is that Marlowe's involvement in Elizabethan newsgathering was strictly lower-level.

How did Marlowe find such employment? Almost certainly through a personal connection. Sir Roger Manwood, a native of Sandwich who established himself in Canterbury and at Hackington, just outside Canterbury, as his career flourished, has often been mentioned as a powerful individual who might somehow have aided Marlowe. However, there is no evidence of any special connection between Marlowe and Manwood. It has also been suggested that Thomas Walsingham, Sir Francis's cousin and later Marlowe's patron, might have helped Marlowe secure a place in government service. After all, Thomas worked for his cousin Sir Francis between 1580 and 1589, spending much of his time carrying letters to and from France and making some minor contribution to the exposure of the Babington plot before inheriting his father's estate in 1589. Unfortunately, we have nothing to indicate that Marlowe knew Thomas Walsingham before 1592–93.

A far more likely connection for Marlowe to have used in seeking government-

[38] See Julia Briggs, "Marlowe's *Massacre at Paris*: A Reconsideration," in *Review of English Studies* 34 (1983): 257–78, for a discussion of possible French sources.

ment work was Nicholas Faunt, the secretary of Sir Francis Walsingham. Although the *Dictionary of National Biography* incorrectly states that Faunt was from Norfolk, it is clear from Cambridge records and other sources that he was a native of Canterbury. A Nicholas Faunt is identified as one of Mr. Gresshop's scholars at the King's School—a contemporary of Stephen Gosson—in the *Registrum Matthei Parker, Diocesis Cantuariensis*.[39] Like a number of other King's School graduates, Faunt proceeded to Cambridge in 1572 at the age of eighteen, where he first matriculated at Caius. The college admission book identifies him as a pensioner, the son of John Faunt of Canterbury, and a graduate of Canterbury school. Later the same year he obtained a scholarship and moved to Corpus Christi College, where he completed his B.A. in 1575–76. Evidently he secured some government employment, for he spent the next few years in France (perhaps, like Marlowe, making use of the French he had first learned in Canterbury). While there, he met Anthony Bacon, who became his friend and regular correspondent, and witnessed the Saint Bartholomew's Day Massacre. Sir Francis Walsingham was also in France during the massacre, and not long afterward, in about 1580, Faunt became his secretary.

Although Faunt left Corpus Christi before Marlowe arrived, Marlowe would surely have known about him and was probably acquainted with his family. Since Faunt had secured a rather glamorous secular post after graduation from Marlowe's college and shared so much of his background with Marlowe, he was an ideal contact for Marlowe to use in his quest for similar (if less steady) employment. In other words, he was likely to prove a "friend" in the distinctly Elizabethan and Jacobean sense—"someone who can be helpful in advancing one's career or prospects."[40] There is no reason to speculate, as Nicholl does, that Faunt came to Cambridge to recruit agents and met Marlowe there.[41] The ties between the two men were much older and ran far deeper.

The Privy Council's letter in support of Marlowe took immediate effect. He received his degree in July, as planned, and moved on to London anticipating still greater triumphs. Later, perhaps, he would remember his Cambridge years as a golden age, because, for all his brash Machiavellian cynicism, Marlowe had spent most of his first twenty-three years swathed in a

humanist cocoon, his pride and ambition continually fed by and literary success. In London he would confront another, les predictable world whose malign power and indifference he had sensed in childhood, a world that could have little respect for l even less regard for his life.

---

[39] *Registrum Matthei Parker, Diocesis Cantuariensis*, ed. W. H. Frere (Oxford, 1928), 535.

[40] Miriam Slater, *Family Life in the Seventeenth Century* (London, 1984), 34–35.

[41] According to Nicholl, *The Reckoning*, 119, Faunt returned briefly to France in early 1587, at about the same time Marlowe was absent from Cambridge. However, the entry on Faunt in the *Dictionary of National Biography* dates Faunt's trip to Paris in 1588.

prefer to live near a theater. In 1587, only one neighborhood preeminently satisfied this requirement—the large suburb just north of the old city wall outside Bishopsgate, sometimes called Shoreditch after a section of its principal thoroughfare. Soon if not immediately after leaving Cambridge, Marlowe settled in this area, specifically in the liberty of Norton Folgate, which was directly adjacent to Shoreditch. This location was not only suitable for a budding playwright, but also offered certain advantages to those who trafficked in information.

Shoreditch, like Norton Folgate, was one of the areas known as liberties, which became preferred sites for the theaters in Elizabethan London. Although the sheriff, aldermen, and lord mayor of London had jurisdiction over most of the city, certain areas both inside and outside the city walls were traditionally exempt from municipal control. These liberties became natural havens for activities that the more sober and puritanical citizens of London—or other political interest groups—wanted to suppress. The south bank of the Thames, also known as Bankside or Southwark, was a rowdy entertainment district notorious for its bull-and bearbaiting rings, taverns, and houses of prostitution. Within the next decade and a half, most of the London playhouses, including Shakespeare's Globe, would locate there, but in early 1587 the first of these, the Rose, had hardly advanced beyond the planning stage.

During the 1580s, theatrical activity in London was centered in the liberty of Halliwell or Holywell, north of Bishopsgate and adjacent to Norton Folgate. There James Burbage built the Theatre in 1576 as an alternative to the established practice of staging plays in inn yards. When this venture flourished, another playhouse, the Curtain, named after a nearby section of the city wall, sprang up just south of the Theatre. A community of actors, managers, and playwrights quickly gathered around these playhouses. Shakespeare, the comedians Tarlton and Kempe, and many other actors and writers associated with the theaters lived in this area in the late sixteenth and early seventeenth centuries.

Probably our most revealing source of information about this neighborhood is a section of a map engraved by Franciscus Hogenborg in about 1559. The area it shows may be somewhat less densely populated than it was by the time Marlowe settled there in 1587, and the theaters, which were built to the north of the area shown on the map, did not yet exist, but in general the area's physical features would have remained the same.

The Hogenborg engraving depicts an open, park-like suburban area with a row of houses lining both sides of a wide north-south thoroughfare. This street was divided into three subsections, only two of which are identified on the engraving: Bishopsgate Street extends north to Norton Folgate, which is not labeled, and Norton Folgate almost immediately becomes Shoreditch. A short distance north of Bishopsgate stands the church of St. Botodolph without Bishopsgate, where Edward Alleyn, the great actor who played Marlowe's Tamburlaine, Faustus, and Barabas, was baptized. A short distance north of St. Botodolph's is Bedlam mental hospital, and scattered around these major landmarks are several large houses with spacious attached gardens. Other details suggest the quality of the residents' daily life. Grossly oversized horses and a cow graze in fenced pastures. Numerous garden plots are visible, separated by fences and hedgerows, one of which contains an apiary. A sow and her piglets trot along Hog Lane. Several large formal pleasure gardens lie next to St. Mary's Hospital, one of which appears to be terraced. Two wells are located in the main street for the convenience of residents. Two windmills grind in Finsbury Fields, and numerous paths crisscross the spacious open greens. The recreational uses of the fields are clearly indicated on the map: archers practice in Moorfields and Finsbury Fields to the west of Bishopsgate Street, and also in Spitalfields to the east. In the western section of Spitalfields is the musket range known as the Artillery Yard, prudently enclosed by a high wall; within it marksmen fire their muskets into thick, banked targets.

A 1607 pamphlet, *The Pleasant Walkes of Moore-fields* by Richard Johnson, provides more information about this area. According to Johnson, Moorfields and Finsbury Fields were given to the city of London by the two daughters of Sir William Fines, a knight of Rhodes during the reign of Edward the Confessor (more probably, Edward I). These women, Mary and Katherine, became nuns in the priory of the Order of Sisters and Brothers of the Star of Bethlehem (later Bedlam hospital). On their deaths, they left their lands to the city "for an ease to the Cittizens, and a place for their servants to dry clothes in," specifically "Merchants' maides . . . which want necessary gardens at their dwellings," and also, according to the pamphlet, "builded the two crosses, the one at Bedlem gate, the other at Shoreditch."[2] The cross at Shoreditch is clearly visible in Hogenborg's engraving at the corner of Shoreditch and Hog Lane. We can also see a number of maids spreading their linen out to dry in the southern portion of Moorfields. Johnson mentions several improvements to these properties in the early seventeenth century which Marlowe did not live to see: the creation of formal, walled paths; the planting of over two hundred trees by various citizens; and the installation of stocks to punish anyone who would "lay any filthy thing within these

---

[2] Richard Johnson, *The Pleasant Walkes of Moore-Fields* (1607), reprinted in *Illustrations of Early English Popular Literature*, ed. John Payne Collier (London, 1864), 6.

fields, or make water in the same, to the annoyance of those that walke therein; which evil savors in times past have much corrupted man's senses, and supposed to be a great nourisher of diseases."[3] In Marlowe's time, it seems, the breezes wafting through Moorfields were not always sweet. Indeed, "this field, until the third year of King James, was a most noysome and offensive place, being a generall laystall . . . burrowed and crossed with deep stinking ditches and noysome common shewers, and was of former times held impossible to be reformed."[4]

Demographically this neighborhood had a decidedly mixed character. According to Stow's *Survey of London*, the section near St. Mary's Hospital, just southeast of Hog Lane in the small liberty of Norton Folgate, contained "many faire houses" belonging to "worshipful persons."[5] The Hogenborg engraving confirms Stow's account, for in it this area looks particularly well appointed and prosperous. The fact that local maids needed the open spaces of Moorfields to dry their linen suggests that a number of merchants lived in the area. However, not all the residents of Shoreditch were equally "worshipful." The theaters were created by, and also attracted, a freewheeling, anarchic breed, as the men who tried to collect money from the Burbages in 1589 quickly discovered. When the would-be collector first approached them, he was threatened and driven away by a volley of "great and horrible oaths" from James and Cuthbert Burbage.[6] He returned with reinforcements, but Richard Burbage and his mother were unimpressed. Instead of paying up, they "beat him with a broom staff, calling him a murdering knave"; and when his companion protested, "the said Richard Burbage, scornfully and disdainfully playing with this deponent's nose, said that if he dealt in the matter, he would beat him also."[7]

The area also harbored characters even more unsavory than these roguish theatricals. Robert Greene's mistress Em Ball, described as "a woman of verye bad reputacion," and by Gabriel Harvey, more incisively, as "a sorry ragged queane," lived very near the theaters in Holiwell Street.[8] Em's brother "Cutting" Ball—presumably a cutpurse who worked the crowds in and around the theaters—was eventually hanged. According to Harvey, Greene employed him and a gang of toughs "to guarde him in daunger of Arrestes."[9]

[3] Ibid., 8–9.

[4] John Stow's *Survey of London*, quoted in Fran C. Chalfant, *Ben Jonson's London: A Jacobean Placename Dictionary* (Athens, Ga., 1978), 131.

[5] Quoted in A. D. Wraight, *In Search of Christopher Marlowe; A Pictorial Biography*, photography by Virginia F. Stern (New York, 1965), 106; the Hogenborg engraving is reproduced on 106–7.

[6] John Bakeless, *Christopher Marlowe: The Man in His Time* (New York, 1937), 100.

[7] Ibid.

[8] Mark Eccles, *Christopher Marlowe in London* (Cambridge, Mass., 1934), 124–5.

[9] Ibid., 124.

The area was in fact notable for prostitution, and one or more of the large houses with attached gardens shown on Hogenborg's engraving may have been upscale bawdy houses. Indeed, no form of entertainment was overlooked. In Hoxton, just to the north of the theaters, Roger Holland kept a house specializing in male prostitution.[10]

The plays staged in this area, when added to its numerous other attractions, were a powerful magnet for habitual troublemakers, including apprentices on holiday. Incidents such as the one Justice of the Peace William Fleetwood reported to Lord Burghley in June of 1584 were not unusual: "Very nere the Theatre or Curten, at the tyme of the playes, there laye a prentice sleping upon the grasse and one Challes alias Grostock dyd turne upon the too upon the belly of the same prentice; whereupon the apprentice start up, and after wordes they fell to playne bloues."[11]

Often the connection of these disturbances to the playhouses was more direct. Burbage, for example, was indicted in 1580 for creating "unlawful assemblies" (stage performances) which incited "affrays and tumults leading to a breach of the peace."[12] McMullan's characterization of such neighborhoods as "thriving deviant centers" seems well supported by the evidence.[13]

The comparatively lax law enforcement in Middlesex County also made the area surrounding the playhouses a convenient locale for assorted covert operations. In May 1586, about a year before Marlowe moved to London, Mrs. Francis Browne lent her house in Hog Lane, a narrow street running east from Norton Folgate, to Father William Weston, a Catholic priest carrying out his mission in England.[14] Weston, like Marlowe, was a native of Kent; some fourteen years older than Marlowe, he was ordained in 1579—the same year Richard Baines arrived at Rheims. Weston traveled extensively on the continent, visiting Douai, Rome, and Spain before returning to England in 1584 to begin his ministry. Probably not coincidentally, one of Walsingham's most cunning and successful spies, Robert Poley, was living in the vicinity at the same time, where he was actively engaged in the exposure (or was it entrapment?) and arrest of the Babington conspirators. When Weston was arrested on 3 August 1586, the two agents who apprehended him were lying in wait for Anthony Babington and John Ballard, two key figures in the Babington conspiracy, who, at the time, were hiding in Poley's house.[15] Ballard was

[10] McMullan, *The Canting Crew*, 139.

[11] E. K. Chambers, *The Elizabethan Stage* (Oxford, 1923), 2:396.

[12] Ibid., 2:397.

[13] McMullan, *The Canting Crew*, 20.

[14] William Weston, *An Autobiography from the Jesuit Underground*, trans. Philip Caraman (New York, 1955), 75 n. 3; 78–79 nn. 18, 19.

[15] Ibid., 79 n. 21.

arrested the following day. Presumably this house of Poley's was the same one where young Thomas Walsingham, later Marlowe's patron, received messages from his cousin Sir Francis Walsingham through Poley, and also met the conspirator Ballard.[16] Poley was still living in Shoreditch in 1591 and writing from nearby Hogsdon in 1597.[17] Not coincidentally, one suspects, Anthony Bacon, who took charge of the Earl of Essex's intelligence operations in 1593, settled in Bishopsgate in 1594. However, its proximity to the Bull Inn, which was regularly used as a playhouse, so alarmed Bacon's mother that he was obliged to move to Chelsea the following year.[18]

Even after the Rose on Bankside became the theater where Marlowe's plays were most often performed, the liberties of Norton Folgate and Holywell remained an attractive location for Marlowe. The neighborhood retained some of its original pastoral character, yet provided easy access to everything the city had to offer. Bishopsgate Street led south through London and down to the Thames. It became Gratious Street, Grace Church Street, Fish Street, and eventually crossed London Bridge into Southwark, providing a relatively direct route to the Rose. While strolling south, Marlowe would have passed the Bull, the Bell, and the Cross Keys Inn, where *The Jew of Malta* was performed in late 1589.[19] A turn to the right would take him to St. Paul's Churchyard, a bustling marketplace and cultural center. There one could buy tobacco, browse in the booksellers' stalls, listen to sermons and proclamations at Paul's Cross, meet and converse with friends, or seek employment. A turn to the left, on the other hand, would lead along Little Eastcheap and Tower Street to the Tower, where Marlowe could admire the ordinance and the forbidding architecture and muse on the power of the crown.

While we lack a detailed record of Marlowe's daily life during the years he lived and worked near the Theatre and Curtain, we can draw some reasonable inferences from what we do know. Since he maintained a steady and substantial literary output, he must have spent a fair amount of time writing. *Tamburlaine the Great, Part 1*, his first major play, may have been staged at the Theatre even before he moved to London. If it was not performed until he arrived, he must have written the sequel very quickly, for, as the prologue to part 2 states, "The general welcomes Tamburlaine receiv'd / . . . Hath made our poet pen his Second Part" (ll. 1–3). If the incident reported in Philip Gawdy's letter to his father dated 16 November 1587 indeed refers to the exe-

[16] John Bakeless, *Tragicall History of Christopher Marlowe* (Cambridge, Mass., 1942), 1:162.
[17] Ibid., 1:178; Eccles, *Christopher Marlowe in London*, 127.
[18] *Dictionary of National Biography* (London, 1921–27).
[19] Quoted in Bakeless, *Tragicall History*, 1:105.

cution of the Governor of Babylon in *Tamburlaine, Part 2*, then the sequel was already on the stage within months after Marlowe's arrival in London:

> My L. Admyrall his men and players having a devyse in ther playe to tye one of their fellowes to a poste and so shoote him to deathe, having borrowed their Callyvers one of the players handes swerved his peece being charged with bullett missed the fellowe he aymed at and killed a chyld, and a woman great with chyld forthwith, and hurt an other man in the head very soore.[20]

Gawdy did not actually witness this incident, but his description corresponds closely to this episode in part 2 of *Tamburlaine*. However, even if *Tamburlaine* is not the play referred to in Gawdy's anecdote, Robert Greene certainly had part 2 in mind when he referred scornfully to "daring god out of heauen with that Atheist *Tamburlan*" in his preface to *Perimedes the Blacksmith*, licensed on 29 March 1588.[21] Nashe, Marlowe's former fellow student at Cambridge, may also have been alluding to Marlowe in his preface to Greene's *Menaphon* (published in 1589, and possibly first in 1587), in which he scoffed at "idiote art-masters" who are "mounted on the stage of arrogance" and vent their "cholerick incumbrances" in "the spacious volubilitie of a drumming decasillabon."[22] In less than a year of Marlowe's graduation, then, both parts of *Tamburlaine* had been successfully performed on the London stage, and he had excited the vehement envy of at least one established playwright, Robert Greene, who immediately linked him to the expression of unorthodox views. From all indications this was a banner year for Marlowe.

Between 1588 and 1592, Marlowe's career continued to flourish. He wrote *Doctor Faustus, The Jew of Malta, The Massacre at Paris*, and *Edward II* at the rate of slightly less than one a year. Unfortunately, while *Tamburlaine* obviously comes early and *Edward II* late, we cannot determine the exact sequence of these plays. *The Jew of Malta* was being performed in late 1589 and was probably written earlier the same year. The weight of argument in recent publications favors a relatively early date for *Doctor Faustus*, quite plausibly 1588–89,[23] which would leave 1590–91 as the likely slot for *The Massacre at*

---

[20] Ibid., 1:199.
[21] Ibid., 1:195.
[22] Ibid.
[23] John Henry Jones, introduction to *The English Faust Book*, (Cambridge, 1994), 52–72; David Bevington and Eric Rasmussen, introduction to *Doctor Faustus: A-and B-Texts (1604–1616)* (Manchester, 1993), 1–3.

Paris. Probably *Dido, Queen of Carthage*, along with Marlowe's translations of Ovid and Lucan, were completed during Marlowe's years at Cambridge, but one or both of the poetic translations may also belong to the London period. While this was not an enormous output, the quality and theatrical appeal of Marlowe's work was consistently high. All his plays except *Edward II*—which was sold by the company that owned it, Pembroke's Men, after the outbreak of plague in 1592—were popular successes that continued to be revived long after Marlowe's death. During the late 1580s and early 1590s, Marlowe was the most admired, envied, and widely imitated playwright in London.

Given the rowdiness of the theater district, we might expect the author of *Tamburlaine* to be in his element, but during the nearly seven years that Marlowe lived in and frequented this area, he was apparently involved in only two quarrels. The second of these was a relatively minor incident that did not occur until 1592, when Marlowe was experiencing a series of frustrations and disappointments. The first and far more serious clash occurred on 18 September 1589, between two and three o'clock in the afternoon. Most of our information about this episode comes from two documents discovered by Mark Eccles, a gaol delivery and a pardon for Marlowe's fellow poet Thomas Watson, both of which incorporate the text of the coroner's inquest on the death of William Bradley. According to this report a certain Christopher "Morley" of London, gentleman, was fighting with William Bradley in Hog Lane, in the parish of St. Giles without Cripplegate. This parish lay in Finsbury Fields, to the west of the residential section of Hog Lane. Although Finsbury Fields were regularly used for archery practice, as depicted in the Hogenborg engraving, they were also a favorite spot for dueling. According to the coroner's report, Thomas Watson of London, gentleman, alerted by the shouts of the crowd that had gathered around the combatants, approached them, drawing his sword to separate them and restore the queen's peace. Marlowe promptly desisted and withdrew. Bradley, on the other hand, "seeing the same Thomas Watson thus intervening with his drawn sword said to him in the following English words, 'Art thou now come? Then I will have a bout with thee.'" Bradley then attacked Watson with sword and dagger, wounding him so badly that he despaired of his life. Watson tried to cope with the assault by edging away from his furious opponent, but soon he found himself pinned against one of those "deep stinking ditches" that Johnson describes and Hogenborg clearly depicts, which effectively cut off his escape route. In a desperate attempt to save his own life, Watson thrust his sword into the right side of Bradley's chest near the nipple, inflicting a mortal wound six inches deep of which Bradley, in the formulaic language of Elizabethan coroner's reports, "then and there instantly died."[24]

The coroner's report necessarily stresses details suggesting that Watson killed as a last resort, because to secure a pardon Watson had to claim that he had acted in self-defense. Still, since numerous witnesses observed the fight, Watson's claim of self-defense must have been plausible enough that no one ventured to challenge him. This was not an unusual outcome of an Elizabethan street fight, for, according to McMullan, witnesses in Renaissance London were generally reluctant to become involved in legal proceedings— especially, one suspects, in neighborhoods like Shoreditch; for this and other reasons, the rate of prosecutions and convictions was quite low.[25] Furthermore, the "special" pardons granted in pleas of self-defense were profitable to the crown, which made courts quite receptive to such pleas.[26]

As is often the case with the documents that provide our information about Marlowe, these documents discovered by Eccles only raised more questions. Who was William Bradley? Why were he and Marlowe fighting? Why did Watson intervene? And why did Bradley turn so viciously on a man who was merely trying to break up a fight? In an attempt to answer these questions, Eccles found records of Bradley's christening and burial in St. Andrew's parish, Holborn. At the time of the fight he was twenty-six years old. His father, William Bradley Senior, was the host of the Bishop Inn, at the corner of High Holborn and Gray's Inn Lane. The younger William had a history of violent quarrels, and, according to a petition he filed at the court of the Queen's Bench sometime in the summer of 1589, he was in fear of death at the hands of Hugo Swift, John Alleyn, and Thomas Watson, and asked that they be bound to keep the peace.[27] The language of the petition is conventional, but it tells us that Bradley and Watson had been involved in a conflict before they met in Hog Lane. Eccles further discovered that Bradley owed money to John Alleyn, the brother of Edward Alleyn and manager of the Theatre. Hugo Swift was Alleyn's attorney and Watson's brother-in-law, and Watson, a sometime playwright, must have known John Alleyn through his connections with Swift and with the Theatre. The earlier quarrel was probably related to Bradley's failure to pay Alleyn, and Alleyn's attempt to recover his money in court.

This partly explains why Bradley turned on Watson with such fury. It does not explain why he was fighting with Marlowe. Perhaps Bradley was looking

---

[24] The full text of Watson's pardon is transcribed in the appendix.
[25] McMullan, *The Canting Crew*, 46.
[26] Ibid., 47.
[27] Eccles, *Christopher Marlowe in London*, 57–58.

for Watson and found Marlowe instead, as Eccles suggests,[28] but this is only one possibility. Bradley's irrational behavior not long after lunchtime suggests that he may have been drinking, in which case he might have fought with anyone in sight. Perhaps Watson intervened because he knew Bradley, or perhaps he intervened because he knew Marlowe. Watson and Marlowe were certainly acquainted, and probably well known to one another. They were both poets and playwrights, they lived in the same neighborhood and were associated with the same players; and, as we shall see, they shared other ties as well.

Once Marlowe and Watson realized that Bradley was dead, they waited until the local constable, Stephen Wyld, arrived. Leaving the scene of a killing was generally considered an admission of guilt, so in order to make a plea of self-defense tenable, it was essential to stand one's ground. Apparently it was impossible to hold an inquest on Bradley's death that afternoon, so Marlowe and Watson were confined to Newgate Prison until an inquest could be arranged the next day. The record of their commitment by the local justice of the peace gives us more information: "Thomas Watson of Norton Folgate in Middlesex County, gentleman, and Christopher Marlowe of the same, yeoman, . . . were delivered to jail the 18th day of September by Stephen Wyld, Constable of the same on suspicion of murder, that is, for the death of [blank] and were committed by Owen Hopton, Knight."[29] Marlowe and Watson were evidently near neighbors, since they both resided in the small liberty of Norton Folgate, quite possibly in the densely populated Hog Lane. It is interesting that Sir Owen Hopton recognized Watson as a gentleman, but classified Marlowe as a yeoman. Since Elizabethans tended to gauge a person's status by dress, manner, and appearance, perhaps Watson was the more elegantly outfitted of the two, or perhaps Sir Owen knew him personally. The error was corrected in subsequent records of the case, all of which describe Marlowe as a gentleman. It is also significant that Hopton left a blank space for the name of the victim. Eccles suggests that Marlowe and Watson might have been suspected of malice aforethought because the investigators were aware of the feud between Bradley and Watson,[30] but initially, at least, this was not the case. The constable had no idea who the dead man was, and Watson, for obvious reasons, did not bother to enlighten him.

When the coroner's inquest convened the following day, the coroner and jury accepted Watson's claim that he had acted in self-defense. Marlowe was then eligible for bail, since he had not killed Bradley and was no longer suspected of being an accomplice to murder. After spending twelve more days in

[28] Ibid., 59.
[29] The full text of this record is transcribed in the appendix.
[30] Eccles, *Christopher Marlowe in London*, 59.

Newgate, Marlowe found two bondsmen to stand surety for him, as recorded in the Middlesex Sessions Rolls on 1 October 1589: "Richard Kitchen of Cliffords Inn, gentleman, and Humphrey Rowland of East Smithfield . . . , horner, came before me, William Fleetwood, . . . and put up bail for Christopher Marley of London, gentleman . . . on condition that the same aforesaid Christopher personally appear at the next Newgate Session to answer to all things that may be objected against him on the part of the said Lady the Queen." Each of the sureties agreed to pay a penalty of £20, and Marlowe himself of £40, should he fail to appear.[31]

The speed with which Marlowe secured bail indicates that his stay in prison was probably tolerable. Although conditions in Elizabethan prisons were vile, and Newgate had a particularly evil reputation, a prisoner with money could garnish his way to accommodations that were somewhat more comfortable. The bribes required to secure better quarters amounted to a few shillings, while for ten shillings a week one could purchase abundant food.[32] If this fare proved too expensive, one could buy food from street vendors or beg for handouts from charitable passersby. Only indigent prisoners suffered the direst effects of imprisonment, and Marlowe was far from indigent.

Apparently Marlowe found his stay in Newgate not merely endurable but instructive. In 1592, he told Richard Baines "that he was acquainted with one Poole a prisoner in Newgate who hath greate skill in mixture of mettals and having learned some thinges of him he ment through help of a cuning stamp maker to coin French crownes, pistoletes and English shillinges." This counterfeiter was no doubt John Poole, who, as Nicholl indicates, was also a Catholic.[33] Such a combination of profession and religious affiliation was not unusual. Catholics who clung to their faith were heavily penalized financially under Elizabeth; furthermore, the lives that many led in exile, and the various schemes they entertained to replace Elizabeth with a Catholic monarch, created a demand for funds that would have been difficult to meet legally. Poole was also related by marriage to Ferdinando Stanley, Lord Strange, a suspected crypto-Catholic whose players performed Marlowe's plays.[34] Marlowe would later claim that he was "very well known" to Lord Strange.

Marlowe's first brush with the law ended in uneventful formality. He made his required appearance at the Old Bailey, the central criminal court, on 3 December 1589. The court accepted the findings of the coroner's jury and Marlowe was free from any further legal obligations, while Watson pre-

[31] The full text of this document is transcribed in the appendix.
[32] Gamini Salgado, *The Elizabethan Underworld* (London, 1977), 168.
[33] Charles Nicholl, *The Reckoning* (London, 1992), 240–44.
[34] Ibid., 243.

sumably returned to Newgate to await his pardon. However, the notation "balliatus" by his name in the Newgate calendar suggests that he may eventually have been bailed.

The Bradley incident, and Thomas Watson's involvement in it, is a valuable clue to Marlowe's intricate network of associations in London. Probably Marlowe knew Watson well, and Watson was drawn into the fight with Bradley out of friendship and concern for Marlowe, as Eccles assumed, as well as out of antipathy for Bradley, but how did Marlowe form this friendship with Watson? Their mutual involvement in writing plays and poems does not seem sufficient in itself to explain this. But as we sift through the evidence we find that Marlowe's new London acquaintances were closely allied and interconnected, to the point where a discussion of any one of them leads naturally and almost inevitably into a discussion of another. Before we consider Watson, it seems best to return to Marlowe's probable job contact at Cambridge, the Canterburian and Corpus Christi alumnus Nicholas Faunt.

Faunt, like his master Sir Francis Walsingham and unlike Marlowe, was a staunch Puritan. He was born in Canterbury around 1554, attended the King's School, where he studied with Stephen Gosson under Marlowe's first master Mr. Gresshop, and matriculated at Caius College, Cambridge, in 1572. However, instead of beginning his studies immediately he traveled to France, where he witnessed the St. Bartholomew's Day Massacre and brought news of it back to England.[35] In 1573 he became a scholar of Corpus Christi College, taking his B.A. degree in 1577. By 1580 he was Walsingham's secretary, carrying dispatches to and from France. While in Paris in August of 1580 he met and befriended Anthony Bacon, who was just beginning an extended intelligence-gathering tour of Europe, and subsequently Faunt carried on an extensive correspondence with him. During the following year Faunt traveled to Germany, Italy, and Switzerland, returning to England in March 1582. He settled in London, married a merchant's daughter in the mid-1580s, and did not return to France until February 1587 or 1588. He therefore was approachable in London in 1586–87, when Marlowe must have been giving serious thought to his future. Faunt was a particular favorite of Ann, Lady Bacon. When her son Anthony returned to England in 1592, Faunt met him and escorted him to his brother Francis's lodgings in Grey's Inn. After Walsingham's death in 1590 Faunt continued to prosper, claiming the office of clerk of the signet and receiving a grant of crown lands.

Perhaps Faunt introduced Marlowe to Thomas Watson—the one acquaintance of Marlowe's who seems to share all of Marlowe's most impor-

<hr />

[35] *Dictionary of National Biography.*

tant personal connections—for Watson and Faunt were both associated with Sir Francis Walsingham, and both had been in Paris in 1580. Faunt could have introduced Marlowe to Thomas Walsingham as well, since Thomas Walsingham and Faunt were both carrying messages in France in 1580. In any case Faunt, as Sir Francis's secretary, would have been well acquainted with Thomas Walsingham. Watson also met Thomas Walsingham in Paris in 1580 and recalled their friendship in his elegy on the death of Sir Francis, *Meliboeus* (1590). Thus three men who assisted Marlowe in various ways—Faunt, Watson, and Thomas Walsingham—were all closely connected to Sir Francis Walsingham, and all were well known to each other.

Faunt was a discreet, capable, and highly successful civil servant who presumably had no literary aspirations. However, as a product of humanist education he must have welcomed the opportunity to help a fellow "countryman," King's School scholar, and Corpus Christi College alumnus advance a promising literary career. Although he and Marlowe shared little more than their geographical and educational background, Faunt's firsthand experience of the St. Bartholomew's Day Massacre may have had something to do with Marlowe's decision to write a play on the subject. Watson, on the other hand, was primarily a scholar and a poet. However they met, Marlowe had more interests in common with Watson than with Faunt.

Watson was a Londoner, born around 1556 in St. Helen's parish.[36] He studied at Winchester College and Oxford, but rather than taking a degree, he pursued his studies, particularly of Roman law, by traveling for over seven years on the Continent. The fact that Watson had the luxury of a gentleman's education suggests that his family was relatively well-to-do. In late 1576 and early 1577 he spent several months at the English College at Douai and also visited Paris. He returned to London in 1577, but was back in Paris in 1580, where he made the acquaintance of Sir Francis and Thomas Walsingham, and presumably of Nicholas Faunt. The intelligence report dated 27 April 1580 that lists "sundry Englishmen, Papists, presently abiding in Paris," among them both "Banes" and Clitherowe, includes two Watsons, one of whom is identified as a student, "Watson, son to the Attorney in London."[37] In view of Watson's London origins, his keen interest in law, the money required to support his lengthy peripatetic education, and the many hints of Catholic sympathies in his personal history, this could very well be Thomas

---

[36] Mark Eccles, "Brief Lives: Tudor and Stuart Authors," *Studies in Philology* 79.4 (1982): 130.
[37] *Calendar of State Papers, Foreign Series*, 14:250–52.

Watson the poet. However, Watson himself provides most of our information about his early life in the dedication to his first published work, a Latin translation of Sophocles' *Antigone* that appeared in 1581. Needless to say, Watson does not represent himself as a papist.

Though Watson has now slipped into obscurity, he enjoyed a brilliant reputation in London during the 1580s and early 1590s. Indeed, by 6 September 1585, only a few years after his first publication, he was sufficiently well established to marry Anne Swift, sister of the lawyer Hugo Swift. Much of his published work was in Latin, which partly accounts for his lack of visibility today. In addition to his Latin translation of *Antigone*, he published *Amyntas* (1585), in Latin hexameters, and *Helenae Raptus* (The rape of Helen), translated from Coluthus's Greek (1586). The antiquary Thomas Coxeter claimed that Marlowe produced an English translation of Watson's *Helenae Raptus* in 1587. If this is true, a connection between Marlowe and Watson presumably already existed during Marlowe's first year in London. Unfortunately Marlowe's English version, if there ever was one, has vanished.

Watson's most important English poems were *Hecatompathia, or Passionate Centuries of Love* (1582), which contributed to the vogue for writing sonnet sequences, and *Tears of Fancie, or, Love Disdained*, which was published after his burial on 26 September 1592, as was his last Latin work, *Amyntae Gaudia*. The latter poem, which was licensed approximately six weeks after Watson's death, includes a Latin dedication to the Countess of Pembroke by "C. M." Since Eccles discovered the documents detailing Watson's and Marlowe's clash with Bradley, this prose dedication has generally been assigned to Marlowe. It may well be his, although its florid style is not notably Marlovian, and Marlowe was out of London because of the plague (which perhaps killed Watson) during September and at least part of October of 1593. While Marlowe and Watson were definitely on cordial terms, and Watson may even have considered Marlowe his protégé, a printer's interpretation of initials on a manuscript is weak evidence of authorship, as witnessed by the false attribution of some lines from Gervase Markham's *Devoreux* to Marlowe on the basis of a misread capital *G*.[38] Furthermore, at least two other poets had the initials C. M.: Christopher Middleton and Christopher Morley.[39] Since the dedication is highly formulaic and contains no personal information about the author except that he is a young poet, its authorship is far from certain.

[38] Fredson Bowers, introduction to *The Complete Works of Christopher Marlowe* (London, 1973), 1:viii.
[39] Sakanta Chaudhuri, "Marlowe, Madrigals, and a New Elizabethan Poet," *Review of English Studies*, new series 39 (1988): 214–15.

Watson augmented his combined income from publication, patronage, and tutoring by writing plays. William Cornwallis, a wealthy Catholic who hired Watson to tutor his son William Jr., described him in a letter of complaint to Sir Thomas Henege as a man who could "devise twenty fictions and knaveryes in a play which was his daily practyse and his living."[40] Meres, who praises Watson's poetry, also mentions Watson as one of the best English tragedians. However, none of his plays is known to have survived.

Watson was a man with an impressive circle of acquaintances whose friendship would have been valuable to an aspiring young poet and playwright. Watson knew the poet Matthew Roydon, later identified by Kyd as one of the men Marlowe often conversed with in Paul's Churchyard; Roydon contributed a laudatory poem to Watson's *Hecatompathia*, as did George Peele, who would later praise Marlowe as "the Muses' Darling." Watson knew John Lyly, poet, playwright, and probable Canterburian,[41] who also wrote a commendatory poem for *Hecatompathia*. Like Marlowe, Watson was acquainted with Thomas Nashe, to whom he told amusing tales of Gabriel Harvey while they supped together at the Nag's Head.[42] Harvey, however, like almost everyone else, thought highly of Watson. And of course Watson knew John Alleyn, who was named with Watson and Hugo Swift in William Bradley's complaint, which probably means that Watson wrote plays for the same companies Marlowe initially wrote for—the Admiral's and Lord Strange's Men. If so, perhaps Watson, like Marlowe, could boast of being very well known to Lord Strange. Watson dedicated his *Helenae Raptus* to the Earl of Northumberland, and the dedication evidently attracted patronage, for he later privately presented a second work, *A learned Dialogue of Bernard Palessy; Concerning waters and fountaines, both naturall and artificiall: Translated Owt of French into English*, to the earl, catering to Northumberland's interest in science and gardening. If Marlowe indeed Englished Watson's *Helenae Raptus*, he may have done so in a bid for the earl's attention and patronage, which he somehow succeeded in getting.

Watson's keen interest in music links him to two prominent Elizabethan musicians, William Byrd and his protégé Thomas Morley, both of whom had Catholic leanings. Byrd, a devout Catholic, collaborated with Watson on a book of madrigals published in 1590, which they dedicated to the Earl of Essex. Watson's madrigals were translated and adapted from the Italian, while Byrd's were original compositions.

Morley's connection to Watson, like his Catholicism, was more tenuous

[40] Eccles, *Christopher Marlowe in London*, 42; Nicholl, *The Reckoning*, 189.

[41] William Urry, *Christopher Marlowe and Canterbury* (London, 1988), 10.

[42] Bakeless, *Tragicall History*, 1:139.

than Byrd's. He dedicated his *Canzonets* to the Countess of Pembroke shortly after Watson's posthumous *Amintae Gaudia* was dedicated to her by C. M., and he later published his own books of madrigals modeled on the earlier publication of Watson and Byrd. Thomas Morley's son Christopher was baptized in the parish of St. Helen's in 1599, so he was probably Watson's near neighbor, and it seems likely that Morley also had a younger brother or half-brother named Christopher who was an aspiring poet, and who may well have been the C. M. who wrote the Latin dedication to *Amintae Gaudia*. It is possible that Thomas Morley was temporarily drawn to Catholicism through his association with Byrd, but he undertook anti-Catholic espionage of some kind in the Netherlands in 1591, was caught, and after his return to England allegedly betrayed other Catholics.[43] His presumed brother Christopher Morley took his M.A. from Trinity College the year before Marlowe finished his second degree. He became a fellow of Trinity, but by 1589 a Mr. Morley, quite possibly Christopher, was tutoring Arabella Stuart. In 1592 he grew dissatisfied, complaining of the losses he had suffered by leaving the university and claiming that he had expected a greater reward for his services. Furthermore, his "forwardness in religion" aroused the vehement suspicion of Arabella's guardian Bess of Hardwick, who finally dismissed him in September of 1592, the same month Watson died and left a poem to which C. M. wrote a dedication. This Mr. Morley the tutor may or may not have been involved in one of the many politico-religious intrigues that centered on Arabella.[44]

Nicholl has suggested that "tricky Tom Watson" may also have supplemented his income by dabbling in intelligence.[45] Watson's close connection to the Walsinghams, and the hints of Catholic sympathies in his history, make this a plausible conjecture. He may well have been the Watson who brought a letter to Burghley from France in August 1581.[46] Furthermore, while Watson also sought patronage from Puritans like Essex, two of the patrons with whom he was definitely associated, Lord Strange and the Earl of Northumberland, had numerous Catholic relatives and friends and were suspected of Catholic inclinations. His employer William Cornwallis was a Catholic, his musician-collaborator Byrd was a lifelong Catholic who lived outside London to practice his religion more freely, and of course Watson, rather than taking a degree from Oxford, had gone to Italy and France and

---

[43] Nicholl, *The Reckoning*, 342.

[44] For a discussion of Christopher Morley as the probable author of a group of poems signed Ch. M., see Chaudhuri, "Marlowe, Madrigals," 199–200, 214–15.

[45] Nicholl, *The Reckoning*, 185.

[46] Ibid., 183.

studied at Douai. Nicholl's speculations about Watson's relatives are more doubtful, because Watson is a very common name. It is far from clear that Robert Poley's unfortunate wife, "one Watson's daughter," was Thomas Watson's sister, and Nicholl's suggestion that the Catholic activist William Watson was a relative of Thomas Watson is quite unlikely, since William Watson was born in County Durham.

Given Watson's substantial literary output and other activities, his theoretical involvement in intelligence was probably quite limited. He may well have known Robert Poley, an active intelligence agent and a witness to Marlowe's death, whether or not they were related by marriage; Poley lived nearby in Bishopsgate and Shoreditch, both Poley and Watson had dealings with Thomas and Sir Francis Walsingham, and both were undoubtedly known to Nicholas Faunt. For that matter, since he was in France at the same time as Richard Baines and their two last names appear on the same informer's list, he may have known Baines as well. However, Watson's encounter with the delusive Mrs. Burnell in 1579, and his overzealous matchmaking between his brother-in-law and William Cornwallis's daughter, are not necessarily signs of a corrupt nature.[47] They might just as easily be interpreted in the same light as Watson's intervention in the Bradley affair—unfortunate consequences of an ill-advised attempt to be helpful. Watson may well have carried many more letters than the one mentioned in 1581. He may have kept his eyes and ears open when he was tutoring William Cornwallis Jr., or when he visited the households of Northumberland and Strange, or when he went about his daily business in Shoreditch. He may have been paid regularly for his observations. But if he ever reported anything of great significance, we have found no record of it.

Watson was Marlowe's likeliest link to Henry Percy, Ninth Earl of Northumberland, who has only recently emerged as a highly significant figure in Marlowe's life. Northumberland's name was not known to appear in any Marlowe document until 1976, when R. B. Wernham published a letter written by Robert Sidney to Burghley in which Marlowe was quoted as saying that he was "very well known" to the Earl of Northumberland and Lord Strange. Most early Marlowe biographers assumed a connection between Marlowe and Sir Walter Raleigh, since Raleigh's name was mentioned in a document discovered much earlier, a spy's report headed "Remembrances of wordes & matter againste Ric Cholmeley," and since Raleigh also wrote a reply to Marlowe's "The Passionate Shepherd to His Love." It now appears that any contact Marlowe had with Raleigh probably

[47] Ibid., 185.

occurred because of their mutual association with Northumberland and Thomas Harriot, the mathematician and scientist who worked with both Raleigh and Northumberland.

Northumberland was not such a dashing figure as Raleigh, nor do we know quite so much about him, but he was in certain ways a more suitable patron for Marlowe. Perhaps the salient fact about Northumberland was the tragic effect of the Reformation on his family. Raleigh created many of his own problems; Northumberland inherited his. His grandfather, the Seventh Earl of Northumberland, was beheaded for pro-Catholic activism, and his father, the Eighth Earl, who was also suspected of complicity in a Catholic plot, was murdered in the Tower in 1585 when Northumberland was twenty-one. Partly because of his reserved nature and partly because of this dire family history, Northumberland for the most part remained aloof from politics.

Henry Percy reaped all the benefits enjoyed by young Elizabethan noblemen; he was privately tutored and prudently reared as a Protestant, although this stratagem did not entirely remove him from suspicion of crypto-Catholicism. He traveled to the Continent in 1582 at the age of eighteen, while Marlowe, who was born in the same year as Percy, was completing his second year at Cambridge. In Paris he formed a close friendship with the Catholic exile Charles Paget, to the alarm of his friends at home, but he claimed, probably quite truthfully, that he and Paget had never discussed religion. Northumberland was keenly aware of the benefits of remaining reticent and tolerant in religious matters.

The earl's natural reserve was probably increased by the fact that he stuttered, though this speech impediment never prevented him from doing what he truly wanted to do. His friendship with Raleigh, which lasted until the end of Raleigh's life, apparently began in his early twenties. Shortly after he succeeded to the earldom in 1585, Northumberland's household accounts record the payment of 20 shillings "to Sir Walter Rawley his man, that brought your Lordship a shert of maile," and another 20 shillings "to the man that brought Sir Walter Rawley's pictor."[48] In due course (1595), Northumberland married Dorothy Devereux, sister of the Earl of Essex, and sired a son, but his relationships with his wife and his mother were uncongenial. He took a keen interest in military matters and participated successfully in combat, but never achieved any great distinction as a soldier. He went to the Netherlands in 1585–86, served in the fleet sent against the Armada, and returned to the

[48] *The Household Papers of Henry Percy, Ninth Earl of Northumberland (1564–1632)*, ed. G. R. Batho (London, 1962), 66, 74.

Netherlands in 1600. However, his second stint in the Low Countries was largely spent squabbling with his fellow officers.

By his own account Northumberland spent his youth hunting, gambling, "drinking" tobacco, pursuing mistresses, and indulging in other fashionable pastimes of wealthy young noblemen. However, at last he found his true vocation, learning. This discovery came about in a highly traditional fashion, through the chance opening of a book; however, instead of Homer, Virgil, or the Bible, the book that opened to reveal Northumberland's destiny was a treatise on the atmospheric refraction of light by the Arabian scholar Alhazan. Science and mathematics became Northumberland's consuming passions, although his interests were quite diverse, encompassing literature, philosophy, history, geography, art, architecture, gardening, alchemy, and astrology. He amassed one of the largest private libraries in England and recruited mathematicians and scientists to join him in his search for knowledge.

The first of these was Walter Warner, who lived at Syon House after the earl acquired it in 1595 and received a pension of £40 a year. Thomas Harriot, the most gifted scientist in England at the time, was first associated with Raleigh, but between 1591 and 1595 he conducted business for both Northumberland and Raleigh. In 1593 or not long thereafter, he joined Warner as a member of Northumberland's household, receiving a pension of £80 a year, which was later increased to £100.[49] Robert Hughes, who was best known for cartography, joined Warner and Harriot in 1615, forming the trio known as the "Three Magi" of "the Wizard Earl," as Northumberland was sometimes called. But in Marlowe's time there were only two Magi, Harriot and Warner, and Harriot served Raleigh as well as Northumberland.

The poets associated with Northumberland were Watson, Marlowe, Roydon, Peele, and Chapman—a well-educated, urbane group with distinctly secular inclinations. Chapman was an abstruse speculative thinker, Peele famous for his wit, Roydon a writer of elegies and comedies, Watson a purveyor of fashionable love poems and elegant translations, Marlowe a phenomenally successful, audacious young playwright. While none of these writers was notably or conventionally pious (Watson's probable roots in the old faith notwithstanding), none of them was conspicuously irreligious either; Marlowe was the only member of this literary group who quickly acquired a reputation for what was loosely called "Atheism."

By surrounding himself with scientists, poets, a superb library, and men like Raleigh who shared his enthusiasms, Northumberland effectively cre-

---

[49] John W. Shirley, *Thomas Harriot: Renaissance Scientist* (Oxford, 1974), 25, 30–31; *Household Papers*, 154.

ated his own university, one which fostered lines of thought and inquiry that were not openly pursued at Oxford or Cambridge. The activities he harbored and encouraged evidently included informal gatherings and freewheeling discussions of topics that interested Northumberland, Raleigh, and others in the group, including questions that may well have seemed, like those proposed by Marlowe's unfortunate Cambridge contemporary Evance, "scandalous, foolish, and opprobrious" to more conventional thinkers. These discussions were probably not radically different from many others that occurred privately among students and faculty in Renaissance universities, or among other intellectuals throughout Europe. They may have included "lectures" in which a member of the group presented arguments, which the rest responded to, or discussions of occult science and magic, or even experimental conjurations. Judging from Benvenuto Cellini's story of a conjuration he instigated to obtain information about a woman he loved, such experiments were not uncommon in the Renaissance, although they were best conducted secretly.[50]

It was presumably activities like these, hosted by Raleigh, Northumberland, or both, that gave rise to gossip about a "schoole of Atheisme." Since Raleigh was far more outspoken, politically active, and controversial than Northumberland, and had consequently made more enemies, the accusations centered on him. However, Northumberland had more time and inclination than Raleigh to indulge in purely intellectual pursuits. While Raleigh was fond of ideas, his association with Harriot began largely because Harriot was useful in furthering his political and economic ambitions. Harriot was Raleigh's mathematics tutor, his navigator, his surveyor and observer of the New World, and his financial agent. Northumberland, on the other hand, made somewhat less practical use of Harriot, offering him a position that allowed him to devote most of his time to his own studies.

In 1592, Father Robert Parsons published some of the gossip he had heard about Raleigh and Harriot in his *Responsio ad Elizabethae edictum* (Response to Elizabeth's edicts):

Of Sir Walter Rawleys schoole of Atheisme by the waye, and of the Coniurer that is M.[aster] thereof . . . , and of the diligence vsed to get yong gentlemen to this schoole, where in both Moyses, and our

---

[50] Benvenuto Cellini, *The Life of Benvenuto Cellini: Written by Himself*, trans. John Addington Symonds (New York, 1936), 1:251–56.

Sauior; the olde and new Testamente are iested at, and the schollers taughte amonge other thinges, to spell God backwarde.[51]

Partly as a consequence of such rumors, in March 1594 an investigation into Raleigh's activities and religious beliefs convened at Cerne Abbas, near his residence at Sherborne, Dorset. This inquiry was undoubtedly politically motivated, but it produced no substantial evidence against either Raleigh or Harriot, and nothing came of it. In 1595, an undaunted Raleigh resumed his pursuit of wealth and glory by setting sail for Guyana, once again with the assistance of Harriot. Northumberland was never implicated in the Cerne Abbas investigation, even though his association with Raleigh and Harriot was well known.

In keeping with his ideal image of himself as a scholar, Northumberland liked to assume a contemplative attitude in his portraits. A miniature by Hilliard dating somewhere between 1585 and 1595 shows him reclining on the ground in a formal garden situated on top of a wooded hill.[52] His right cheek is propped up on his palm, his gloves and hat are tossed carelessly aside, and a book lies beside him. It is a conventional pose of the melancholy scholar, but there is a less conventional symbolic object prominently displayed in the picture. Hanging above the earl on the branch of a tree is a scale. On one side—the short arm of the balance—is a sphere, which looks like a globe or miniature world. On the other, longer arm of the balance is a feather, which holds the world in equipoise. Under the feather is the simple Latin inscription "Tanti," meaning, "Worth so much" or, in the context of the iconographic scale, "Thus much I weigh it." Probably not accidentally, Marlowe's Gaveston uses the same motto in Marlowe's *Edward II* to express his scorn for the multitude:

> As for the multitude, that are but sparks
> Raked up in embers of their poverty,
> *Tanti!* I'll fawn first on the wind,
> That glanceth at my lips and flieth away. (1.1.20–23)

When added to the other evidence of a connection between Northumberland and Marlowe, their use of the same Latin motto to express contempt

---

[51] Quoted in Bakeless, *Tragicall History*, 1:130; also in Frederick S. Boas, *Christopher Marlowe: A Biographical and Critical Study* (Oxford, 1940), 113.

[52] Depicted in Nicholl, *The Reckoning*, facing p. 195. A larger plate appears in Roy Strong, *Artists of the Tudor Court: The Portrait Miniature Rediscovered, 1520–1620* (London, 1983), frontispiece.

suggests not just distant acquaintance but a definite conceptual interaction between the two men.

Marlowe's two other patrons, Lord Strange and Thomas Walsingham, were less eccentric and less important historically than Northumberland and his friend Raleigh. Marlowe's involvement with them is not only a probable result of his acquaintance with Faunt and Watson, but is also linked to a series of events that began to unfold in 1589, and that comprise yet another chapter in Marlowe's life.

5

Lord Strange and Thomas Walsingham

❧

I am none of these common pedants, I.

Edward II, 2.1.52

AS WE HAVE SEEN, Marlowe's acquaintance with the Earl of Northumberland was probably the result of a chain or network of personal connections. The same can be said of his relationship with Lord Strange, although in the case of Strange the alliance was a byproduct of decisions made by the acting companies who performed Marlowe's plays, rather than a result of individual benevolence.

When Marlowe launched his career as a professional playwright in 1587, he provided plays for the Lord Admiral's Men, who performed them mainly at James Burbage's playhouse, the Theatre. However, sometime around 1589 the Lord Admiral's Men began to collaborate with Lord Strange's Men, to the point where the two companies staged the same plays and sometimes performed jointly. In 1591, they quarreled with James Burbage over finances and shifted their base of operations to the Rose, Philip Henslowe's new playhouse on Bankside. Marlowe probably became "well known" to Lord Strange as a result of this alliance between or merger of the two companies, which coincided closely with Strange's summons to Parliament in late January 1589, at which time his patronage of the company presumably became more active.[1]

Strange's background was somewhat similar to Northumberland's. Both were scions of prominent northern noble houses. If, as the saying went, there were "no princes but Percys" in Northumberland's domain, Stanley could claim royal blood on both sides of his family. Both Northumberland and Stanley had numerous Catholic relatives and friends. Both were tolerant in

---

[1] E. K. Chambers, *The Elizabethan Stage* (Oxford, 1923), 2:119–20, 136–37; *Dictionary of National Biography*.

religious matters and neither was notably zealous. Both were scholarly. Strange, in fact, had taken an M.A. at Oxford, an unusual, even eccentric, accomplishment for a nobleman. Strange is sometimes linked with Northumberland in an imaginary circle of freethinkers known as the "School of Night," a theory that takes its cue mainly from Father Parsons's remark about Raleigh's "schoole of Atheisme," but there is no compelling evidence that such a group ever existed as a consciously created entity, or even that Strange and Northumberland were on particularly familiar terms.

In spite of the similarities in their backgrounds, their personalities and primary interests were quite distinct. Strange maintained a huge household and lived in an elegant, even princely style. He was more courtly and sociable than Northumberland, and far more interested in politics, although he had to exercise extreme caution in this area. Strange's intellectual enthusiasms were more aesthetic than scientific. He wrote poetry himself and was a generous patron of poets, players, acrobats, and tumblers. In 1579, after completing his degrees at Oxford, he married Alice, one of the Spensers of Althorp whom Edmund Spenser claimed as noble kinsmen. The marriage produced three daughters, but no sons.

While the sins of his father and grandfather were visited on Northumberland, Strange's most dangerous relative was very much alive. This was his cousin Sir William Stanley, who had fought for the queen in Ireland and the Netherlands but had turned traitor and joined the Spanish in 1587. Sir William outraged the English not only by handing a captured town, Deventer, over to the Spanish, but also by becoming one of the principal Catholic exiles plotting against the queen. In early 1591, Stanley suggested to Father Parsons that Lord Strange would be the ideal pretender to the English crown. Emissaries were sent to Strange later that year to persuade him to join a conspiracy, but they were intercepted. From this point on, Strange was no doubt watched closely. A few months after Marlowe's death, another emissary, Richard Hesketh, approached Strange, urging him to claim the crown and threatening him with death if he revealed the plan. After some hesitation, Strange informed on Hesketh, who was executed in November 1593. Strange himself died in April of 1594 at the age of thirty-five. While his death may have been due to natural causes, his symptoms were suspiciously consistent with slow poisoning, which, along with witchcraft, was one of the diagnoses favored by rumor.

Marlowe's connection with Lord Strange's Men, and therefore at least nominally with Strange, continued after Marlowe's death. Although Kyd, as we shall see, alleged that Strange shunned Marlowe after discovering that he was a "reprobate," Marlowe's *Massacre at Paris* was added to the repertory of the companies associated with Strange in January 1594. Any rupture that might have occurred between Marlowe and Strange did not result in Strange's Men ceasing to perform Marlowe's plays, though it may have induced Marlowe to write *Edward II* for another company. The fact that Marlowe and Kyd both wrote plays for Strange's Men brought them into close association for a time. In 1591 they were working in the same room, perhaps because they lodged in the same house in Norton Folgate. As a result, Kyd would later accuse Marlowe of owning a fragment of a manuscript found in Kyd's possession, which Kyd claimed was accidentally shuffled in with his papers.

Thomas Walsingham may also have become Marlowe's patron by 1590. Certainly he could have done little for Marlowe before that, as surviving documents reveal. Thomas was born in about 1563, the youngest of three sons of Sir Thomas Walsingham of Scadbury, Chislehurst, Kent, and as such he was a poor prospect for a patron. His father was a cousin of Sir Francis Walsingham, but according to Conyers Read the relationship between Sir Thomas and Sir Francis was not close. However, one of Sir Thomas's daughters, Ann, married Thomas Randolph, a skilled diplomat who served as ambassador to France and Scotland. Walsingham had the highest regard for Randolph,[2] and perhaps as a result of Ann's or Randolph's mediation, Sir Francis employed two of Sir Thomas's sons in his intelligence network. Thomas's eldest brother, Guldeford, who predeceased his father, was gathering military intelligence in 1578.[3] Young Thomas was a courier to and from France in 1580–84, at which time he made the acquaintance of Thomas Watson and Nicholas Faunt. In 1586, while Robert Poley was busy infiltrating and betraying the Babington conspirators, Thomas went to Poley's house in Bishopsgate to collect messages from Sir Francis, and while there he met the conspirator John Ballard. In 1587, Thomas escorted Poley to a meeting with Sir Francis, and in 1588–89 he was paid a hundred shillings for special services to the queen.[4]

These surviving traces of Thomas Walsingham's news-gathering activities probably represent only a small portion of his actual involvement in intelligence work, which must have been his primary, if not his sole, source of income. After his father's death in 1584, Thomas's older brother Edmund inherited the estate. Young Thomas therefore continued to labor in the trenches for his cousin Sir Francis, and evidently found it difficult to support himself in a style he deemed suitable for a young gentleman. Although he

---

[2] Conyers Read, *Mr Secretary Walsingham and the Policy of Queen Elizabeth* (Oxford 1925), 3:427.
[3] John Bakeless, *Tragicall History of Christopher Marlowe* (Cambridge, Mass., 1942), 1:161.
[4] Ibid., 162.

never attended either university, Thomas was obviously well educated, and like Marlowe he seems to have spent much of his time in St. Paul's Churchyard, for one of the booksellers, William Smith, claimed in a deposition of late 1582 that he was well known to Thomas Walsingham.[5] This was a relatively inexpensive and highly respectable pastime, one that even the youngest son of a knight might enjoy, but Thomas craved fine clothes and other fashionable items, which the hundred shillings we know he earned in 1588–89 would scarcely have provided. Fate seems to have turned in his favor just in time, for in late 1589 his brother Edmund died. The license of entry, which allowed Thomas to inherit his estate, was issued on 27 October,[6] and Edmund's will was proved on 22 November.

At this time Thomas was already deeply in debt. The young heir spent at least part of early 1590 in Fleet Prison over a sizable unpaid account, as revealed by the pardon he secured on 27 May 1590:

> Whereas Thomas Lund recently in our court of the Queen's Bench . . . pled against Thomas Walsingham, late of London, Gentleman, alias Thomas Walsingham of Chiselhurst in the County of Kent, gentleman, . . . concerning a debt of two hundred marks, . . . and because the same Thomas Walsingham did not come before the said Justices, the said Thomas Lund . . . filed a writ of exigent of outlawry in our court of Hustings. . . . Therefore the same Thomas Walsingham was delivered to our Fleet prison for the said reason and in the same remained.[7]

Exactly how long Thomas remained in prison we do not know, but by the time his pardon was issued, his cousin Sir Francis was dead. Since no further records of government payments to Thomas have surfaced, it appears that his active involvement in intelligence ended at this point.

After buying his pardon, paying his debts, and settling into his new role as lord of the manor, Thomas was now in a position to be a benefactor, and Tom Watson, his old acquaintance from Paris, lost no time in recognizing his change in status. Upon Sir Francis Walsingham's death in 1590, Watson dedicated a Latin elegy for Sir Francis to Thomas in hope of receiving a small token of his appreciation and affection. And through Watson, perhaps Marlowe also began a profitable association with Thomas, if they were not al-

[5] Ibid.
[6] PRO C66/1339, m. 26.
[7] PRO C66/1356, m. 35. The full text of this document is included in the appendix.

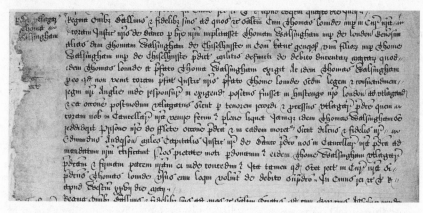

Thomas Walsingham's pardon for outlawry (1590). Photo courtesy of the Public Record Office, London.

ready acquainted. However, even if they had known each other previously, their relationship was now on an entirely new footing.

This unexpected windfall made Thomas Walsingham a highly desirable match, and he probably married Audrey Shelton in the early 1590s, when both were of optimal marriageable age. Audrey was the daughter of Sir Ralph Shelton of Shelton, Norfolk. The Sheltons were an old and distinguished family, related to Queen Elizabeth through her mother Anne Boleyn, and several of Audrey's relatives held positions at court. The fact that the Walsinghams traced their line back to Geoffrey Walsingham, lord of Little Walsingham, Norfolk, perhaps had something to do with the match. A. D. Wraight suggests that Thomas and Audrey were not married until 1598, when a version of Marlowe's *Hero and Leander* was dedicated to each of them, and places the birth of their only child, Thomas, in 1600, on the basis of unspecified evidence.[8] But since Lady Audrey was born in 1568, by 1598 she would have been elderly for an Elizabethan bride (Wraight's highly speculative rationale for her marrying at an advanced age is not convincing), and if her son was not born until 1600, he would have been only sixteen when his first child, Catherine, was born.[9] Assuming that Thomas the younger was at least twenty-one when his first child was born, which is likely, he must have been born in or before 1595. Thomas Walsingham was in all probability married to Audrey by 1597, when the queen visited Scadbury and knighted him,

[8] A. D. Wraight, *In Search of Christopher Marlowe; A Pictorial Biography*, photography by Virginia F. Stern (New York, 1965), 251.
[9] See the Pedigree of Walsingham in ibid., facing page 281.

because, as Wraight points out, Elizabeth's close ties to the Sheltons would have made her favorably disposed to honoring Audrey's husband.

Walsingham was active in coastal defense in 1596 and 1597, which would also have recommended him for knighthood, and he was a member of Parliament for Rochester as well. Several properties were granted him in 1597–98 as further tokens of royal favor, including a house at the lower end of the tiltyard in Whitehall Palace, which he continued to hold into the reign of James I. On 11 August 1615 he was the victim of a burglary in his residence at Whitehall, as recorded in the Middlesex Sessions Rolls:

> in the night of the said day, Robert Chapman, Thomas Jones and John Waterman, all late of London yomen, broke burglariously into the dwellinghouse of the Lord King James called Whitehall . . . and stole therefrom six needle-worke cushions worth eight pounds, six needle worke covers for stooles worth sixe pounds, and forty pounds' weight of silke worth twenty pounds, of the goods and chattels of Sir Thomas Walsingham, Knt.[10]

These costly items, particularly the forty pounds of silk, may well have been related to Walsingham's official duties as guardian and keeper of the robes, a post he shared with his wife Audrey after 1607.[11] By then, living amidst such luxury, Tom Walsingham may almost have forgotten that he himself had once been incarcerated for debt. Chapman and Jones were imprisoned and promptly hanged.

Lady Audrey proved a brilliant match for Sir Thomas. Her career at court had already begun by 1598, for in dedicating his completed version of *Hero and Leander* to her, Chapman addresses her as a lady of the queen's bedchamber. She was a great favorite both of Elizabeth and of Burghley's younger son Sir Robert Cecil, to the point where she was rumored to be Cecil's mistress. She was deeply involved in the intrigues to place James on the throne, which is hardly surprising. Indeed, her husband probably approved and encouraged her in this, for the Walsinghams had long been partial to James, as were Cecil, Northumberland, and Sir Robert Sidney, whose brother Sir Philip had been married to Sir Francis Walsingham's daughter Frances. After the accession of James, Lady Walsingham, Sir Thomas, and their son Thomas the younger flourished. Lands, pensions, lucrative posi-

[10] *Middlesex County Records*, ed. John Cordy Jeaffreson (London, 1887), 2:100.
[11] Bakeless, *Tragicall History*, 1:165.

tions at court, rich presents, and a knighthood for young Thomas rained on them. They were therefore tempting targets for thieves; another Middlesex County true bill of 5 July 1618 includes a list of stolen possessions that provides a vivid glimpse of their wealth:

> at Drury Lane Co. Midd. on the said day, Robert Purefrey late of Drury lane aforesaid gentleman stole a man's hatt worth thirty shillings, a bever hatt worth ten shillings, a black woolen-cloth cloak lyned with velvett worth fifteen pounds, a velvett cloak lyned with sables worth thirty pounds, a cloth cloak lyned with unshorne velvett worth ten pounds, a russett cloth cloke lyned with russett velvett worth ten pounds, a silke grogran cloake worth ten pounds, another cloth cloake lyned with velvett worth five pounds, two pairs of silke stockinges worth thirty shillinges, a night-cap worth twenty shillinges, a bag embroidered with gold worth ten shillings, a silver bason worth nine pounds, and a silver standishe worth ten pounds, of the goods and chattels of sir Thomas Walsingham the elder, Knt., and a blacke silke grogan cloke worth thirty shillings, of the goods and chattels of Sir Thomas Walsingham the younger, Knt. Putting himself 'Not Guilty,' Robert Purefrey was acquitted.[12]

This loss, of course—a few items they kept in one of their town residences—represented only a tiny fraction of the Walsinghams' total worth.

Lady Audrey died in 1624. On 3 May 1630, a few months before his death, the elder Sir Thomas conveyed a piece of property called Rose Acre at Shelton, Norfolk, to Henry Shelton of Shelton—evidently one of his late wife's kinsmen.[13] His signature on the document is rather spidery, but elegant and well formed. Thomas the younger, who from all indications was on excellent terms with his father, dedicated a tablet on the family tomb to his memory, praising him as "most wise in conducting the affairs of his country, most zealous for peace, most friendly to his neighbors, most generous to the poor, most famous for his liberal hospitality to all."[14] If even part of this is true, Marlowe was fortunate in the character of his patron.

But when Thomas (and perhaps Audrey) Walsingham entered Marlowe's life, Walsingham brought with him a trusted servant named Ingram Frizer, who was destined to be the death of Christopher Marlowe. We have no definite information regarding Frizer's origins, but he may have been born in or

---

[12] *Middlesex County Records*, 2:131–32.
[13] Folger MSS Z.c.24 (18).
[14] Wraight, *In Search of Christopher Marlowe*, 279.

Thomas Walsingham's signature: Conveyance of Rose Acre (1630). Photo courtesy of the Folger Shakespeare Library, Washington, D.C.

near Kingsclare, Hampshire. On 9 October 1589, shortly before Thomas Walsingham inherited his estate, Frizer purchased the Angel Inn at Basingstoke near Kingsclere, which he resold, undoubtedly at a profit, within two months. At the time of this purchase, one of the sellers, Thomas Bostock, was bound to Frizer for £250 but defaulted on the loan. Frizer took him to court and obtained a favorable judgment in 1592; however, he was unable to collect and was still resorting to litigation in 1595.[15] This is all we have found on record about Frizer until the day of Marlowe's death. Nevertheless, we can deduce from later evidence that Marlowe knew Frizer in 1593 because Frizer was Thomas Walsingham's servant.

Most of what we know about Frizer was recorded after Marlowe's death. He was quickly pardoned for killing Marlowe, much more quickly than Watson was pardoned for killing Bradley, and almost exactly a month after Marlowe's death, on 29 June 1593, he was arranging a loan of £200 for a young gentleman named Drew Woodleff. Drew was the son of the late Robert Woodleff of Peterley, Buckinghamshire, near Aylesbury. The elder Woodleff had died on 7 January 1593, leaving a sizable estate to his son Drew, who was then, according to the inquisition post mortem, fully of age. However, it appears from the inquisition that much of Woodleff's property was acquired by marriage to Anne Drury, the daughter of Robert Drury, knight, and sister of Drew Drury. If or how this family is related to the prominent courtier Drew Drury is unclear.

Unfortunately, Drew Woodleff and his mother quickly found themselves in debt—quite possibly because the family's finances had been in decline even before Robert Woodleff's death. Unfortunately, neither Drew nor his mother seemed capable of remedying the situation. In an attempt to repair his fortunes, Drew approached a man named Nicholas Skeres, who introduced him to Frizer. Frizer persuaded Woodleff to sign a bond for £60,

[15] Bakeless, *Tragicall History*, 1:166–67.

promising to produce the money later, but when Woodleff urgently needed the money and demanded it, Frizer claimed not to have that amount on hand and instead offered Woodleff a commodity of ordinance on Tower Hill.

This ploy appears to be a variation on a common extortionate lending practice in which the lender induces borrowers to accept worthless commodities as part of the loan arrangement. Shakespeare alludes to this practice in *Measure for Measure* as Pompey muses on the plight of "young Master Rash, . . . in for a commodity of brown paper and old ginger, ninescore and seventeen pounds, of which he made five marks ready money" (4.3.4–7). The practice was apparently rife on the Continent as well, for Molière's Harpagon in *The Miser* nearly defrauds his own son by engaging in it.

Woodleff, who obviously had no idea what to do with ordinance on Tower Hill, then asked Frizer to sell it for cash, but Frizer claimed he was able to get only £30 for it, leaving Woodleff with a £30 loss and Frizer with 100 percent interest, the only difficulty being that Woodleff was unable to pay. At some point Woodleff was also induced to sign a bond for 20 marks, supposedly to help Skeres pay a debt to Frizer. Skeres no doubt promised to pay Woodleff before the note fell due, but in the end Woodleff owed Frizer £30 and 20 marks, along with other debts he was still unable to pay. Frizer therefore arranged a loan of £200 from his master Thomas Walsingham, which Woodleff presumably used to pay off Frizer and other creditors, but of course he was then unable to pay Walsingham and was taken to court for it. Walsingham has sometimes been criticized for his involvement in this shady business, but he probably did not fully understand Frizer's game. Frizer used Woodleff, in effect, to squeeze money from his master; Walsingham knew only as much as Frizer told him, and all he gained from the transaction was Woodleff's bad debt. Frizer might be compared to Chaucer's Reeve, who could steal subtly from his master and still "have a thank."

This was not the end of the matter. On 30 April 1596, the Woodleffs (one suspects that Frizer referred to them privately as the Woodcocks) sold Frizer part of their land in Great Missenden, Buckinghamshire, which he resold, no doubt for a tidy profit, sometime before June 1599. In the same year, according to the Patent Rolls, they were issued a pardon for selling other lands without a license and were granted a license to sell the manor of Peterly to Sir Robert Dormer. By 1598 they were still in debt, and at last filed a complaint against Frizer, hoping to regain some of the money they had foolishly lost in their earlier dealings with him.[16] In response, Frizer merely invoked a techni-

---

[16] J. Leslie Hotson, *The Death of Christopher Marlowe* (New York, 1965), 45–49.

cality: they were outlawed for debt, and therefore he was not obliged to respond to their complaint.

In later records, Frizer's name is linked to Lady Walsingham as well as to Sir Thomas. In 1603, a lease in reversion of lands in Lancaster was granted to him under King James at her suit, one of several royal grants of the use of lands in which he was involved with her. Shortly before this, in 1602, he had left London and settled in Eltham, Kent, not far from Scadbury, where Sir Thomas had been granted reversion of the keepership of the royal park. There he lived in eminent respectability, doing duty as a churchwarden, assisting in the measurement of church lands, and serving as an assessor and a commissioner. He was allowed to dig a well in the vicar's close to supply water for brewing at his house, but, characteristically, he managed to avoid paying for the privilege.[17] On 2 June 1608 he marched in the funeral procession of Sir James Deane, to whom he had sold the inn at Basingstoke thirty-nine years before; he received a legacy of £20 in Deane's will and was forgiven a debt of £5. Not long afterward, Deane's nephew Andrew Chamberlain also bequeathed Frizer £20.[18] A "Mrs. Ingreram," probably Frizer's wife, was buried at Eltham on 25 August 1616, and two children of one of his daughters, Alice Dixon, were interred there in 1625. Frizer himself was buried on 14 August 1627, having lived into his sixties. He was survived by his daughter Alice Dixon, a grandson John Banckes, and probably by a second wife who remarried the following year.[19]

Though Frizer has regularly been cast as a villain by Marlowe's biographers, he seems on the whole an unlikely assassin. He was shrewd and sometimes unscrupulous in money matters, as was many another Elizabethan, but those who profited from their dealings with him, including Sir James Deane and the Walsinghams, evidently thought highly of him. His struggle with Marlowe is, as far as we know, the only recorded involvement in personal combat of a man who clearly preferred litigation and cunning to physical confrontation. Everything we know about Frizer, including his grasping nature and his disinclination to deal generously with others, is completely consistent with the official version of Marlowe's last day on earth, as recorded in William Danby's coroner's report. Why ascribe Marlowe's death to the hypothetical malice and connivance of powerful adversaries when other forces working against him, both external and internal, can plausibly explain what happened in Deptford?

<hr>

[17] Bakeless, *Tragicall History*, 1:169–71.
[18] Arthur Freeman, "The Deptford Killer," *Times Literary Supplement*, 28 May 1993, 30.
[19] Bakeless, *Tragicall History*, 1:171.

6

Fortune Turns Base

Base Fortune, now I see that in thy wheel
There is a point to which, when men aspire,
They tumble headlong down.

Edward II, 5.6.58–60

ALTHOUGH MARLOWE'S ACQUAINTANCE with Ingram Frizer would soon put an abrupt end to his life and career, in the first few weeks of 1592 his prospects had never looked brighter. The enormously popular *Jew of Malta* rivaled the successes of the *Tamburlaine* plays and *Doctor Faustus*, and probably not coincidentally, the actors who performed Marlowe's plays, the Admiral's–Lord Strange's Men, were also flourishing in late 1591 and the first six months of 1592. They appeared six times at court in late December, early January, and early February, more than any other acting company during the same time period. On 19 February they initiated a series of performances at the Rose that ran six days a week for eighteen weeks. Among the most profitable plays in their repertory were *The Jew of Malta*, Kyd's *The Spanish Tragedy*, and Shakespeare's *Henry VI, Part 1*.[1]

The Jew of Malta is the first of Marlowe's plays to make use of his daily experiences in London. *Dido* is largely an academic exercise, while the *Tamburlaine* plays are characterized by a rather pedantic exoticism, couched in sonorous, stylized blank verse. *Faustus* benefits from Marlowe's direct knowledge of the university, but *The Jew of Malta*, although it is set on a remote Mediterranean island, incorporates many recognizable features of London life—cunning politicians, prosperous and often unscrupulous merchants, a multinational population, religious factionalism and bigotry, rigid social strat-

---

[1] E. K. Chambers, *The Elizabethan Stage* (Oxford, 1923), 2:122.

ification, and an urban jungle of cony-catchers and cutpurses, prostitutes and pimps, burglars and blackmailers. Its dialogue, in contrast to the stately rhetoric of *Tamburlaine*, is racy, vigorous, and colloquial, drawn directly from life.

During the first six months of 1592, Marlowe was presumably working on *The Massacre at Paris* or *Edward II*, or both. Neither of these plays seems to have been performed in London in early 1592 or before, and, as fate would have it, neither could be performed in London later that year. By the end of June a long siege of plague began. In an attempt to prevent the spread of infection, the Privy Council issued an edict on 23 June suspending public performances of plays in London until Michaelmas (October 10). If the actors wanted to continue performing they would have to travel outside London—unwelcome news both for them and for the playwrights.

However, the plague and the closing of the theaters were not the only setbacks Marlowe experienced in 1592. A series of incidents occurred throughout the year that suggest his personal life was beginning to follow a somewhat more erratic and ominous course than his literary career. The first of these is recorded in a letter from Sir Robert Sidney, who had succeeded his brother, the late Sir Philip, as governor of Flushing, to Lord Treasurer Burghley. On 26 January 1592, Sidney wrote to report that he was sending back to England "one named Christofer Marly, by his profession a scholer," and a goldsmith named Gifford Gilbert, both arrested in Flushing for "coining," specifically for counterfeiting English and Dutch coins and passing a Dutch shilling. At this point Richard Baines makes his first appearance in documents bearing directly on Marlowe's life:

> The matter was revealed unto me the day after it was done, by one
> Ri[chard]: Baines whome also my Ancient shal bring unto yowr
> Lo[rdship]: He was theyr chamber fellow and fearing the succes, made
> me acquainted with all. The men being examined apart never denied
> anything, onely protesting that what was done was onely to se the
> Goldsmiths conning: and truly I ame of opinion that the poore man
> was onely browght in under that couler, what ever intent the other
> twoe had at that time. And indeed they do one accuse another to have
> bin the inducers of him, and to have intended to practis yt
> heerafter. . . . The scholer sais himself to be very wel known both to
> the Earle of Northumberland and my lord Strang. Bains and he do
> also accuse one another of intent to goe to the Ennemy [Spain] or to
> Rome, both as they say of malice one to another.[2]

[2] PRO SP 84/44, f. 60; R. B. Wernham, "Christopher Marlowe at Flushing in 1592," *English Historical Review* 91 (1976): 345.

Since Sidney's letter is the only account we have of this episode, it is impossible to tell what lay behind the events he records, although it is obvious that neither Baines nor Marlowe was being completely forthright.

Once again the only recourse is to fill the gap with speculation—a challenge that Marlowe biographers have rarely failed to meet. Nicholl proposes that Marlowe was sent to Flushing as a "projector" or provocateur to coin counterfeit money, make contact with English Catholic exiles plotting to put his patron Lord Strange on the throne, and gather incriminating information.[3] Unfortunately, this intriguing theory overlooks the fact that Marlowe was in Flushing with Baines, who, along with the goldsmith, was Marlowe's "chamber fellow." Sidney obviously believed that Baines was actively involved in the counterfeiting scheme, and, "fearing the success," informed on his accomplices to escape arrest. But since Baines was a government agent like Marlowe, he was presumably in Flushing on business, and if counterfeiting was part of that business, why would Baines inform on Marlowe, since doing so would abort the operation and incense his superiors? Even if Baines harbored extreme malice toward Marlowe, this would be a perilous way to satisfy it.

Nicholl also suggests that Marlowe might have been inviting arrest in order to gain "a credential" and win the trust of English Catholic exiles.[4] This also seems rather unlikely. Unless such an arrest were arranged in advance, the outcome would be dangerously unpredictable, and Sidney's letter makes it clear that no prior understanding existed between him and Burghley. Furthermore, Marlowe was sent immediately back to England and was still there in May. No elaborate covert operation materialized for which he was supposedly trying to acquire credentials.

To fill this gap one could readily construct a less thrilling but more economical scenario that might come closer to approximating what actually happened. For example, we can begin with the fact that Marlowe and Baines were in Flushing at the same time, either jointly or separately, by design or by chance, and were sharing the same chamber. Since neither man's name has yet been linked to a major intelligence operation, the likeliest explanation for this is that they were in Flushing on routine business. Perhaps they were already acquainted, since Barabas's plot to poison an entire nunnery in *The Jew of Malta* does bear some resemblance to Baines's fantasy that the English College in Rheims might be destroyed by poisoning the well. This association might have been based not only on their mutual involvement in intelli-

---

[3] Charles Nicholl, *The Reckoning: The Murder of Christopher Marlowe* (London, 1992), 234–49.
[4] Ibid., 247.

Map of Groningen, ca. 1572, one of a series of drawings detailing the fortifications used to defend Dutch towns in the later sixteenth century. Like Flushing (Vlissingen), where Marlowe was arrested on suspicion of counterfeiting in 1592, Groningen was equipped for seige warfare with moats, walls, bastions, and a star fortress, a design which insured that every angle of approach was covered by artillery fire. Kraus Collection #36, Monumenta Cartographica, Harry Ransom Humanities Research Center, The University of Texas at Austin. Reproduced with permission.

gence work but also on their similar backgrounds, and possibly on certain shared attitudes. If this Richard Baines is the Cambridge graduate, both he and Marlowe were products of humanist education who probably considered their exceptional merit shabbily rewarded. Both, in different ways and to different degrees, were hostile to authority. Both had a taste for danger and intrigue. Perhaps these and other imponderable similarities convinced them that they were kindred spirits—at least for a time.

While they were in Flushing, a remote English outpost where government oversight was ostensibly weaker than in London, Marlowe recalled his conversation with the counterfeiter Poole. He then proposed to Baines that they experiment with counterfeiting to supplement their chronically insufficient incomes. Or, if we assume prior acquaintance, perhaps he proposed this to Baines before they embarked. In either case, Marlowe, because of his knowledge of counterfeiting methods, would presumably have initiated the scheme, and he would not have approached Baines unless he had reason to believe that he would be receptive. Baines, of course, if he is the Baines who became rector of Waltham, had apparently remained active in intelligence, at least occasionally, as a supplement to his none-too-lavish income. Marlowe's combined earnings from plays, patrons, and intelligence work probably provided him with little more than a modest living and occasional luxuries. Either man could have viewed counterfeiting as a way of beating an inequitable system, and the prospect must have been inviting. After all, if the experiment failed they could always claim that they had no serious intentions of counterfeiting—which is the ploy Marlowe and the goldsmith ultimately used.

Baines agreed to the experiment, but at some point lost his nerve. Given what we are assuming was his personal history, such a development would not be surprising. Marlowe's experiences with imprisonment had been quite different from Baines's. His incarceration in Newgate was brief, relatively endurable, even enlightening, while Baines's imprisonment at Rheims was a nightmare. Baines knew what it was like to be detained indefinitely and tortured to obtain a confession that would justify even longer detainment. Probably he was not eager to repeat the experience. Better to be poorly rewarded than maimed and crippled for life—or worse. Traitors were hanged, drawn, and quartered, and counterfeiting could be considered a form of treason. Although Baines probably turned against Marlowe primarily out of fear, as Sidney reports, Marlowe's claim that Baines harbored malice toward him is also plausible, particularly when we consider Baines's gratuitous and cunning charge that Marlowe intended to defect to the enemy and Rome with his bad coin.

What inspired this malice we can only guess. Perhaps Marlowe taunted Baines when he showed signs of wavering, which would hardly be out of character, or perhaps Marlowe was already in the habit of making outrageous and blasphemous remarks, as Baines and Kyd later accused him of doing. Roy Kendall has pointed out that Baines himself, in his confession at Rheims, admitted to making similarly irreverent remarks. However, the outrageous remarks Baines confessed to making differed significantly from those he ascribed to Marlowe. Baines's comments were mainly scornful of specifically Catholic practices and beliefs and probably reflected his growing resentment of life in the seminary at Rheims, which was highly regimented and ascetic. Marlowe's remarks were contemptuous of conventional Christian belief in general, "utterly scorning both God and his ministers," as Baines would later describe them.

Richard Baines, the rector of Waltham, while he could not wholly accept either Anglo-Catholic or Catholic doctrine, may well have found these scabrous and irreverent remarks disturbing and offensive. Or perhaps it was a comment about "tobacco and boys," or a lewd suggestion about the relationship between Christ and St. John, that irked him. The thought that this sacrilegious rogue, this sodomite, could expose him to mortal peril may well have generated an intense antipathy on Baines's part. This animus not only underlay his treachery in Flushing but also pulsed through the list of allegations he would make against Marlowe in London more than a year later.

When we reframe the incident in Flushing as a psychodrama rather than a spy novel, it begins to look less like a secret mission than like a debacle. A chastened Marlowe was escorted back to England to face trial for a misdeed from which he gained nothing, and to make matters worse, Sir Robert Sidney seemed to regard Marlowe and Baines not with indignation, but with a mixture of amusement and contempt. Only a Dutch shilling was "uttred," Sidney noted with satisfaction, and that "plain peuter and with half an ey to be discovered." However, he did show some respect for the goldsmith, "an eccellent worckman." To make sure this trifling matter was adjudicated properly, Sidney delivered the malefactors to Burghley, who was probably more than a little annoyed to see them. If Baines hoped Marlowe would be severely punished for his transgression, he must have been bitterly disappointed. He had exposed the scheme at such an early stage that the evidence was inconclusive. Marlowe's story that he was only testing the goldsmith's skill could not be disproved—although we may doubt that Burghley believed it. However, Burghley, as one of the Privy Councilors who had urged the Cambridge authorities to grant Marlowe's M.A., and possibly as Marlowe's employer, knew Marlowe well. While he had shown poor judgment in this matter and made a nuisance of himself, Burghley knew he was no threat to the queen, whatever Baines might say about his intention to defect, and, more important, Marlowe was still potentially useful to Burghley. Probably Marlowe's punishment was limited to a few tart remarks by the lord treasurer and forfeit of payment for any services he was supposed to be performing in Flushing.

It is quite possible that Marlowe's misadventure in Flushing led to the breach Kyd recalled between Marlowe and Lord Strange. Strange's distaste for Marlowe did not necessarily develop, as Kyd believed, because Strange discovered that Marlowe was irreligious, nor, as Nicholl suggests, because Strange found out that Marlowe was a projector and spy.[5] Perhaps it occurred simply because Strange learned that Marlowe had been arrested for counterfeiting, was accused of intention to defect to Catholicism, and then claimed to be "very well known" to Lord Strange. After Sir William Stanley's attempt to lure his cousin into Catholic succession schemes in 1591, Strange must have been anxious to avoid association with anyone who was suspected of disloyalty or complicity in Catholic plots. While this loss of his patron did not end Marlowe's association with Strange's players, it deprived him of favors from Strange that he was probably loath to lose, and may have encouraged him to turn (or turn more often) to Thomas Walsingham for support.

After Flushing we hear no more of Marlowe for three and a half months, but on 9 May 1592, he was bound to keep the peace by Allen Nichols, the constable of Holywell Street, and his subconstable Nicholas Elliot. We do not know exactly what Marlowe's offense was, but in itself this was a trivial incident. Being bound to keep the peace was extremely common in Elizabethan England. One could be bound to keep the peace for making threats, brandishing a weapon, pushing and shoving, or otherwise behaving in a potentially dangerous way. One could even be bound to keep the peace for being in the company of someone who was behaving in a manner perceived as threatening. Marlowe, however, is the only person named in this recognizance.

Although being bound to keep the peace was not unusual, it seems worth noting that this was Marlowe's second arrest for transgressive or antisocial behavior in less than four months. Nothing like this had happened to him before. In the fight with Bradley in 1589, the innkeeper's son appears to have been the aggressor. Marlowe stopped fighting as soon as Watson appeared, and Watson killed Bradley only when Bradley turned on him. Now Marlowe was the instigator and antagonist. Since this was only a minor infraction, he could escape further consequences by posting a bond of £20, keeping the peace toward the constables, and appearing in court during Michaelmas

[5] Ibid., 249.

term to avoid forfeiting his bond. However, to a person in Marlowe's position £20 was a substantial sum, and this time he seems to have put up the money out of his own pocket, since no bondsmen were involved. If he had recently lost a generous patron and was in danger of losing a market for his plays, it was not an opportune time to forfeit £20.

By the end of June, plays were no longer being performed publicly in London because of the outbreak of plague, and the city was an increasingly hazardous place to live. Marlowe undoubtedly began to consider leaving until the actors returned, but in the meantime yet another annoyance was in store for him. In late August, his old rival and critic Robert Greene was nearing the end of his disreputable life. After Greene's death on 3 September, Henry Chettle tried to exploit his notoriety by publishing a pamphlet called *Greene's Groatsworth of Witte*, which ostensibly consists of Greene's lament for his misspent life, written on his deathbed. This lugubrious work also contains an attack on actors and an exhortation to certain unnamed fellow playwrights to profit from Greene's example.

Greene, of course, had entertained doubts about Marlowe's orthodoxy and moral rectitude since 1588, when he declared in his preface to *Perimedes the Blacksmith* that he would not stoop to "daring God out of Heauen with that Atheist *Tamburlan*" and that he deplored "impious instances of intolerable poetry" and "such mad and scoffing poets . . . bred of Merlin's race."[6] Greene's most successful play, *Friar Bacon and Friar Bungay* (ca. 1591), appears to be a transparent comic rejoinder to Marlowe's *Tragical History of Doctor Faustus*, emphasizing repentance and redemption rather than despair and damnation. Even Greene's ponderously moralistic cony-catching pamphlets, which were written without a thought of Marlowe, stand in stark contrast to Marlowe's gleeful ironic romp through a maze of Machiavellian deceit in *The Jew of Malta*. The author of *Groatsworth* avoids mentioning Marlowe by name, but since only one "famous gracer of Tragedians" had recently written a play with a prologue spoken by the ghost of Machiavel, no one would have doubted who was meant:

> Wonder not, (for with thee wil I first begin), thou famous gracer of Tragedians, that Greene, who hath said with thee (like the foole in his heart), There is no God, should now giue glorie vnto his greatnes: for . . . his hand lies heavie vpon me, . . . and I have felt he is a God that can punish enemies. Why should thy excellent wit, his gift, bee so

[6] Quoted in John Bakeless, *Tragicall History of Christopher Marlowe* (Cambridge, Mass., 1942), 1:95–96, 123–24.

blinded, that thou shouldst giue no glorie to the giuer? Is it pestilent
Machivilian pollicy that thou hast studied? O peevish follie![7]

Greene was the first person we know of to accuse Marlowe of atheism in print,
albeit indirectly; the author of *Groatsworth* not only repeated the allegation
but also embellished it, and he would certainly not be the last of his line.

Marlowe was irked by this latest public accusation, which, unlike
Greene's earlier, more oblique references to "that Atheist *Tamburlan*" and
"impious instances of intolerable poetry," was unambiguously directed at
him. He was joined in his annoyance by a relative newcomer to playwriting,
generally believed to be Shakespeare, who was also stung by one of the author's comments:

> there is an upstart Crow, beautified with our feathers, that with his
> Tygers hart wrapt in a Players hyde, supposes he is as well able to
> bombast out a blanke verse as the best of you: and being an absolute
> Iohannes fac totum, is in his owne conceit the onely Shake-scene in
> the countrey.[8]

Word of the playwrights' displeasure soon reached Henry Chettle, the minor
author and publisher who admitted to preparing this "scald trivial lying
pamphlet," as Nashe later called it, for publication.[9] Marlowe and Shakespeare evidently suspected Chettle of writing part or all of the pamphlet
himself, a suspicion now shared by some scholars.[10] In his preface to *Kind
Heart's Dream* (registered 8 December 1592), Chettle observes dryly that
Greene's "letter written to divers play-makers is offensively by one or two of
them taken, and because on the dead they cannot be avenged, they wilfully
forge in their conceites a living Author: and after tossing it two and fro, no
remedy, but it must light on me."[11] Chettle claims that he was not acquainted
with either man, "and with one of them [Marlowe] I care not if I never be."
Yet he is obviously anxious to pacify this individual he has no desire to meet,
and therefore claims that far from authoring the offensive material, he
deleted some of the passage addressed to Marlowe, "whose learning I reverence": "[I] stroke out what then in conscience I thought he in some displeasure writ: or had it been true, yet to publish it, was intollerable." In a further

---

[7] *Greene's Groatsworth of Wit* (Binghamton, N.Y., 1994), 80.
[8] Ibid., 84–85.
[9] Quoted in Bakeless, *Tragicall History*, 1:124.
[10] D. Allen Carroll, introduction to *Greene's Groatsworth of Wit*, 6–7.
[11] Henry Chettle, preface to *Kind-Hartes Dreame* (New York, 1966), 5–6

attempt at mollification, Chettle adds that he hopes Marlowe "will use me no worse than I deserve."[12] It is unlikely that Marlowe was satisfied with this convenient tale, since Chettle knew very well that what he was publishing was offensive.

At some point between the closing of the theaters and mid-September, Marlowe left London for Canterbury. Whether he simply returned home to visit his friends and family and avoid the plague, or whether he received another assignment and stopped in Canterbury on his way to or from his destination, we do not know. The agent Robert Poley was carrying letters from the court to Dover and back between approximately the twelfth and twenty-fourth of September 1592; if Poley was sent to Dover, Marlowe may have been sent there as well.[13] In any case, while Marlowe was in Canterbury he was involved in yet another quarrel resulting in his arrest, and once again he appears to have been the instigator or aggressor.

This time his adversary was William Corkine, a tailor and part-time chorister in the cathedral. All we know about the encounter is contained in the suit for damages filed by Corkine in the Canterbury civil court:

> William Corkyn sues Christopher Marlowe, gentleman, on a plea of transgression. . . . And hence the same plaintiff, by Giles Winston his attorney, makes plaint that the foresaid defendant on the fifteenth day of September, in the thirty-fourth year of the reign of our lady Queen Elizabeth . . . in the city of Canterbury aforesaid, in the parish of St. Andrew and in the Ward of Westgate of this same city, by force of arms, that is to say with staff and dagger, assaulted the same plaintiff, and then and there struck, wounded, and maltreated this same plaintiff. And then and there inflicted other outrages on the said plaintiff to the grave damage of the same plaintiff and against the peace of the said lady the Queen, wherefore the said plaintiff says he has suffered loss, and has incurred damages to the value of £5.[14]

According to Urry,[15] Marlowe's father paid the sum required for his son's surety to appear in court, and in a recognizable variation of the strategy he used in Flushing, which was a common practice for anyone disputing charges, Marlowe proceeded to bring countercharges against Corkine. However, instead of waiting to do this in civil court, Marlowe and his lawyer

---

[12] Ibid., 6.
[13] William Urry, *Christopher Marlowe and Canterbury* (London, 1988), 68–69.
[14] Ibid., 66, 131. This document is transcribed and translated in its entirety in the appendix.
[15] Ibid., 66.

brought charges against Corkine before a grand jury at the Canterbury Quarter Sessions held on 26 September. The indictment uses formulaic language similar to that of Corkine's plea, claiming that Corkine "assaulted a certain Christopher Marlowe, gentleman, and then and there struck, wounded, and maltreated the same Christopher Marlowe, and then and there inflicted other outrages on the said Christopher Marlowe, to the grave damage of the same Christopher and against the peace of the said lady the queen, etc."[16] No weapon is specified, however, and the grand jury dismissed the indictment, presumably because Marlowe failed to produce convincing evidence against Corkine.

In all probability, any initial assault Corkine may have made on Marlowe was verbal, provoking Marlowe to respond with a physical attack. Since Corkine was not wounded seriously enough to justify criminal charges, Marlowe's staff and dagger were very likely used to pummel Corkine over the head, "breaking his coxcomb" in classic Elizabethan fashion. Corkine no doubt retaliated with his fists and feet, but whatever the extent of the damage he inflicted, Marlowe could not specify in his indictment that a weapon had been used against him. It is little wonder the grand jury took no action.

Why did Marlowe risk such an embarrassment? Perhaps he was merely trying to intimidate Corkine, or perhaps he was eager to have the case settled. His required appearance at Finsbury court in London was pending, and the Privy Council's ban on the performance of plays in London was about to expire. Nevertheless, he had to wait until Corkine's plea was presented in civil court on 2 October. He was given a week to respond, and when he returned to court on 9 October the suit was dropped by mutual consent.

Marlowe apparently missed his day in court at Finsbury, but he may have returned to London by late October, where some of the news awaiting him was encouraging. On 22 October, Edward Alleyn married Philip Henslowe's stepdaughter Joan Woodward, further consolidating the alliance between the Admiral's–Lord Strange's Men and Henslowe. By late December all the actors were back in London. Strange's men were again playing at court, and Marlowe's *The Massacre at Paris*, which Henslowe called "The Tragedy of the Guise," was added to the Admiral's-Strange's repertory.[17] A new company called Pembroke's Men had emerged and was playing at court in late December. This company was apparently an offshoot of Admiral's–Lord Strange's Men that had formed earlier in 1592, when the actors left London for the provinces. Somehow they were in possession of Marlowe's *Edward II*, either

---

[16] Ibid., 66–67, 131. This document is transcribed and translated in its entirety in the appendix.
[17] Chambers, *The Elizabethan Stage*, 2:122–23.

because Admiral's-Strange's Men let them have it or because Marlowe had sold it to them. The fact that the play has no part that seems to be meant for Edward Alleyn suggests that it was written expressly for Pembroke's Men. But the new company found it difficult to establish themselves under such adverse conditions, and after the second wave of plague struck they were forced to sell *Edward II* to a printer in July 1593. By 28 September, according to a letter from Henslowe to Alleyn, they were inactive: "As for my lorde a Penbrockes wch you desier to knowe wheare they be they are all at home and hausse ben this v or sixe weackes for they cane not saue ther carges wth trauell as I heare & weare fayne to pane ther parell for ther carge."[18]

The rest of the news waiting for Marlowe in London was less pleasant. His friend Tom Watson had died, perhaps at St. Bartholomew's Hospital, since he was buried in the churchyard of St. Bartholomew the Less on 26 September. Even though Marlowe's career was well launched, losing Watson was a blow. Moreover, the "scald trivial lying pamphlet" attributed to Greene was now on sale in St. Paul's Churchyard. In spite of its questionable authorship and its coy refusal to name names, Marlowe could hardly ignore the attack, because those who wrote and published it believed they could profit from publicly criticizing Marlowe. The pamphlet was a warning, though not precisely of the kind its author intended. It was an irksome reminder that acquiring a reputation for unorthodoxy could be a serious liability for a Renaissance author. Although the pamphlet purported to know what Marlowe was saying in his heart, its criticism seemed to be based mainly on the content of his plays. And if the indirect expression of unconventional ideas in dramatic form could inspire such an attack, more direct expression of them was out of the question. Thought was free, but speech was not, particularly when it crossed the fine line between private and public utterance. If Marlowe had indeed written a manuscript that would later be variously described as "the Atheist lecture," "a book against the Scripture, how that it was all of one man's making," and a list of "contraieties oute of the Scripture," the appearance of this pamphlet meant that the manuscript had to remain in private circulation.[19] In its modest way, *Groatsworth* made it clear that Marlowe could not take the world's respect and approval, much less its tolerance, for granted. If he crossed the invisible but firmly drawn line that separated acceptable from unacceptable expression, even a contemptible literary hack would venture to patronize and admonish him.

All in all, 1592 had been a bitter year for Marlowe. Since leaving the uni-

---

[18] Ibid., 2:128.
[19] These allegations are discussed in detail in chapter 8.

versity he had gradually come to realize that it was relatively easy to imagine a superman, and virtually impossible to be one—a shift in attitude reflected in the gradual diminution of his heroes from the colossal Tamburlaine to mere fallible, ineffectual mortals. But if Marlowe was gaining experience and wisdom, his actions, particularly in the pivotal year 1592, suggest that he was also growing resentful and angry, and developing an explosive temper. Marlowe was far too intelligent and practical to deny reality, but his humanist education, privileged status, and competitive spirit made him too proud to suffer frustration and adversity patiently. He might make a joke of Barabas's indignant "What tell you me of Job?" and still understand Barabas's attitude perfectly (*The Jew of Malta*, 1.2.184). Several times during the year he had lashed out at perceived threats to his dignity and autonomy, and each time he had suffered a humiliating defeat. The more he tried to assert his power and control, the more he was forced to confront his limitations. It would have been an ideal time for quiet reflection and a mature reassessment of inflated expectations, but other, more alluring projects monopolized Marlowe's attention, and in less than a year he would have no more expectations to revise.

Perhaps Marlowe consoled himself by writing the Latin dedication to Watson's posthumous *Amintae Gaudia*, entered in the stationer's register on 10 November—if Thomas Morley's brother Christopher had not already composed it and added the initials C. M. Either man would have welcomed the countess's favor. Not long thereafter, Marlowe certainly wrote the charming Latin epitaph on Sir Roger Manwood, who died on 14 December 1592. Perhaps this poem was commissioned, although it was never placed on Manwood's tomb. Perhaps Marlowe eulogized Manwood to repay some favor, although the poem says nothing about Manwood's generosity. Or perhaps Marlowe simply admired his countryman's success as a politician and the power he wielded on the bench as a "just and dreadful punisher of sin," in spite of the charges of corruption that tainted his career (*Tamburlaine the Great, Part 2*, 3.3.4).

Manwood, like Marlowe, was a native of Kent; the son of a Sandwich draper who settled in Canterbury just outside Westgate, he eventually built a manor at nearby Hackington. He was one of the justices sitting on the bench at the Old Bailey when Marlowe appeared there to be formally cleared in the death of William Bradley, but since the outcome of that case was not in doubt, neither this nor Manwood's worldly success seems to explain the epitaph. The poem has a delicate, playful tone entirely lacking in the stilted rhetoric of the dedication to *Amintae Gaudia*, as if Marlowe felt that the spirit of a sophisticated Latinist would relish a witty tribute to the power he once wielded. It is also possible that Thomas Walsingham asked Marlowe to write the poem. A connection of some kind existed between the Walsinghams and the Manwoods; Thomas Walsingham's son, Thomas the Younger, would marry Sir Roger's granddaughter Elizabeth, daughter of Sir Peter Manwood of Hackington, Kent.

Certainly Marlowe would increasingly rely on Thomas Walsingham for refuge and support in 1593. The brief revival of drama in London lasted only a month. By the end of January, a resurgence of plague brought a new ban on public performances. The actors had no choice but to return to the provinces, and Marlowe headed for Scadbury, Thomas Walsingham's estate at Chislehurst, Kent. There he would begin and partly complete his great Ovidian minor epic *Hero and Leander*. And there he was believed to be staying when he was caught up in a series of events that have inspired more frenzied speculation than any other part of Marlowe's life.

7

A Trim Reckoning

❧

What is that honor? Air. A trim reckoning! Who hath it?
He that died a' Wednesday.

Shakespeare, *Henry IV, Part 1*, 5.1.135–36

A SUDDEN DEATH, even one that occurred four centuries ago, is an affront to normalcy. Such seemingly absurd events violate our sense of order and coherence, disturb us so profoundly that the need to probe and analyze them is as automatic as breathing. If we cannot undo what has happened, we can at least try to comprehend it. Marlowe's death is a source of endless fascination precisely because we lack sufficient information to file it tidily away. We weave fictions around Marlowe that we know are fictions, resigned to the fact that our desire for resolution can never be satisfied. It is an activity rather like thumb sucking—all forepleasure, with no end pleasure in sight. Nevertheless, it is a ritual that no biography of Marlowe can do without.

A number of well worn but serviceable narrative genres have been deployed in this quest for a satisfying explanation. Early commentators on Marlowe like Thomas Beard, Francis Meres, Edmund Rudierd, and William Vaughan were partial to the moral fable. To such writers the reason for Marlowe's sudden death is obvious: Marlowe was stabbed in the eye with the dagger he was wielding because it was God's will to punish him: "Herein did the iustice of God most notably appeare, in that hee compelled his owne hand which had written those blasphemies to be the instrument to punish him, and that in his braine, which had deuised the same."[1] The idea of divine retribution has little appeal, however, for twentieth-century writers, who prefer complex answers to simple ones, and favor theories that reflect more

---

[1] Quoted in John Bakeless, *Tragicall History of Christopher Marlowe* (Cambridge, Mass., 1942), 1:145.

contemporary attitudes and preoccupations. Man has now replaced God as the causal agent. Political conspiracy, espionage, imposture, and polymorphous sexuality figure prominently in books written on Marlowe during the twentieth century. While these fictions are considerably more imaginative and entertaining than Beard's strident moralizing, they may come no closer to the truth.

So many fanciful and speculative theories have been concocted about Marlowe's death, including the predictable denials that he died in Deptford at all, that there is little point in adding to them.[2] It is difficult enough already to disentangle fact from fiction. Since criteria such as reasonable probability and interpretive economy have fallen into disuse, perhaps it would be helpful to dust them off and see where they lead. Perhaps we should ask what the likeliest (rather than the most ingenious or sensational or titillating) explanation of Marlowe's death is. This is the question I will consider in this chapter, without pretending to offer an absolute answer.

Virtually all writers on Marlowe do agree that the circumstances surrounding his death were part of a chain of events that began several months earlier. In 1930, C. F. Tucker Brooke noted the probable significance of the dispirited mood prevailing in London in the spring of 1593. The plague, which provided an eerily appropriate backdrop for Marlowe's death, had also generated a diffuse anxiety, and one of the products of this "nervous tension," Brooke concluded, was "the brutal spirit of persecution manifested during this spring by Archbishop Whitgift."[3] Rigorous prosecution of dissenters was no novelty for Whitgift, but in 1593 his efforts seemed to intensify. On 21 March he indicted two Puritans who had been in prison for six years, Henry Barrow and John Greenwood—the same "Sr Greenwood" to whom Marlowe had yielded his place in commons in 1581. Greenwood and Barrow were promptly tried, convicted, and hanged on 6 April. Meanwhile, Whitgift was vigorously pursuing John Penry, Marlowe's (and briefly, Green-

---

[2] Theories that Marlowe died for political reasons or as the result of a conspiracy begin with Samuel A. Tannenbaum's *The Assassination of Christopher Marlowe* (Hamden, Conn., 1928) and continue unabated through Charles Nicholl's *The Reckoning: The Murder of Christopher Marlowe* (London, 1992). Many of them are shrewdly assessed by Kenneth Friedenreich, although he draws no distinction between a psychological theory based on literary and extra-literary evidence and highly fictionalized speculation based on a few inconclusive documents and conveniently isolated facts. Kenneth Friedenrich, "Marlowe's Endings," in *"A Poet and a filthy Play-Maker": New Essays on Christopher Marlowe*, ed. Friedenreich, Roma Gill, and Constance Kuriyama (New York: AMS Press, 1988), 361–69.

The even more bizarre theories that Marlowe wrote Shakespeare's plays after his supposed death began in 1819 with an article by an anonymous author in *Monthly Review* and continue to the present. Like all anti-Stratfordian fantasies, the claims for Marlowe are based on deliberate selection and highly partial interpretation of evidence.

[3] C. F. Tucker Brooke, *The Life of Marlowe and The Tragedy of Dido, Queen of Carthage*, in *The Works and Life of Christopher Marlowe*, ed. R. H. Case (New York, 1966), 52.

wood's) contemporary at Cambridge. Since Whitgift believed Penry to be the author of the Marprelate tracts, he was intent on punishing him. Penry was captured on 22 March, brought to trial on 21 May, three days after Marlowe was summoned by the Privy Council, and hanged on 29 May, the day before Marlowe died. By further coincidence, Penry was executed at St. Thomas a'Watering, about two and a half miles from the house in Deptford where Marlowe was killed.

To Brooke the "demoralizing" effects of the plague also underlay the wave of anti-alien sentiment that swept through London in the spring of 1593.[4] Nicholl mentions other probable sources of popular disaffection, such as the continuing threat from Spain, the prolonged military engagement in the Low Countries, and high unemployment and inflation.[5] To these one might add the renewed ban on popular entertainments such as bull-and bearbaiting and the performance of plays, which normally served to release pent-up aggression and relax social tension. The emotional climate was ripe for scapegoating, and "strangers" and Puritans, who were readily cast as dangerous others, were obvious targets. "Atheists"—a loose term for all those whose beliefs were heterodox—were also vulnerable, and as we shall see, some accusations of atheism and adventitious inquiry into it did occur. But misgivings about atheists, who posed only an abstract threat to divinely ordained authority, did not have such powerful political and economic rationales as the attacks on Puritans and foreigners. Activist Puritans were dangerous to church and state because they unintentionally abetted the Catholics by undermining the authority of the English church. Resident aliens posed a different kind of danger. English merchants and craftsmen perceived strangers as an immediate threat to their livelihood, and therefore the status of foreigners was an explosive economic issue, hotly debated in Parliament and elsewhere. In March 1593, a bill was introduced in the House of Commons prohibiting foreigners from selling imported goods at retail.[6] In response, another bill was passed offering the strangers extended privileges. Overall, the English government favored immigration, which increased the Protestant population and was believed to strengthen the economy as a whole.[7] However, passage of the second bill further alienated English merchants and craftsmen.

The debates in Parliament on strangers ended on 24 March. In mid-April, to the Privy Council's alarm, anti-alien "libels" containing intemperate at-

[4] Ibid., 53.
[5] Nicholl, *The Reckoning*, 39.
[6] Brooke, *The Life of Marlowe*, 54.
[7] Nicholl, *The Reckoning*, 39, 290–91.

tacks on resident aliens began to be posted in the streets of London. Although one arrest was made immediately, the libels continued to appear. Therefore, on 22 April the council ordered Dr. Julius Caesar and four other commissioners "to examine by secret means who may be authors of the said libels, and by your industries to discover what the intentions are of the publishers thereof."[8] These discreet measures were not immediately effective, for on 5 May another of the "lewd and malicious libels," one which "doth exceed the rest in lewdness," was posted on the wall of the Dutch Churchyard in Broad Street.[9] The text of this libel, which was recovered in full in 1971, poses some intriguing questions. It takes the form of a doggerel poem, a fifty-three-line screed of complaints and threats signed "Tamburlaine" that also alludes to Marlowe's *The Jew of Malta* and *The Massacre at Paris*. Although "Tamburlaine" is an obvious pseudonym, and no reasonably literate investigator would mistake the poem for Marlowe's, the author of the libel reads Marlowe's plays as a blueprint for violent action: "We'll cut your throats, in your temples praying / Not Paris massacre so much blood did spill."[10] It is the kind of misguided admiration that might well make an author wince—especially under such volatile social and political conditions.

On 10 May a proclamation was read at the Guildhall offering a reward of 100 crowns in gold to anyone providing information about the libels. The following day, the Privy Council drafted a letter authorizing the lord mayor's commissioners to search the property and papers of any suspected persons. The commissioners were also urged to arrest any who were "duly to be suspected," and, should these suspects fail to provide information about the "seditious libels," to put them to torture in Bridewell "as often as you shall think fit."[11] On 12 May, Marlowe's fellow playwright Thomas Kyd was subjected to such a search. Among his papers the investigators found no libels, but they did find a suspicious manuscript containing heretical ideas. When Kyd failed to confess to involvement in the libels or to provide useful information, he was arrested and tortured.

The first question that arises is, of course, why Kyd? Was it, as Nicholl suggests, because of the allusions to Marlowe's plays in the Dutch Church libel, and the fact that Kyd had once worked in the same room with Marlowe?[12] This is one possibility. It is even possible that Kyd was believed to be involved in the writing of Marlowe's plays, since authors of plays in the sixteenth cen-

---

[8] Dasent, *Acts of the Privy Council*, quoted in Brooke, *The Life of Marlowe*, 54–55.
[9] Ibid., 55.
[10] Quoted in Nicholl, *The Reckoning*, 41.
[11] Dasent, quoted in Brooke, *The Life of Marlowe*, 55.
[12] Nicholl, *The Reckoning*, 42.

tury were about as little known outside circles of enthusiasts as authors of screenplays are today. It is worth recalling that Marlowe's name did not appear on the title page of *Tamburlaine*, and that apparently none of his plays was published under his name in his lifetime. But possible though it may be, this theory is not necessarily correct. Kyd was obviously suspected of involvement in the posting of one or more of the libels, but we do not know which ones (there were "divers"), or how he was believed to be involved, or who decided that he was a suspicious person. Kyd might conceivably have been suspected of anti-alien sympathies. Kyd's *The Spanish Tragedy* is sharply (if obliquely) critical of ruling elites—the group in England that most enthusiastically supported the immigrants. But there is a more practical reason why Kyd might have been suspected in connection with the libels, one that has nothing to do with Marlowe.

It is no accident that the one man whom we know was pilloried, fined, and imprisoned for posting a libel against strangers was a scrivener named Shore. Libels had to be written, and while their authors were necessarily literate, a document intended for public display would be more impressive (and legible) if copied in a fair hand. This was a skill possessed by very few craftsmen, because most had never progressed beyond petty school. Some scriveners were obviously active in this paper war, if not as authors then certainly as copyists, and a number of them must have been questioned about libels that had a suspiciously professional look. Kyd's father was a scrivener, and Kyd himself, who never attended a university, was one of those "shifting companions" Nashe scoffs at in his preface to *Menaphon*, who "leave the trade of Noverint [scrivener], whereto they were borne, and busie themselves with the indevours of Art."[13] While it is possible that Kyd's connection with the theater and with Marlowe brought his name to the commissioners' minds, the fact that Kyd had been a scrivener, and perhaps still plied his old trade on occasion, was a more plausible reason for questioning him and searching his papers. It may be significant that in the letter he wrote to Sir John Puckering after his release, Kyd never says that he was suspected of authoring the libel, which bears no more resemblance to his style than to Marlowe's. Instead he declares, "I was neither agent nor consenting thereunto,"[14] as if his suspected involvement were more indirect. Furthermore, though Kyd accuses Marlowe of being irreligious in order to distance himself from suspicion of atheism, he never indicates that he was investigated for libel because of his association with Marlowe, nor does he accuse Marlowe of sedi-

[13] Thomas Nashe, *Works*, ed. R. B. McKerrow and F. P. Wilson (Oxford, 1958), 3:315.
[14] The complete texts of Kyd's letter and note to Puckering are transcribed in the Appendix. Quoted in Brooke, *The Life of Marlowe*, 106.

tious intent. Rather he says, "if I knewe eny whom I cold justlie accuse of that... mutinous sedition towrd the state I wold... willingly reveale them."[15]

The ostensibly heretical fragment of a manuscript found in Kyd's lodgings might be taken as confirmation of the investigators' suspicions, because to an Elizabethan atheism and sedition were closely allied rebellions against divinely sanctioned authority. While a heretical document wasn't nearly as impressive as the foul papers of a libel, it might pass for probable cause. Kyd was therefore "duly to be suspected," and when he continued to maintain his innocence and failed to provide information about the libels, he was tortured in accordance with the Privy Council's directive. At some point Kyd decided that this troublesome atheistic manuscript must have belonged to Marlowe, and his ascription may well have been correct. To claim, as Nicholl does, on the basis of no evidence whatsoever, that the manuscript was planted by one of the investigators is pure whimsy. Nicholl offers no clear explanation of who this person was, except to hint that Walsingham's master spy Thomas Phelippes, who was now working for the Earl of Essex, might have engineered the plant.[16] He does not explain exactly how Phelippes was involved in the investigation of Kyd, why he decided to plant the document in Kyd's papers rather than somewhere else, or why he did not plant a much more damaging document if his intent was to incriminate Marlowe. This manuscript is in any case not particularly incriminating, since it is a copy of part of a book refuting anti-trinitarian views (John Proctour's *Fall of the Late Arrian*). Marlowe's Canterbury schoolmaster Mr. Gresshop had a copy of this book, which was presumably not obscure, in his library, and once its source was identified the manuscript would have endangered no one. On this point and on many others, Nicholl's elaborate conspiracy theory suffers for lack of evidence.[17]

When the Privy Council summoned Marlowe on 18 May, almost two weeks had elapsed since the Dutch Church libel was posted, and almost a week had passed since Kyd's arrest. If Marlowe was suspected of mutinous sedition or inciting to rebellion, the council's dilatory manner of summoning him is inexplicable. A messenger of Her Majesty's chamber, Mr. Henry Maunder, was dispatched "to the house of Mr. Tho. Walsingham in Kent, or to any other place where he shall understand Christofer Marlowe to be re-

---

[15] Ibid.

[16] Nicholl, *The Reckoning*, 300.

[17] Nicholl's discussion of a false "Raleigh" poem in *The Reckoning*, 298–99, is interesting, but the fact that this tactic was used against Raleigh in 1603 in no way proves that a roughly similar tactic was used against Marlowe in 1593. Raleigh was a major political figure who might have been worth making the target of such an elaborate ploy. Marlowe was not.

maining," for the purpose of apprehending Marlowe and bringing him to the court, "and in case of need to require aid." The language of the directive, including the last phrase, is formulaic, and, as Brooke demonstrated long ago, such summonses were not unusual.[18] On the other hand, it probably is significant that the entry makes no mention whatsoever, as many others do, of Marlowe's being summoned "to answer such matters as should be objected against him." When Marlowe arrived in court on 20 May, he was simply instructed to give his "daily attendance"—in other words, to be ready to appear at each meeting of the Privy Council until his presence was no longer required. This was also a routine procedure. During the ten days between his arrival and his death, the Privy Council showed no special interest in Marlowe. He was not arrested and tortured; his papers were not searched and seized. If we compare his treatment to that of Kyd, who was presumably still languishing in Bridewell, or to Penry, whose arrest, trial, and execution progressed with lightning speed, the difference is telling. Brooke's suggestion that Marlowe was being summoned as a material witness, not as a suspect, is the most reasonable conclusion we can draw from these facts. While Marlowe was no doubt on guard, he was in no immediate danger.

In the meantime, an acquaintance of Marlowe's named Richard Cholmeley was experiencing difficulties of his own that seem at least remotely connected to Marlowe's. We can trace this thread of the story back to 13 May 1591, when the Privy Council ordered the apprehension of Thomas Drury and his companions Roen and Cholmeley. However, on 29 July Cholmeley and another man, Burrage, were paid for bringing Drury in to face charges on "divers great and fond matters."[19] On 19 January 1592, Richard Cholmeley's brother Sir Hugh Cholmeley wrote to Sir Robert Cecil concerning his and Richard's activities on behalf of the queen.[20] Apparently both were involved in the detection and capture of Catholics.[21] No more is heard of Cholmeley until 19 March 1593, when a warrant was issued to George Cobham to apprehend Richard Cholmeley and Richard Strong and bring them before the council. This time Cholmeley remained at large until 28 June, when, after petitioning Archbishop Whitgift, he turned himself in to one of Justice Richard Young's officers named Wilbrom.

Two informer's reports, which are preserved among the Harleian manuscripts along with the Baines note, clarify the basis for this second warrant. These manuscripts are tidily executed clerical copies in the same hand, not

---

[18] Dasent, quoted and discussed in Brooke, *The Life of Marlowe*, 58–60.
[19] Quoted in Frederick S. Boas, *Marlowe and His Circle* (Oxford, 1931), 80.
[20] Ibid., 80–81; Bakeless, *Tragicall History*, 1:126.
[21] Nicholl, *The Reckoning*, 271–73.

signed originals. The informer remains anonymous, but both documents seem to have been composed by the same person. Nicholl claims that the author was Drury,[22] but the crisp style of these reports bears little resemblance to surviving samples of Drury's disjointed prose, and it is obvious from the second report that the informer was not a former companion of Cholmeley, as Drury was. The first document, headed "Remembrances of words & matter against Ric Cholmeley," is a list of allegations in which each item, according to a formula widely used in state papers for recording reported statements, begins with "That." The other is a letter further describing Cholmeley and detailing his activities.

The two documents also differ in that the first is mainly concerned with documenting Cholmeley's indiscreet and disparaging remarks about the Privy Council and other prominent government figures, as well as his arrogant boasts about himself. Item one, for example, reads, "That hee speaketh in generall all evill of the Counsell; sayenge that they are all Atheistes & Machiavillians, especially my Lord Admirall."[23] After more allegations in the same vein, the informer includes an item of special interest to Marlowe biographers: "That he saieth & verely beleveth that one Marlowe is able to shewe more sounde reasons for Atheisme then any devine in Englande is able to geve to prove devinitie & that Marloe tolde him that hee hath read the Atheist lecture to Sir Walter Raliegh & others." We can gather from this report that Cholmeley had been an agent of the Privy Council working against the Catholics. However, according to the informer, Cholmeley had only contempt for his masters, boasting "that hee can goe beyonde & cossen them as he liste."

The second document aggressively depicts Cholmeley as a dangerous, seditious person and an atheist: "Their practise is after her Majesties decease to make a kinge amonge them selves & live accordinge to their owne lawes. . . . his manner of proceedinge in seducinge the Queenes subjectes is firste to make slannderous reportes of most noble peeres & honorable Counsailors. . . . his second course is to make a jeste of the Scripture with these fearefull horrible & damnable speeches, that Jhesus Christe was a bastarde St Mary a whore & the Anngell Gabriell a Bawde to the holy ghoste." The informer ends the letter with a warning: "This cursed Cholmeley hath Lx of his company & hee is seldom from his felowes & therefore I beeseech your worship have a speciall care of your selfe in apprehendinge him for they bee resolute murderinge myndes."[24]

[22] Ibid., 306.
[23] BL Harleian MS 6848, f. 190. The full texts of both of these reports on Cholmeley are transcribed in the appendix.
[24] BL Harleian MS 6848, f. 191.

Like Sir Robert Sidney's letter from Flushing reporting the coining incident, these reports raise more questions than they answer. The informer seems to believe what he says—with some allowance for politic exaggeration. After all, the more dangerous he represents Cholmeley as being, the more credit he can take for exposing him. But what do we make of Cholmeley? Was he a disaffected megalomanic agent who seriously believed he could create his own state? If we recall the radical underground groups and cults that flourished in the 1960s and 1970s in a similar climate of contempt for authority, this seems possible. The leaders of such groups typically take a grandiose view of themselves and what they can accomplish. No doubt some of the exaggeration in the document originated with Cholmeley, who must be the source of the claim that he had sixty followers.

Or perhaps Cholmeley, who had pretended to be a Catholic in the past, was now on a fishing expedition of a different sort, pretending to be a malcontent and atheist, the better to catch malcontents and atheists. If so, he was no longer working for the Privy Council or for Burghley and his son Sir Robert Cecil. And there is a third possibility, which may be the likeliest of all. Perhaps Cholmeley was a loose cannon, a man with no true loyalties who actually had more than a little sympathy for atheism and rebellion (the bitterness of his reported remarks about the Privy Council seems genuine), and who cynically played the political game purely for his own advantage. Perhaps he was a sincere admirer of Marlowe and his plays. This is consistent with the informer's report "that beinge imployed by some of her Majesties prevy Counsaile for the apprehension of Papists & other daungerous men hee used as he saieth to take money of them & would lett them passe in spighte of the Counsell." In this case Cholmeley was working for someone who would have supported him had he gotten into trouble, but he was also ready to capitalize on whatever opportunities for additional profit his work provided. He was the classic double-dealing agent, except, perhaps, for the size of his ego and the scope of his ambition. If chance had made Cholmeley king, Cholmeley would not have refused.

Cholmeley's employer at the time of the informer's report was apparently the Earl of Essex. As F. S. Boas was the first to point out, Essex wrote a letter to Sir E. Littleton, Sir E. Aston, and R. Bagot on 13 November 1593, thanking them for their work on behalf of his servant Cholmeley and urging them to continue their efforts to establish his innocence.[25] Since Cholmeley was a disaffected agent of the Privy Council and Sir Robert Cecil, it seems likely that he entered Essex's service to spite his former employers. Essex had re-

[25] Boas, *Marlowe and His Circle*, 83.

cently recruited Anthony Bacon to direct his own private intelligence network, which he hoped would surpass the one the Cecils had inherited from Sir Francis Walsingham—the operation with which Marlowe was probably still connected. A number of the men Essex employed, like Cholmeley and Thomas Phelippes, had previously worked for Walsingham, the Privy Council, and the Cecils. Cholmeley was therefore building his fanciful atheist empire while in Essex's employ. We may never know exactly what was afoot, but perhaps Cholmeley was not acting on his own initiative.

At this time Essex, who had just been appointed a Privy Councilor, was eager to increase his credit with the queen. It was therefore to his advantage to weaken rivals like Sir Walter Raleigh and Sir Robert Cecil. Raleigh was already out of favor with Elizabeth, who had discovered his secret marriage to Elizabeth Throckmorton, one of her maids of honor, in August 1592. By the spring of 1593 Raleigh had retired to his estate in Dorset and was no longer competing with Essex in court, but Essex knew from his own marriage to Frances Walsingham that Elizabeth's displeasure with her favorites' unapproved marriages tended to be temporary. Essex needed to strengthen his position with the queen while Raleigh was out of contention, and if possible undermine the Cecils.

Raising the specter of an uprising of atheists and malcontents by unleashing someone like Cholmeley might have served Essex's purposes. Miscellaneous heresy was an area of relatively minor concern to the Cecils and to Archbishop Whitgift, who were mainly preoccupied with containing Catholics and radical Puritans. No one knew how many atheists lurked in England or how dangerous they were, but the implicit working assumption was that they were too few and too disorganized to pose a serious threat. By employing an experienced agent provocateur like Cholmeley, Essex could find out if a heterodox power base existed, and, if so, how extensive it was. Depending on these findings, he could then decide what use to make of his knowledge of this new sect. It is worth recalling that Essex eventually destroyed himself because he believed he could mount a successful coup d'état by riding through the streets of London and mobilizing the discontented rabble. Evidently he believed reservoirs of discontent existed in London that could be tapped for his purposes.

If conventional wisdom proved correct and relatively few atheists surfaced, Essex could always exaggerate the threat, gaining the queen's favor by exposing a potential danger that other councilors had overlooked because of their preoccupation with Catholics and radical Puritans. If we recall Essex's successful attempt to aggrandize himself by incriminating Dr. Roderigo Lopez in 1594, this conjecture seems more than possible. In the Lopez case,

Essex exploited the animus against an outsider and potentially dangerous "other" (both a Jew and a foreigner) to further his own ambitions. If he could conjure up an atheist menace, Essex could not only aggrandize himself, but also discredit the Cecils and other members of the council for ignoring it. He might even suggest, as Cholmeley allegedly did, that they were atheists themselves: "the Lord Threasorer the Lord Chamberleyn the Lord Admirall, Sir Robrt Cecill. Those saieth hee have profound wittes, bee sounde Athiestes & their lives & deedes showe that they thinke their soules doe ende vanishe & perishe with their bodies." And if Raleigh resurfaced as a threat, Essex could also align him with this dangerous sect. In executing this hypothetical maneuver, Essex would have collaborated with another member of the Privy Council, Sir John Puckering, Lord Keeper of the Privy Seal (chancellor), who was also a recent addition to the council, having been appointed in 1592.[26] Puckering and Essex had a long acquaintance as a result of Puckering's former service as sole justice of the Carmarthen circuit, one of Essex's Welsh territories, and Essex often asked Puckering for favors. However, Puckering also had ties to Essex's rivals, which would have limited his ability and willingness to support Essex.[27]

This argument may seem consistent with Nicholl's argument that Essex's purpose was to destroy Raleigh by attacking Marlowe,[28] but if Essex was plotting at all, he probably had a far grander goal in mind than using Marlowe to discredit a single rival. That he was primarily targeting Raleigh seems especially unlikely since Raleigh was already in eclipse, and Essex had begun to forge an "extraordinary rapprochement" with him.[29] If Essex's intent was rather to conjure up bugbears and hobgoblins to enhance his status with the queen, Marlowe seems to figure in the plan incidentally rather than centrally. He would have been useful because he had already acquired some reputation as an "Atheist," his plays had an enthusiastic following among the rabble who frequented the theater, he had worked for other members of the Privy Council, and he had had some contact with Raleigh. Thus Cholmeley refers in passing to Marlowe and Raleigh but devotes far more attention to discrediting members of the Privy Council, notably Burghley and Sir Robert Cecil.

Nicholl believes that Cholmeley wrote the Dutch Church libel, since he boasted of writing libelous verses in praise of virtuous priests at Sir Robert Cecil's request, and also claimed to have written a libel against Sir Francis

---

[26] Paul E. J. Hammer, *The Polarisation of Elizabethan Politics* (Cambridge, 1999), 290 n. 121.

[27] Ibid., 290.

[28] Nicholl, *The Reckoning*, 291–301.

[29] Paul E. J. Hammer, "A Reckoning Reframed: The 'Murder' of Christopher Marlowe Revisited," *English Literary Renaissance* 26 (1996): 236–37; see also Hammer, *The Polarisation of Elizabethan Politics*, 116.

Drake and Justice Young on his own initiative.[30] Perhaps Cholmeley did concoct the Dutch Church libel—and other anti-alien libels besides. Fomenting anti-alien sentiment would certainly have been consistent with this hypothetical strategy of Essex's. Popular unrest directed at aliens might make Raleigh, who had spoken against the strangers in Parliament, look like an instigator, and it would also throw Essex's fellow Privy Councilors on the defensive. The references to Marlowe's plays in the Dutch Church libel may have been less an attack on Marlowe than a crude attempt to tap the same emotions aroused by his plays and channel them into political unrest. Essex had great faith in the power of drama to arouse popular sentiment, as indicated by his tactic of commissioning performances of *Richard II* before his abortive coup.

Like most theories about Marlowe in the weeks leading up to his death, this is pure circumstantial speculation. There is no direct evidence of any such plot on Essex's part, though he was heavily engaged in an intrigue of some kind in June 1593, possibly a prelude to the Lopez case.[31] It seems rather unlikely that Essex would target anyone for religious reasons. He may have been ambitious and competitive, but he was remarkably tolerant in matters of faith, and it is possible that Cholmeley was merely following his own inclinations and expressing his own beliefs in the conversations reported in the "Remembrances." He did, after all, claim that he had written some libels on his own initiative.

At some time during May, Cholmeley's remarks about Marlowe's atheism and the "Atheist lecture" were supported by the testimony of Richard Baines. Baines was involved in some obscure dealings with Cholmeley's former associate Thomas Drury in mid-May, but his activities around the time of Marlowe's death are more obviously significant. On the Saturday evening preceding Marlowe's fatal encounter with Ingram Frizer on Wednesday, 30 May, someone delivered a document signed by Richard Baines with the heading "A note containing the opinion of on Christopher Marly concerning his damnable judgment of religion and scorne of gods word."[32] At some point during the following weeks, an edited copy of this note was made to alert the queen to the atheist menace. The endorsement on the copy declares that Baines's note was delivered on "whitsun eve last," and that Marlowe "within iii dayes after [i.e., after Whitsunday, which the author crossed out and then forgot to include in the revised sentence] came to a soden & fearfull end of his life." Since Whitsunday fell on 2 June 1593, four days after Marlowe's

[30] Nicholl, *The Reckoning*, 287.
[31] Hammer, *The Polarisation of Elizabethan Politics*, 156–63.
[32] BL Harleian 6848, f. 154.

death, the author of the endorsement was apparently confused: Marlowe's life ended three days after the Sunday before Whitsunday. Such faulty recollection is perfectly understandable, since Whitsunday is a moveable feast.

The heading and body of the manuscript are in a legible secretary hand. Baines's name appears to be signed at the end in a bolder script used specifically for signatures, a common practice in manuscripts of the period. Whether any part of the note is actually in Baines's hand, or whether it was dictated to a scribe or copied from another manuscript, is uncertain. The copy of the note sent to the queen is also apparently signed, but the hand is entirely different and the document is clearly identified as a copy. While the Baines Note is often forcefully phrased and quite lucid, it has the appearance of being composed or written quickly. It is not a fair copy and contains occasional corrections, as if the author or scribe were conscious of the style and anxious to be precise. In the heading, for example, a repetition of "opinion" is struck out in favor of "judgment"; in line three, "Moyses is found" is amended to "Adam is proved." The bulk of the manuscript, like other similar reports, consists of a list of alleged statements, each beginning with "that," seemingly jotted down in the order in which they came to mind. The list of allegations is followed by a concluding paragraph in which Baines generalizes about Marlowe's conduct and promises to produce "honest" witnesses to corroborate his allegations. He also promises to name some "great men" to whom Marlowe has supplied "a number of contrarieties oute of the Scripture."

One notable feature of the manuscript is that the last item in the list appears to have been added later. It is written in two visibly cramped lines between the list of allegations and the closing paragraph, and also has more corrections than any other item in the list, suggesting that it might have been written in even greater haste: "<That {illegible}> That on Ric Cholmley <hath Cholmley> hath confessed that he was perswaded by Marloes reasons to become an Atheist." Perhaps this item was inserted specifically to corroborate the earlier report on Cholmeley. Similarly, the last sentence concerning the "contrarieties," which is reminiscent of Cholmeley's "Atheist lecture," has, as Roy Kendall points out, the air of an afterthought.[33] Baines's note and the two copies of reports on Cholmeley, which are preserved in the same collection of papers, were all in the possession of the same person, Lord Keeper Sir John Puckering, to whom Kyd later addressed his letter and note containing further allegations about Marlowe.

[33] Roy Kendall, "Richard Baines and Christopher Marlowe's Milieu," *English Literary Renaissance* 24 (1994): 538–39.

Most of the statements Baines attributes to Marlowe attack the authority of the Bible and discredit prominent biblical figures. Some of them, such as "Christ was a bastard and his mother dishonest," are atheistic commonplaces similar to the remarks ascribed to Cholmeley. Others, such as "Crist deserved better to dy than Barrabas," or "St John the Evangelist was bedfellow to Christ," have a distinctly Marlovian flavor. Two of the reported statements are wild cards. "All they that love not Tobacco & Boies were fooles" is manifestly a joke, but one that Baines deemed shocking enough to report. The claim "that he had as good Right to Coine as the Queen of England" obviously dates back to conversations in Flushing, but is only marginally relevant to the issue at hand. Perhaps Baines was still smarting from his failure to hang Marlowe on charges of counterfeiting. And of course the final paragraph includes Baines's notorious recommendation that Marlowe's mouth be "stopped."

The reliability of Baines's allegations has long been questioned, usually on the basis of an ad hominem attack. Although we now know that Baines the author of the note was probably not the felonious Richard Baines who was hanged in 1594, the fact that he was an informer has also been frequently mentioned as sufficient grounds for doubting his word. However, an informer who provided false or misleading information would soon be out of work, and Baines had apparently been working for Walsingham and the Privy Council at least since 1586. This probably indicates that his performance was satisfactory and his information considered generally reliable. Indeed, the fact that Thomas Drury was instructed to seek him out suggests that for some purposes he was in demand. More recently, Kendall has suggested that since Baines confessed to duplicity at Rheims, we should doubt his testimony against Marlowe.[34] Actually we do not know how much of Baines's confession in Rheims we can believe, since it was obtained under duress; furthermore, the situation in Rheims was not directly comparable to that in London in 1593. Lying to protect oneself, or to achieve some other arguably worthy goal, as Baines did when he pretended to remain a devout Catholic, is not the same as lying to injure another person. Baines apparently harbored malice toward Marlowe and may have lied about him in Flushing—unless, of course, he actually believed that Marlowe intended to defect, which is possible. And even if he acted against Marlowe out of malice, perhaps he did not need to lie, for telling the truth can often do more damage than lying.

The only reasonable test of Baines's allegations is whether or not they can

[34] Ibid., 515.

be corroborated. And in fact much evidence exists to suggest that Marlowe did voice unorthodox opinions and was acquiring a reputation for atheism, and that the other charges Baines made were true. The allusions to Marlowe and his works in *Groatsworth of Wit*, in Chettle's preface to *Kind-Hartes Dreame*, and in works that are certainly by Greene, consistently represent Marlowe's opinions as unorthodox. And indeed Marlowe's plays, while not openly blasphemous (which would be impossible in a climate of established religion and state censorship), seem to embody attitudes very different from those expressed in an orthodox moralistic play like Greene's *A Looking Glass for London and England*. Greene, I believe, grasped the implications of Marlowe's plays quite well and knew an intellectual enemy when he saw one. Cholmeley's remark about Marlowe's "Atheist lecture," even if the incident were fabricated, would hardly be believed unless it conformed to a known profile. And lest we suspect that Marlowe was falsely accused by Cholmeley and Baines of acquaintance with Thomas Harriot and Sir Walter Raleigh, we have Marlowe's own word that he was very well known to Raleigh's friend and Harriot's patron the Earl of Northumberland. We know from Sir Robert Sidney's letter, and from an informer's report on the counterfeiter John Poole, that Baines's allegation about counterfeiting was true.[35] And it is particularly hard to dismiss the confidence with which Baines offers to produce more witnesses:

> These thinges with many other shall by good & honest witnes be
> aproved to be his opinions and comon speeches. . . . almost into every
> company he cometh he perswades men to Athiesm willing them not
> to be afeard of bugbeares and hobgoblins, and utterly scorning both
> god and his ministers as I Richard Baines will Justify & approve both
> by mine oth and the testimony of many honest men, and almost al
> men with whome he hath conversed any time will testify the same.

A man whose continued employment depended on his credibility would be foolish to make promises he was unable to keep, and Baines, whatever else he may have been, was no fool.

During the ten days following Marlowe's prompt appearance at the Star Chamber on 20 May, the Privy Council met only three times—on the 23rd, 25th, and 29th. Perhaps, as Brooke suggests, they were preoccupied with the trial of John Penry, which began on 21 May.[36] During this period of benign

---

[35] Bakeless, *Tragicall History*, 1:101.
[36] Brooke *The Life of Marlowe*, 69.

neglect Marlowe probably remained in or close to London, but we do not know his exact whereabouts until Wednesday 30 May. On that day, according to William Vaughan's *Golden Grove* (1600), one of the more reliable Elizabethan accounts of Marlowe's death, he was invited to a feast in Deptford by "one named Ingram."[37] As we now know, thanks to Leslie Hotson's discovery of the coroner's report on Marlowe's death, this was Ingram Frizer, Thomas Walsingham's servant, who was already in the process of appropriating Drew and Anna Woodleff's money and property. Also present at the feast were Nicholas Skeres, who assisted Frizer in his dubious dealings with Drew Woodleff, and Robert Poley, who had just returned from The Hague carrying letters.

According to the coroner's report, this feast lasted most of the day and into the evening. Frizer and his guests gathered in a room at the house of a certain Widow Eleanor Bull in Deptford at around 10 A.M. They dined there, remained quietly together in a room, took a long walk in the garden belonging to the house, and returned at 6 P.M. for supper. After the second meal, a quarrel arose between Marlowe and Frizer over "the sum of pence, that is, le recknynge," during which the two men "publicaverunt," or loudly exchanged, "divers malicious words."[38] After this dispute, Marlowe lay on a bed or couch in the room, while Frizer sat on a bench nearby, wedged between Skeres and Poley with his back to Marlowe. The three were probably, as Vaughan reports, playing "tables" or backgammon. Suddenly Marlowe, "moved by ire towards the aforesaid Ingram Frizer on account of the aforesaid words that had passed between them," seized the dagger hanging at Frizer's back and inflicted two superficial scalp wounds—probably by hitting him over the head with the hilt of the dagger, as he did in the case of Corkine. Frizer panicked, and, fearing for his life, struggled with Marlowe to recover the dagger. In the course of this struggle, Marlowe received a mortal wound above his right eye.

Hotson's recovery of the coroner's report was a brilliant piece of investigative scholarship. However, today we can only smile ruefully at G. L. Kittredge's naive assertion in his brief introduction to Hotson's book that "the mystery of Marlowe's death . . . is now cleared up for good and all on the authority of public records of complete authenticity and gratifying fullness."[39] Virtually every conceivable reason for objecting to the coroner's report, ranging from healthy skepticism to irrational denial, has been advanced. More than one author has suggested that Poley, Skeres, and Frizer were lying,

[37] Quoted in Bakeless, *Tragicall History*, 1:147.

[38] The full text of the coroner's report is transcribed and translated in the appendix. J. Leslie Hotson, *The Death of Christopher Marlowe* (New York, 1965), also provides a transcription and translation, although his version (overall quite accurate) differs in a few details from mine.

[39] Hotson, *The Death of Christopher Marlowe*, 7.

that Marlowe was assassinated, and that the coroner's report is at least misleading, and possibly an official cover-up. More bizarre scenarios propose that the body in Widow Bull's house was not really Marlowe's—that the young playwright's apparent death was a ruse that allowed him to escape to the Continent, where he wrote Shakespeare's plays.

Some of these conjectures are more plausible than others, but without exception they are highly speculative theories or outright fictions based on tenuous, selective, or nonexistent evidence. As a result, the conspiracy-and-assassination scenarios, the latest being Charles Nicholl's equivocal fingering of the Earl of Essex and Sir Robert Cecil, never agree on the alleged instigator of Marlowe's murder. It is of course possible that a number of people besides Richard Baines, known and unknown, might have wanted Marlowe dead. But until we have direct evidence that someone not only wanted him dead but acted on this desire, we are only guessing. The simplest and most probable hypothesis is that Marlowe was not assassinated at all, and that the coroner's report is a reasonably accurate account of what happened. Nicholl is correct to remind us that what is plausible is not necessarily true,[40] but in the absence of conclusive evidence, plausibility has distinct virtues. A plausible interpretation may or may not be true, but idle speculation and fanciful theories have no credibility at all.

Most of the grounds for suspicion about Marlowe's death seem baseless on dispassionate examination. We have no reason to suppose, for example, that Marlowe was lured to Deptford. For a person waiting for a summons from the Privy Council while London was still ravaged by plague, Deptford was a convenient and agreeable place to while away a day. A small port town on the bank of the Thames just three miles south of London, it was surrounded by open green fields and flanked on the east by ships lying at anchor. The *Golden Hind*, the ship in which Sir Francis Drake had sailed around the world, was anchored there, now doing duty as a tourist attraction and restaurant.

Nor was Marlowe's company at Widow Bull's house as suspicious and sinister as biographers with a taste for melodrama have tended to make it. Marlowe and Frizer were both servants of Thomas Walsingham, in rather different capacities; they were certainly well acquainted, and Marlowe may even have admired Frizer for his shrewd, brazen pursuit of his own financial interest. Skeres, Frizer's accessory, had once been employed—like Poley, Thomas Walsingham, Watson, and probably Marlowe—in carrying official packets and letters. Although Skeres had some connection to Essex, he appears to have

---

[40] Nicholl, *The Reckoning*, 21.

lived mainly by his wits. He was no skillful manipulator of law like Frizer and was not notably law-abiding, but as far as we know he was never involved in a violent assault, which makes him an unlikely candidate for the role of assassin in which Nicholl attempts to cast him. Poley was a professional government agent of rare and varied accomplishments, whose well-documented escapades have been thoroughly traced by Marlowe biographers without bringing us any closer to knowing what happened in Deptford. Poley was frequently employed as a messenger to the Low Countries and Scotland and had just returned from one of these journeys when he joined Frizer's party. He had also been active in a number of intelligence operations directed by Sir Francis Walsingham, playing a crucial role in the unfolding of the Babington plot, in which Skeres and Thomas Walsingham were also peripherally involved.

Marlowe probably knew all three of these men well and had no reservations about spending a day with them. Exactly what they were doing at Widow Bull's house—apart from feasting, strolling amicably in the garden, playing backgammon, and eventually fighting—we do not know. Nor do we know exactly what kind of establishment Widow Bull's house was. It was neither a licensed tavern nor a brothel and was probably not a safe house for intelligence operations either, since all the men's activities specified in the coroner's report and in Vaughan's account were ostensibly recreational. The men may have discussed some unknown business, or the gathering may have been purely social. Mrs. Bull was the widow of Richard Bull, a former manorial sub-bailiff; she was also a cousin of Blanche Parry, one of the queen's favorite waiting-women, and she was somehow related to Burghley, though probably not closely enough to be strongly suspected of involvement in his intrigues. The fact that the men did not gather there until 10 A.M. suggests that she was not a landlady. Probably she was an upscale victualer and caterer to private parties with whom Frizer had made arrangements for his feast. What he was celebrating we will probably never know.

The claim that Marlowe and Frizer began quarreling over the bill is perfectly consistent with what we know about Marlowe, particularly during the last year and a half of his life. Elizabethans in general were quick to quarrel over trifles, but this account seems even more credible because of Marlowe's immediate circumstances. The closing of the theaters and the cost of waiting for the council's summons had probably left him even shorter of cash than usual, which might have made a few shillings seem much more than a trifle. Furthermore, if Frizer had invited him to a feast but then insisted that he pay part of the bill, this could certainly have angered him. If Marlowe and Frizer had been drinking heavily with their meal, as Elizabethans frequently did, this would not have made either more accommodating. And finally, according to the coroner's report, Frizer and Marlowe exchanged insulting and disparaging remarks loudly enough to be heard by others in the house. Under such circumstances, the sight of Frizer's dagger hanging carelessly at his back as he sat at the table playing backgammon might have been tempting, even to a man of less volatile temper than Marlowe. To a proud, ambitious man who had been repeatedly thwarted during the previous year and who was demonstrably subject during that period to transgressive impulses, it might have been irresistible.

Unfortunately, Elizabethan coroners' reports never specify who was questioned or what information they provided as the coroner pieced together the sequence of events. Critics of the coroner's report on Marlowe's death therefore assume that the only witnesses were Frizer, Skeres, and Poley,[41] but this assumption may be incorrect. Other witnesses must have supplied or confirmed details such as the description of the men's quiet demeanor earlier in the day. And the coroner's use of the verb "publicaverunt" (they made public) to describe how Marlowe and Frizer spoke their malicious words suggests that the quarrel was audible to others, either in the room or throughout the house.

It is entirely possible that someone else was in the room when the attack occurred. The men had eaten a meal. Someone served it, removed the dirty trenchers, and brought more to drink. Even if no witnesses were there when Marlowe snatched Frizer's dagger, the noise of a struggle after a loud argument might have brought some witnesses to the room quickly. Certainly within a few minutes after Marlowe was wounded, everyone on the premises would have known what had happened. This leaves little room for theories that this was a planned, professional murder. Why kill a man in a place full of potential witnesses? Surely there were plenty of dark alleys, desolate highways, deserted stretches of riverbank in and around London that would have served the purpose of assassination far better, with no danger of being apprehended, and no need for Frizer to enter a plea of self-defense and secure a royal pardon.

The coroner's description of the wound Marlowe sustained and its effects has also become an issue in arguments about the circumstances surrounding his death. S. A. Tannenbaum, one of the earliest promulgators of an assassination theory, insisted that such a wound could not possibly have caused instant death, even though one of the authorities he quoted plainly stated that it could.[42] Later scholars have emphasized that such a wound could indeed

[41] For example, ibid., 84.
[42] Tannenbaum, *The Assassination of Christopher Marlowe*, 66.

damage major cerebral arteries or veins, causing hemorrhage or embolism and rapid death.[43] Yet another debate concerns whether such a wound would result from an assassination attempt. Common sense suggests that it would not. Assassins using a dagger normally strike at the heart or the throat, not the eye socket. Nicholl argues that the eye and face were targets for fencers,[44] and indeed the eye is a target in other forms of combat besides fencing, for good reason: it is highly vulnerable, and a strike at the eye or face is intimidating. However, an assassin is not a fencer. He relies on the element of surprise to effect quick and certain death, and the eye socket does not meet either of those requirements reliably enough. While it is doubtful that Frizer (or anyone else) planned to murder Marlowe by stabbing him in the eye, it is possible that Marlowe deflected a thrust aimed at another vital spot during a struggle. However, this only leads back to the point that victualing houses are not popular sites for assassinations. It is more likely that, if the hit was intentional, Marlowe's eye was the only target available to Frizer, which might well have been the case if, as the coroner reports, Frizer was attacked from behind while sitting on a bench between two other men, pinned against a table.

What we know about the four men immediately involved in Marlowe's death is far easier to reconcile with the coroner's report than with a conspiracy or assassination theory. Frizer was a financial opportunist who knew how to use the law to his own advantage; while he was not particularly ethical, he was no hired killer, nor was he the sort who would lend himself casually to anything dangerously illegal. Skeres, assuming that all the references we have found to Nicholas Skeres refer to the same person, was a surety for a loan to Marlowe's friend Matthew Roydon. He was also a low-level government agent somehow involved with Poley in the Babington conspiracy, a messenger carrying letters to Essex, and a go-between in Frizer's deceptive financial dealings with Drew Woodleff. Perhaps he was also the man described in 1585 as one of the masterless men "whose practice is to robbe Gentelmen's Chambers and Artificers' shoppes in & about London," and the Nicholas Skeres arrested in "very dangerous company" in 1595 and identified as a servant of the Earl of Essex. This same man was jailed again after the Essex uprising.[45] But as far as we know, the closest Nicholas Skeres ever came to a violent act was sitting next to Frizer when he killed Marlowe. Nicholl's suggestion that he was the assassin purely because of his connection to the Earl of Essex is unconvincing. Like most theories about Marlowe, this idea

[43] William Urry, *Christopher Marlowe and Canterbury* (London, 1988), 91–92; Nicholl, *The Reckoning*, 18.
[44] Nicholl, *The Reckoning*, 85.
[45] Bakeless, *Tragicall History*, 1:181–82.

feeds on the inverse dynamics of information and speculation: the less we know, the more we are tempted to speculate.

Poley was an adulterer, a skillful deceiver, a betrayer of others' trust, a highly efficient informer and messenger who managed to provide well for himself in this often distasteful line of work. However, he obviously preferred to deliver his victims to state violence rather than perpetrate violence himself. Once again, as in the case of Skeres, we have found no record of Poley ever being involved in physical combat with another person. Unlike Marlowe, he was never arrested on suspicion of murder, or sued for assault, or bound to keep the peace by his local constables. Far from being impulsive and volatile, Poley was cool, pragmatic, and discreet. Like Frizer, he favored methods of manipulating and destroying others that were intellectual rather than physical. He was far more likely to have been in Deptford on 30 May to report on Marlowe's conversation than to supervise his assassination. But if he ever filed such a report, it has yet to be discovered.

Although some will undoubtedly continue to resist the conclusion most forcibly suggested by the available evidence, the one person in the party at Deptford who was most likely to attack another person physically was Christopher Marlowe. Why is this conclusion so difficult to accept? Perhaps a certain celebrity status attaches to major authors that makes us reluctant to acknowledge their human weaknesses; or perhaps we still cling unconsciously to Victorian notions of the genteel poet, who pens odes to nightingales as his life ebbs softly away. Whatever the reason, it seems easier to blame Marlowe's death on his uncouth companions than on Marlowe himself. Or perhaps the plain tale in the coroner's report simply is not glamorous enough. Marlowe undoubtedly gained stature in the twentieth century partly because he was perceived as a daring, transgressive figure—the designated bad boy of Elizabethan drama. Perhaps we do not want to admit that this dashing creature of our imagination could attack another man for frivolous reasons and then botch it disastrously. But considering the series of embarrassing reversals Marlowe had experienced during the preceding year, hardly anything could be more plausible.

Unfortunately, the lives of artists, even some of the most eventful ones, are never as extraordinary and admirable as their works. Artists can be just as petty, fallible, and rash as anyone else, and can squander their lives just as foolishly. Perhaps fanciful theories about Marlowe's death persist in general because we are reluctant to admit that artists, apart from their genius, are no better or worse than the rest of us. Authors must be special, beautiful people, if only by being made the center of a murderous plot or the victim of a conspiracy. Such arguments have a powerful appeal in a century when ingeniously plotted mystery novels, Cold War intrigues, and sensational conspiracy theories are popular literary forms, but the fact that we find these narrative modes intriguing does not make them true. On the contrary, the more biographers tailor Marlowe's life to suit our current taste, the more likely they are to distort it.

Significantly, no one before the twentieth century saw Marlowe's death as the result of a conspiracy. Gossip about political intrigues and secret murders was common enough in the sixteenth and seventeenth centuries. Such gossip arose in connection with the death of Marlowe's former patron Lord Strange, but Marlowe's death failed to inspire any comparable rumors. However, a sizable body of material commenting directly or indirectly on Marlowe did accumulate after his death. While none of it either confirms or contradicts the evidence we have already considered, it does tell us a great deal about how his contemporaries perceived Marlowe.

8

The Dead Shepherd

❧

When a man's verses cannot be understood, nor a man's good wit seconded with the forward child, understanding, it strikes a man more dead than a great reckoning in a little room.

Shakespeare, *As You Like It*, 3.3.12–15

AS SOON AS THE CORONER'S inquest was complete, Marlowe's body was prepared for burial and carried from Widow Bull's house to nearby St. Nicholas's Church. The parish register records the date of interment, and also notes the unusual cause of death, as parish registers sometimes did: "Christopher Marlow slaine by Francis Frezer; the ·1· of June." The vicar's or clerk's slip of "Francis" for "Ingram" is easily explained, since Frizer was not a local resident.

We do not know exactly where in the churchyard Marlowe was buried, who attended the ceremony, or what rites were performed, but custom required that even strangers be buried decently. At the very least, someone would have provided a winding sheet, since "only animals were buried naked."[1] Marlowe's family, who would normally have provided for his burial, had probably not yet learned of his death. Indeed, they may still have been unaware of it when his sister Ann married John Cranford in Canterbury on 10 June. According to local tradition, Marlowe's grave was located near the north side of the twelfth-century Norman tower of St. Nicholas's, the only part of the original church still standing.[2] Most of the present church was erected during the seventeenth century, as was the charnel house where many of the bones in the churchyard were stored and later burnt, probably

---

[1] David Cressy, *Birth, Marriage, and Death* (Oxford, 1997), 429–30.
[2] A. D. Wraight, *In Search of Christopher Marlowe; A Pictorial Biography*, photography by Virginia F. Stern (New York, 1965), 326.

including Marlowe's.[3] Even the part of St. Nicholas's dating from the seventeenth century was partly rebuilt after World War II, to repair damage done in 1940 by German bombs intended for the nearby Royal Naval Yard, one of which landed squarely in the middle of the church. A plaque inside St. Nicholas's identifies it as Marlowe's burial site.[4]

The earliest responses to Marlowe's sudden death divided along predictable lines: his friends and admirers praised his works and lamented his untimely end; others gossiped about him or denounced him. However, contemporary accounts of Marlowe's death substantially agree on several points. They all indicate that Marlowe died suddenly and violently, that he quarreled with another man, attacked him, and was killed by him. No one questioned these details. At the same time, charges of atheism or blasphemy continued to be leveled at Marlowe, and no one who had known him disputed them. Although Puritans such as Thomas Beard were in the vanguard of the attacks on Marlowe, they were not the first to see Marlowe's death as a manifestation of divine vengeance.

The first known critical reference to Marlowe after his death occurs in the heading of the revised copy of the Baines Note. This document, which is endorsed "Copye of Marloes blasphemes. As sent to her H," appears to be the rough draft of a copy sent to the queen.[5] The heading, which the writer composed with some difficulty, reads, "A note delivered on Whitsun eve last of the most horrible blasphemes and damnable opinions uttered by Xpofer Marly who <since Whitsunday dyed> within iii dayes after came to a soden & <vyolent deathe.> fearfull end of his life." Although the author fussed over his exact wording, his basic meaning is clear: Marlowe's end, whether violent or fearful, "since Whitsunday" or three days after, was a direct result of his horrible blasphemies and damnable opinions. The reviser also pointedly deleted some material from Baines's note, striking out a reference to Sir Walter Raleigh and omitting Marlowe's alleged remarks about tobacco, boys, and counterfeiting, along with the last paragraph in which Baines promises to produce more witnesses and to name certain "great men" with whom Marlowe shared his views. Whoever edited the note, presumably Sir John Puckering or one of his assistants, seems to have been mainly interested in documenting an atheist menace. Therefore he deleted unrelated allegations and supplied a heading that emphasizes this issue.

Sometime in June, Puckering received a letter from Thomas Kyd that tended to confirm his negative view of Marlowe's "damnable opinions." Kyd

[3] William Urry, *Christopher Marlowe and Canterbury* (London, 1988), 95.
[4] Depicted in Wraight, *In Search of Christopher Marlowe*, 327.
[5] The text of this copy of the Baines Note, complete with heading, is included in the appendix.

had finally been released from prison, only to be rebuffed by his patron Lord Strange. Strange, because of his own delicate political position, was probably anxious to avoid the appearance of harboring anyone suspected of sedition, as may have been the case with Marlowe. We can infer from the letter that Kyd had asked Puckering to intervene with Strange on his behalf, and that Puckering had refused. Kyd therefore wrote to the lord keeper in a desperate attempt to convince Puckering of his innocence.[6]

The first suspicion about himself that Kyd tries to dispel is that of atheism, which suggests that Kyd knew this issue was of special concern to Puckering. Kyd repeats the story he told in prison—that the anti-trinitarian manuscript found among his papers was Marlowe's. He and Marlowe had been working in one room together two years previously; therefore the paper must have been accidentally shuffled in with his at that time. Kyd also claims that the opinions expressed in the manuscript were "affirmed by Marlowe to be his." In other words, Marlowe did not believe in the divinity of Christ, a view expressed more crudely in some of the remarks Baines ascribes to Marlowe. In an obvious attempt to distance himself from these opinions and increase his credit with his former patron, Kyd contrasts both himself and Lord Strange to Marlowe, claiming, "For never could my Lord endure his name, or sight, when he had heard of his conditions, nor would in deed the forme of devyne praier used dulie in his lordships house, have quadred with such reprobates." He himself, Kyd insists, could never "love or be familiar friend, with one so irreligious." Kyd claims he saw nothing to admire in Marlowe, neither "for person, quallities, nor honesty," and furthermore, "he was intemperate & of a cruel hart." If Puckering wishes to confirm that Kyd is not an atheist, "which some will sweare he [Marlowe] was," Kyd suggests that Puckering question "such as he conversed withall," namely "*Harriot, Warner, Royden* and some stationers in Paules churchyard." Kyd disingenuously claims that he is not accusing these men of sharing Marlowe's opinions, but then proceeds to argue that if he had held the same views as they hold, he would have been one of their company.

Kyd was obviously aware of Marlowe's death when he wrote this letter, for he concedes that one should not upbraid the dead except in "the greatest cause." He then offers comments about Marlowe's intemperance and cruelty which seem directly inspired by the news from Deptford, for they have no obvious or necessary connection to atheism. Still, the fact that Kyd's remarks were prompted by recent events does not mean that they are insincere or

[6] The texts of Kyd's letter and note to Puckering are included in the appendix.

fabricated. The earnest Kyd may well have found Marlowe a baffling and somewhat repellant roommate.

In the last section of his letter, Kyd insists that he had nothing to do with the libel and offers to take a sacred oath on his innocence. He also suggests that the lives and actions of his false accusers should be examined, and declares that if he knew anyone whom he could justly accuse of libel or atheism, he would do so. This last statement seems a bit devious, since Kyd has already obliquely implicated several people. Viewed in the best possible light, his letter is a desperate and rather confused attempt to save himself by casting suspicion on others. Marlowe was a safe target, since he could no longer defend himself, nor could he be harmed except in name, but Kyd was obviously reluctant to accuse anyone else unequivocally. Nevertheless, he had said enough that Puckering smelled blood in the water, and consequently prodded Kyd to provide more specific information about Marlowe's opinions and associates.

Kyd responded with a terse, unsigned note. While his manner is ostensibly compliant, compared to his letter the note seems evasive and somewhat rueful. He avoids naming names and reports only four of Marlowe's "monstruous opinions," protesting weakly that "I cannot but with an agreved conscience think on him or them," and can "particulariz fewe in the respect of them that kept him greater company." Actually Kyd names no one in the note except Roydon, whom he had already mentioned in his letter. Furthermore, the statements he attributes to Marlowe seem mild compared to those reported by Baines. Kyd corroborates Baines on three points: Marlowe habitually ridiculed conventional Christian beliefs, he said that St. John was "our savior Christs Alexis," and he characterized a prominent biblical figure (in Kyd's case St. Paul rather than Moses) as a "jugler." However, the particulars of Kyd's note are sufficiently different from those of the Baines note that they seem to be completely independent recollections.

The other remarks Kyd attributes to Marlowe hardly qualify as "monstruous opinions." The statement that "the prodigall Childe's portion was but fower nobles" is humorous banter at the expense of conventional religious pictures, while the statement that "things esteemed to be donn by devine power might have aswell been don by observation of men" is no more than a shrewd observation of the sort that Sir Francis Bacon would soon be freely making in print. Kyd ends with the assertion that Marlowe "wold perswade with men of quallitie to goe unto the King of Scotts"; this issue was of no particular interest to Puckering, and as a result the item is not assigned a number. Not surprisingly, Kyd's note was not copied and sent to the queen, nor, apparently, did it help Kyd regain his patron's favor. Later in 1593, Kyd dedicated *Cornelia*, his translation of Garnier's *Cornélie*, to the Countess of Sussex. He was dead by December 1594. Perhaps the "paines and undeserved tortures" he complains of in his letter to Puckering had undermined his health, or perhaps he simply fell victim to one of the many hazards of living by one's wits in Elizabethan London, where dying in one's thirties was a routine event.

In his note Kyd also mentions Marlowe's "other rashnes in attempting soden pryvie injuries to men." Nicholl correctly points out that "injuries" may mean taunts or sly insults, not physical attacks.[7] After all, Kyd's note is mainly concerned with Marlowe's verbal behavior. However, verbal aggression and physical aggression are often closely allied; one can quickly lead to the other, as apparently happened in Deptford after Marlowe and Frizer loudly exchanged "divers malicious words." This may be partly why Kyd considered Marlowe's behavior rash. Even if the "pryvie injuries" Kyd had in mind were verbal, they were aggressive acts arguably related to Marlowe's attack on Frizer.

Kyd's letter and note raise a number of questions, partly because we know so little about their context. However, they do combine with other evidence to form a reasonably consistent picture of how Marlowe was viewed by his contemporaries. Far more puzzling is a letter written by Thomas Drury on 1 August 1593 to Anthony Bacon, Essex's new director of intelligence.[8] Drury never mentions Marlowe by name in this letter, nor, contrary to Nicholl's suggestion, is there any compelling reason to believe that he avoids mentioning Marlowe.[9] Since Marlowe had been dead over two months and his death was fairly notorious, Drury had no reason to be coy about naming him. Drury's letter has been the object of considerable speculation, but it may, like Gabriel Harvey's "goggle-eyed sonnet,"[10] actually have nothing to do with Marlowe. However, since it does allude to the libels and to the investigation of atheism, it has definite interest, as does its author.

Drury, we will recall, was an associate of Richard Cholmeley whom Cholmeley managed to have arrested in July 1591. In late 1592 Drury, who was still in prison, or back in prison, was recruited by Lord Buckhurst and Puckering to perform certain unspecified services for them, evidently intelligence

---

[7] Charles Nicholl, *The Reckoning* (London, 1992), 86.

[8] This letter (Lambeth Palace Library 649, f. 246) is transcribed almost in its entirety by S. E. Sprott in "Drury and Marlowe" (*Times Literary Supplement*, 2 August 1974, 840); all subsequent quotes are from Sprott's transcription, although I have modernized Drury's bizarre spelling for the reader's convenience. However, the name "Bayns," which Sprott renders as conjectural, is perfectly legible, considering Drury's idiosyncratic penmanship.

[9] Nicholl, *The Reckoning*, 303.

[10] Thomas Nashe, *Works*, ed. R. B. McKerrow and F. P. Wilson (Oxford, 1958), 3:133.

related.[11] On 1 August, however, Drury wrote a letter to Bacon complaining that his most recent services had not been properly rewarded. He promised to provide new information, but instead of seeking employment with Essex, he asked Bacon to recommend him to Burghley so that he could receive "some reward and favor in his sight." This was a reasonable request to make of Bacon, for Burghley was Bacon's uncle by marriage, and Bacon had been of great use to Burghley during his extended travels on the Continent in 1580–92. He was therefore a potentially influential intercessor for Drury.

Several points need to be made at once about Drury's letter, in addition to the fact that it never mentions Marlowe. Drury's handwriting is bizarre, his syntax is disjointed and ambiguous, his diction is vague, his spelling, which I have modernized for clarity, is odd even by Elizabethan standards, and his letter is "a narrative," as Nicholl sees it, only in the loosest sense of the word.[12] Essentially Drury's letter is a rambling list of boasts, complaints, and promises, ending in a request for a recommendation and the proposal of a face-to-face meeting. Drury's obvious difficulty in making himself clear may well have contributed to his recurrent difficulties with his employers on the Privy Council.

In his letter Drury first declares that he was ordered to seek out "one Mr. Bayns which did use to resort unto me," in order to procure "the desired secret." This secret, he says, was one for which the city of London had promised a hundred crowns by proclamation—in other words, the reward offered for information concerning the recent libels. Nicholl speculates that Baines told Drury that the author of the Dutch Church libel was Cholmeley.[13] But if Baines could identify the author of this libel, he would probably have collected the reward himself. Perhaps "the desired secret" was another piece of information, one that might lead indirectly to the author or authors of the libels. Drury's claim is too vague to permit any definite interpretation, and evidently he did not collect the reward—perhaps because the authorities did not consider his "secret" sufficiently valuable. Informers habitually claimed that their discoveries were more important than they actually were. Which person named Baines had previously had contact with Drury is open to conjecture, but Drury refers to him by the polite title "Master." Quite possibly he was Richard Baines of Cambridge, Master in Arts and gentleman.

Drury's litany of complaint continues: "After there was a libel by my means found out and delivered a vile book also by my decyphering taken

[11] Letter of Buckhurst to Puckering, BL Harleian 6995, f. 137 (f. 100 in catalogue). My thanks to David Riggs for sharing with me his transcript of this letter, which he discovered.
[12] Nicholl, The Reckoning, 304.
[13] Ibid., 305.

and a notable villain or two which are close prisoners and bad matters against them of an exceeding nature and yet no reward." Kendall connects the "secret" mentioned in the previous sentence to this discovery,[14] but Drury draws no clear connection between the two. Instead he uses the ambiguous preposition "after," which normally means "and then" rather than "therefore." Since there were "divers" libels posted in London, and no doubt more than one search and seizure of papers, Drury might be referring to any one of a number of events. Actually, his "after" seems to suggest that this was a different libel from the one to which the "secret" pertained, and that its discovery was an additional accomplishment. Furthermore, because of Drury's habit of using "and" and "also" as all-purpose connectives, we cannot be certain that the book Drury mentions is associated with this second libel. The fact that Drury puts the libel, the book, and the notable villain or two in the same sentence might be taken to suggest that these three items were closely connected, but this is far from certain. And what could Drury mean by his "decyphering," which in intelligence referred specifically to the decoding of cryptograms?

Nicholl connects this second complaint of Drury's to the spy's report concerning Cholmeley, documents in which the informant alleges that Cholmeley claimed he wrote pseudo-Catholic libels at Cecil's request and was given a Catholic book by Cecil to use as a source.[15] But if Cholmeley did compose libels at Cecil's bidding, then they would hardly constitute damning evidence against him. Either Drury was not fully aware of Cholmeley's activities, or he was referring to an entirely different situation in which the libel and the "vile book" were indeed incriminating evidence leading to the arrest of the unspecified "villain or two." Judging from the Remembrances, Cholmeley was in trouble not because he wrote libels and had a book Cecil gave him, but because he was suspected of sedition, of "Atheism," and of slandering members of the Privy Council. If Drury helped bring the libel and book to light as evidence against Cholmeley, it had no value, which might explain the absence of a reward.

Drury proceeds to claim yet another accomplishment: "Then after all this there was by my only means set down unto the Lord Keeper [and?] the Lord of Buckhurst the notablyst and vyldist articles of Atheism that I suppose the like were never known or read of in any age all which I can show unto you they were delivered to her highness and command given by her self to prosecute it to the full but no recompense no not of a penny." Both Kendall and

[14] Roy Kendall, "Richard Baines and Christopher Marlowe's Milieu," *English Literary Renaissance* 24 (1994): 537.
[15] Nicholl, *The Reckoning*, 305. Both of these reports on Cholmeley are included in the appendix.

Nicholl assume that this refers to the Baines Note, although Kendall is more tentative.[16] Several facts seem to support this conjecture: Baines was an acquaintance of Drury's from whom Drury succeeded in obtaining a secret, Baines's note was submitted to Drury's handler Puckering to document the atheist menace, and an edited copy was forwarded by Puckering to the queen. But if the "articles of Atheism" are the Baines Note, whose prosecution did the queen order? Certainly not Marlowe's, whose recent death is prominently mentioned in the revised heading of the copy of the note sent to her. The only person named in the note whose prosecution she could have ordered was Richard Cholmeley—Drury's treacherous acquaintance. And the reference to Cholmeley in the Baines Note does look suspiciously like a later insertion. It is quite likely that the person whom Drury was trying to incriminate was Cholmeley, who was still alive, and against whom Drury had reason to seek revenge, since Cholmeley had been instrumental in Drury's arrest earlier.

According to Drury, the "book that doth maintain this damnable sect" is sought after, and he alleges that he can produce a man who knows who wrote it, and to whom it was delivered, and who also knows "who read the lecture and where and when." Nicholl identifies the "book" Drury mentions with the "lecture," although it is far from clear that Drury uses these words to refer to the same item. Of course the word "lecture" immediately suggests to both Sprott and Nicholl the "Atheist lecture" that Marlowe, according to a statement ascribed to Cholmeley by the informer in the Remembrances, read to Raleigh and others.[17] But perhaps these are not the same lecture. It is highly unlikely that only one lecture of skeptical tenor was produced in England in the early 1590s. And since Marlowe was already alleged to have written the "Athiest lecture," which has long been identified with those "contraieties oute of the Scripture" mentioned by Baines as being Marlowe's production, why should Drury promise to produce a man who can reveal who wrote it, especially if he procured the Baines Note? Nicholl's suggestion that "wrote" means "copied" is unconvincing in this context; the word means exactly what it says. Furthermore, Marlowe had already been accused in the Remembrances of reading this lecture, so if the lecture referred to is Marlowe's, why should anyone need to discover who read it? If these comments refer to Marlowe, then Drury is trying to sell information he knows the authorities already possess, which makes no sense.

Finally, Drury alleges that the man he will produce knows "diverse such

[16] Kendall, "Richard Baines and Christopher Marlowe's Milieu," 537; Nicholl, *The Reckoning,* 306–7.
[17] Sprott, "Drury and Marlowe"; Nicholl, *The Reckoning,* 307.

other secrets as the state would spend a thousand pounds to know," and also says he can name aldermen and their agents who convey money to the enemy (namely, Catholics), and reveal "a device intended against the state by a captain." Like most traffickers in intelligence seeking employment or a reward, Drury appears to be grossly exaggerating what he has accomplished and what he can deliver. Perhaps his letter is ambiguous not because he is being discreet, or simply because he is inarticulate, but because he actually has much less to offer than he would like Bacon to believe. We can reasonably infer from the letter that Drury did know Richard Baines and that he was asked to obtain some information from him concerning the recent libels, which he claims he did. When Marlowe's name came up in connection with Kyd's arrest, Drury may have gone to Baines again, this time on his own initiative, since he knew that Baines disliked Marlowe and had some damaging information about him. This information would have satisfied Puckering's seeming desire for evidence of an atheist threat, earning Drury and Baines a reward. Baines was more than willing to comply, and he may even have added the allegation linking his note to the Remembrances against Cholmeley at Drury's suggestion.[18] However, most of the note seems to consist of recollections or paraphrases of statements Marlowe actually made that Baines obviously felt he could verify if challenged.

Nicholl has suggested that Drury was the author of the Remembrances against Cholmeley,[19] but this is impossible. The author of the report that accompanies the Remembrances stresses that he had to win the confidence of Cholmeley and his gang. They were initially suspicious of him, but "yesterday hee sente two of his companions to mee to knowe if I woulde joyne with him in familiaritie & be one of their dampnable crue." Cholmeley, of course, already knew Drury, and knew very well that he could not trust him. Furthermore, whoever drafted the Remembrances and the accompanying report had a polished and lucid prose style totally unlike Drury's in his letter to Bacon. Drury may have heard something about the Remembrances after they were sent to Puckering, and realized that he had an opportunity to earn another reward while settling the score with his treacherous former friend. Securing the Baines Note was not only an attempt to document an atheist presence, but also an effort to confirm the charges against Cholmeley in the Remembrances. Unfortunately, the financial reward Drury expected did not materialize, even after Cholmeley turned himself in on 28 June.

We can only speculate as to why Drury was not rewarded, but the likeliest

---

[18] Kendall, "Richard Baines and Christopher Marlowe's Milieu," 541.
[19] Nicholl, The Reckoning, 306.

reason is that his information against Cholmeley was worthless. Puckering was already in vigorous pursuit of Cholmeley, and had been since March. Nor does Drury seem to have succeeded with Bacon, for he was soon in prison again, this time for abusing the lord chamberlain. He appealed to Cecil in a typically obscure letter, claiming that his speech had been misunderstood, which, considering the surviving samples of his prose, is completely credible.[20] He was released by 17 August and presumably returned to work. On 15 June 1595, Burghley paid him for bringing letters from France.

Drury's letter to Bacon is far too vague to interpret confidently without the aid of further evidence, but we can gather from it and from the two versions of the Baines Note that Marlowe's reputation for atheism could be turned by people such as Baines, Drury, and Puckering to their own purposes. To these people, with the possible exception of Baines, Marlowe was not so much a target as a tool, a card that could be played, an individual whose usefulness did not end with his life. Marlowe's fame and notoriety had made him both an icon and an exemplum, and the power to assign significance to Marlowe was now completely out of his own hands.

While Marlowe's name was turning up in state papers to serve a variety of personal and political ends, it was also being bandied about in public. In the closing months of 1593, Thomas Nashe and Gabriel Harvey were engaged in a diverting and mutually profitable pamphlet war in which Marlowe's name was mentioned on several occasions. Two of Harvey's pamphlets contain references to Marlowe, suggesting that he was an unbeliever and, like all unbelievers, came to a bad end. In *Pierce's Superogation*, Harvey mentions "no religion but precise Marlowisme," while in *A New Letter of Notable Contents* he moralizes, "*Plinyes*, and *Lucians* religion may ruffle, and scoffe awhile: but extreme *Vanitie* is the best beginning of that brauery, and extreme *Miserie* the best end of that felicity. *Greene*, and Marlow might admonish others to aduise themselues."[21] However, the "goggle-eyed" sonnet attached to the *New Letter*, which Marlowe biographers long mistook for an attack on Marlowe, is actually directed at Nashe and at the eccentric Peter Shakerley, the "Tamburlaine" of St. Paul's Churchyard.[22]

In his responses to Harvey, Nashe also refers to Marlowe. Perhaps, as Nicholl suggests, Marlowe's recent death was already preying on Nashe's mind as he wrote *Christs Teares Over Jerusalem*, entered in the Stationer's Register on 8 September 1593.[23] *Christs Teares* contains a lengthy meditation

[20] Ibid., 316–17.
[21] Quoted in John Bakeless, *Tragicall History of Christopher Marlowe*, 1:127, and C. F. Tucker Brooke, *The Life of Marlowe and The Tragedy of Dido, Queen of Carthage*, in *The Works and Life of Christopher Marlowe*, ed. R. H. Case (New York, 1966), 112.
[22] Nicholl, *The Reckoning*, 60–64.
[23] Ibid., 56–57.

on atheism in which Nashe mentions several of the stock atheistic arguments included in the Baines list:

> Impudently they persist in it, that the late discouered Indians are able to shew antiquities thousands before Adam.
>
> With Cornelius Tacitus, they make Moyses a wise prouident man, well seene in the Egiptian learning, but denie hee had any diuine assistance in the greatest of his miracles. The water (they say) which he strook out of a Rocke in the Wildernes, was not by any supernaturall worke of God, but by watching to what parte the Wild-asses repayred for drink.
>
> With Albumazar, they holde that his leading the Chyldren of Israell ouer the Red-sea, was no more but obseruing the influence of Starres, and wayning season of the Moone that with-dreweth the Tydes.[24]

Nashe furthermore touches on the theme of the "heretical conceits" found in Kyd's chamber: "Some there be that fantasie phylosophicall probabilities of the Trinities vnexistence."[25] He concludes, "Discourse ouer the ends of all Atheists, and theyr deathes for the most parte haue beene drunken, violent, and secluded from repentance."[26] Yet Nashe does not name Marlowe or attack him personally, and in response to Harvey's criticisms, he adds a new epistle "To the Reader" to the next printing of *Christs Teares* (1594). "Maister Lillie," Nashe fumes, "poore deceassed Kit Marlow, reuerent doctor Perne, with a hundred other quiet senslesse carkasses before the conquest departed, in the same worke he hath most notoriously & vilely dealt with"; in retaliation for Harvey's grave digging, Nashe promises "to stretch him [Harvey] forth limbe by limbe on the racke, and . . . baite him to death with darts."[27]

Among the darts Nashe launches at Harvey in *Have with You to Saffron-Walden* (1596) is an assault on the credibility of Harvey's attacks on Marlowe and Greene: "Those things which hee might haue related truely hee would not, and those which he would hee could not, for want of good intelligence. How he hath handled Greene and Marloe since their deaths, those that read his Bookes may judge."[28] But instead of directly refuting Harvey's allegations about Marlowe, as he does many of Harvey's criticisms of Greene and himself, Nashe simply proclaims that he has never abused Marlowe: "I never

[24] Nashe, *Works*, 2:116.
[25] Ibid., 2:115.
[26] Ibid., 2:121.
[27] Ibid., 2:180.
[28] Ibid., 3:132.

abusd Marloe, Greene, Chettle in my life, nor anie of my frends that vsde me like a frend; which both Marloe and Greene (if they were aliue) vnder their hands would testifie."[29] Rather than answering Harvey's charges, Nashe quotes Marlowe with devastating effect while assailing Harvey's younger brother Richard: "Dick, Pastor of Cheselhurst, that was wont to pen Gods iudgments vpon such and such a one, as thicke as Water-men at Westminster bridge."[30] Marlowe may well have heard "little and little witted Dicke" deliver some of his diatribes at Chislehurst during one of his visits to Scadbury, and the comment Nashe credits him with, like the remark Kyd recalls about the prodigal son's purse, has an authentic ring: "This is that Dicke of whom Kit Marloe was wont to say that he was an asse, good for nothing but to preach of the Iron Age."[31] But however apt the description of "little witted Dicke" may be, citing it hardly disproves Harvey's charges.

Unfortunately, Nashe's elegy on Marlowe, which was prefaced to an edition of *Dido, Queen of Carthage*, has been lost.[32] It might have revealed more about the friendship between Nashe and Marlowe, but judging from the sketchy descriptions we have of the poem, Nashe probably confined himself to praising Marlowe as a poet, as he does when introducing his inspired burlesque of *Hero and Leander* in *Nashes Lenten Stuffe* (1599): "Hath any bodie in Yarmouth heard of Leander and Hero, of whome diuine *Musaeus* sung, and a diuiner Muse than him, *Kit Marlow?*"[33] Nashe's failure to mount a specific defense of Marlowe in response to Harvey's attacks, as well as his general comments on atheism, suggest that he was not completely comfortable with Marlowe's religious ideas; however, he liked and admired Marlowe too much to fault or abuse him for them.

One of the most influential early responses to Marlowe's death is the moralized account of the Puritan Thomas Beard, first published in 1597 in his *Theatre of God's Judgments*. Beard's account is remarkable for its detail and accuracy, considering the fact that it seems to rely solely on hearsay. Beard declares that Marlowe was "by profession a scholler,"[34] the vocational description Marlowe himself used when he was questioned by Robert Sidney at Flushing. He also correctly identifies Marlowe's alma mater as Cambridge and notes his activities as a "play-maker" and "a Poet of scurrilitie"—the latter doubtless referring to the *Amores* and possibly *Hero and Leander*. Beard provides a reasonably accurate summary of Marlowe's alleged opinions, in-

29 Ibid., 3:131.
30 Ibid., 3:84.
31 Ibid., 3:85.
32 Ibid., 2:335–37.
33 Ibid., 3:195.
34 Quoted in Bakeless, *Tragicall History*, 1:144.

cluding his doubts about the Trinity, his scoffing at Christ and Moses, and his Machiavellian claim that religion was "but a deuice of pollicie."[35] He also reports that Marlowe wrote books detailing his blasphemous ideas. The fight in Deptford is described as occurring in a manner quite consistent with the coroner's report, except that it is erroneously placed "in London streets." This error probably resulted from Beard's confusing London Street in Greenwich, which was near Deptford, with the city of London.[36] The phrase was dropped in the second edition, probably because someone brought the error to Beard's attention. Beard knew that Marlowe had died of a head wound inflicted by the dagger he himself was wielding, and provides a sensational detail that may or may not be true: "hee euen cursed and blasphemed to his last gaspe, and togither with his breath an oth flew out of his mouth."[37]

Beard's moralized account tells us a great deal about the rumors that were circulating a few years after Marlowe's death. It indicates that some details of the fight, and Marlowe's alleged religious views, were common knowledge, to the point where a proselytizer like Beard could incorporate them into his book without making any special effort to investigate. Beard appears to have simply repeated what he had heard—or at least the part of it that best suited his purposes.

The sport of moralizing Marlowe had a remarkably long and vigorous life. Beard's tale was perpetuated in later editions and became a favorite source for authors of later publications. Edmund Rudierd, another fervent Puritan, incorporated a more concise version of Beard's story in his *Thunderbolt of Gods Wrath* (1618). Rudierd devotes less space to Marlowe's opinions, but keeps the story of the fight intact and adds some colorful adjectives, such as "filthy Play-maker" and "stinking breath," to insure that the "prophane wretch" Marlowe is made sufficiently repellant.[38] Samuel Clarke's *Mirrour, or Looking-Glass both for Saints and Sinners* (1646) closely paraphrases Beard's account, which was reprinted in editions of 1654, 1657, and 1671. R. B.'s *Wonderful Prodigies*, published in 1682 and 1762, simply quotes Beard's account in a section detailing judgments of atheists.

Shortly after Beard's first edition of *Theatre of God's Judgments* was published, a slightly different description of Marlowe's death appeared in William Vaughan's *Golden Grove* (1600). Vaughan deliberately exploits the same material as Beard and seems to be using Beard's book, but because he also has access to other sources, his narrative is more accurate in several re-

[35] Quoted in ibid.
[36] Quoted in ibid., 1:145.
[37] Quoted in ibid., 1:144–45.
[38] Quoted in ibid., 1:145.

spects. Vaughan is even less interested in Marlowe's specific beliefs than Rudierd, only briefly mentioning "a booke against the Trinitie"; however, he correctly places Marlowe's death "at Detford, a litle village about three miles distant from London." He also cites the name of Marlowe's killer, "one named Ingram, that had inuited him thither to a feast, and was then playing at tables [backgammon]."[39] Unlike the coroner or others present at the inquest, neither Beard nor Vaughan knew that Marlowe had used Frizer's dagger to attack him—a detail with definite legal significance given Frizer's plea of self-defense. However, Vaughan does mention intimate details that are at best only implicit in the coroner's report, such as exactly what Frizer was doing when he, Skeres, and Poley sat at a table with their backs to Marlowe. Vaughan seemingly had access to information that could have originated only with someone who was actually present at Widow Bull's house when the fight occurred—someone who knew Frizer's given name, how Marlowe came to be at Widow Bull's, and exactly what Frizer was doing when Marlowe attacked him. Beard's information, on the other hand, seems to originate with someone who knew something about the Baines Note but had no direct knowledge of the details of Marlowe's death. Since Vaughan was related to the Earl of Northumberland by marriage,[40] this may explain how he acquired such minute details of the day's events.

Both Marlowe's work and the circumstances of his death were sufficiently well known that Shakespeare could allude to them on the public stage in 1599 and be confident that at least part of his audience would understand the allusion. *As You Like It* contains two references to Marlowe's death: Phoebe's apostrophe to the "dead shepherd" as she quotes a famous line from *Hero and Leander*, and Touchstone's rueful comment, "When a man's verses cannot be understood . . . it strikes a man more dead than a great reckoning in a little room" (3.3.12–15, 3.5.81–82). Though neither Beard nor Vaughan mentions it, the quarrel over the reckoning as a circumstance contributing to Marlowe's death seems to have been fairly well known.

A good story rarely escapes embellishment in the retelling. After reading Beard's account, which makes no mention of the reckoning, Francis Meres felt obliged to explain the "grudge" that inspired Marlowe's attack. He therefore adds a new character when he re-creates the scenario in *Wit's Treasury* (1598): "As the poet Lycophron was shot to death by a certain riual of his: so Christopher Marlowe was stabd to death by a bawdy Servingman, a riual of his in his lewde loue."[41] The Elizabethan mania for historical parallels obvi-

---

[39] Quoted in ibid., 1:147.
[40] Nicholl, *The Reckoning*, 80.
[41] Quoted in Bakeless, *Tragicall History*, 1:148.

ously played a part in Meres's invention of a love triangle to explain the conflict, though he seems to have heard that Frizer was someone's servant. By 1691, Meres's "lewde loue" had blossomed into throbbing romantic passion in Anthony Wood's *Athenae Oxonienses*: "He being deeply in love with a certain Woman, had for his rival a bawdy serving man, one rather fit to be a Pimp, than an ingenious *Amoretto* as *Marlo* conceived himself to be."[42] These fanciful and censorious accounts of the incident persisted well into the twentieth century.

Many of those who praised Marlowe must have had conflicting feelings about him, admiring his work while deploring his alleged actions and ideas. The anonymous author of *The Return from Parnassus* (1601) expressed precisely such a divided response in a crisp antithesis:

> *Marlowe* was happy in his buskine muse,
> Alas vnhappy in his life and end,
> Pitty it is, that wit so ill should dwell
> Wit lent from heauen, but vices sent from hell.[43]

Others, like Nashe and Shakespeare, kept any reservations they may have had about Marlowe to themselves—or quarreled with Marlowe's ideas obliquely in their works, as Shakespeare seems to be doing when he depicts cultural conflict between Christians and Jews in *The Merchant of Venice*. When Marlowe's contemporaries praised him, they stressed his literary achievement rather than his exemplary life. The same Francis Meres who implicated Marlowe in a lewd love affair in *Wit's Treasury* paid tribute to him in *Palladis Tamia* (1598) as one of the English poets who had embellished their native language, just as the greatest ancient poets had advanced Greek and Latin: "The English tongue is mightily enriched and gorgeously inuested in rare ornaments and resplendent abiliments by Sir Philip Sydney, Spenser, Daniel, Drayton, Warner, Shakespeare, Marlowe, and Chapman." Meres also agreed with the author of *The Return from Parnassus* that Marlowe was "happy in his buskine muse," ranking him among "our best for Tragedie."[44]

While it was fashionable to praise other poets lavishly in the Renaissance, especially for their "wit" (ingenious invention), the references to Marlowe repeatedly suggest that his contemporaries felt there was something inimitable and preternaturally sublime about his poetry. Marlowe himself might have been a reprobate, but his genius was "lent from heauen." In *The Honor of the*

[42] Quoted in ibid., 1:149.
[43] Quoted in ibid., 1:147.
[44] Quoted in ibid., 1:186.

Garter, a poem commemorating the induction of Marlowe's acquaintance the Earl of Northumberland into the Order of the Garter in June 1593, George Peele suggested that Marlowe had enjoyed special divine favor, referring to him as "Marley the Muses darling." In *Lenten Stuffe* (1599) Nashe capped Marlowe's reference to "divine Musaeus" in *Hero and Leander* by applying it to Marlowe: "Hero, of whome diuine *Musaeus* sung, and a diuiner Muse than him, *Kit Marlow*."[45] George Chapman similarly refers to Marlowe's "divine wit."[46] Michael Drayton produced the most elaborate encomium of this kind in "Of Poets and Poesie" (1627), describing Marlowe's verse as pristine and celestial, a product of "that fine madness . . . / Which rightly should possesse a Poet's braine":

Neat *Marlow*, bathed in Thespian springs
Had in him those braue translunary things,
That the first poets had, his raptures were,
All ayre, and fire.[47]

The publisher Thomas Thorpe, in his dedication to the *First Book of Lucan* (1600), similarly referred to Marlowe as "that pure Elementall wit."[48]

Henry Petowe, who made an earnest if feeble attempt to complete *Hero and Leander*, preferred sublunary metaphors. To Petowe, Marlowe was "that king of poets, / Marlo admired, whose honney-flowing vaine / No English writer can as yet attaine."[49] Even if Marlowe was neither divinely inspired nor a king of poets, Petowe's comment on his inimitability was undoubtedly true. None of the many Renaissance writers who tried to emulate Marlowe's poetic style, including the young Shakespeare, ever succeeded. The author of the preface to Bosworth's *Chast and Lost Lovers* (1651), while commenting on Bosworth's frequent echoes of *Hero and Leander*, credits Ben Jonson with characteristically ambivalent praise of Marlowe's "mighty lines": he "was often heard to say, that they were Examples fitter for admiration than for parallel."[50] Jonson knew as well as Petowe did that no one had ever replicated the sound of Marlowe's verse; therefore he praised Shakespeare in "To My Beloved Master" for surpassing rather than mastering the mighty line.

Perhaps the most unusual of the published references to Marlowe is Edward Blunt's dedication of *Hero and Leander* to Sir Thomas Walsingham

---

[45] Nashe, *Works*, 3:195.
[46] Quoted in Bakeless, *Tragicall History*, 1:186.
[47] Quoted in ibid., 1:188.
[48] Quoted in ibid., 1:186.
[49] Quoted in ibid., 1:187.
[50] Quoted in C. F. Tucker Brooke, *The Reputation of Christopher Marlowe* (New Haven, 1922), 364.

(1598). Blunt actually says very little about Marlowe, except for a brief reference to his being "unhappily deceased," nor does he say much about the poem, though he obviously thought it was good enough to publish. The dedication appears to be an elaborate conceit in which Blunt compares himself to a devoted friend of Marlowe who, by publishing Marlowe's unfinished poem, is acting as his executor and carrying out his last wish. This is probably no more than a figure of speech, since there is nothing in the dedication to indicate that Blunt had direct knowledge of Marlowe, yet Blunt's statements are sometimes taken quite literally.[51] Blunt does make it clear that Thomas Walsingham was a liberal patron to Marlowe, because he seems to hope he will be rewarded for having published the last work of a poet Walsingham admired and encouraged. The dedication actually tells us very little, except that Blunt wanted to collect some of the reward Marlowe might have received by dedicating his finished poem to Walsingham.

These published comments and references, of course, hardly represent the entire spectrum of opinions about Marlowe in Renaissance England. Published statements, whether their tenor is positive or negative, involve covert negotiations between the writer and the anticipated audience, as well as between the writer and the subject, and therefore they can rarely be taken at face value. Fortunately, the commonplace books of one of Marlowe's seventeenth-century admirers have survived, providing us with somewhat less calculated responses to Marlowe. Henry Oxinden's jottings on Marlowe were almost completely private, and consequently they are free of any attempt to please or impress an audience, such as self-imposed censorship or hyperbole. In fact, on the cover of the commonplace book preserved in the Folger Shakespeare Library Oxinden wrote, "Let nobody see this booke."

Oxinden was a Kentish gentleman, born in Canterbury on 18 January 1609. By the early 1640s, when he kept his commonplace books, he was living at Barham, near Canterbury, in a house called Madekyn. Oxinden was a connoisseur of literature and an amateur poet who had amassed a large library. He enjoyed the learned conversation of his neighbor Simon Aldrich, a retired clergyman of about sixty-five who lived in the house called Little Madekyn, which Oxinden rented to Aldrich's son-in-law John Swan. Possibly Aldrich, a Canterbury native and a Cambridge graduate who was approximately ten years younger than Marlowe, had actually known Marlowe, but certainly he had heard a great deal about him. He told Oxinden that Marlowe was a shoemaker's son of Canterbury, which impressed Oxinden sufficiently that he made note of it several times, not only in his commonplace books but also in

[51] Wraight, *In Search of Christopher Marlowe*, 178.

the margins of his copies of *Hero and Leander* and Beard's *Theatre of God's Judgments*. These marginalia eventually led scholars, who had no idea where Marlowe was born, to discover the Marlowe documents in Canterbury.

Some of Oxinden's information about Marlowe could have come both from Aldrich and from his copy of Beard. An entry dated 10 February 1640 contains several details that Aldrich and Oxinden might have read, but its content is not limited to a particular printed source:

> He [Aldrich] said that Marlo who wrot Hero, & Leander was an Athe-ist, & had wrote a book ag[ain]st. the Scripture, how that it was all one mans making, & would have printed it but would not be suffered. He was the son of a shoemaker in Cant: he said hee was an excellent scholler & wrote excellent verses in Latin. Died aged about 30. He was stabd in the head with a dagger, & dyed swearing.[52]

Here Beard's book against the Trinity becomes a treatise on the spurious authorship of the Bible, and we get additional information about Marlowe's desire to publish this book, as well as comments on his superior scholarship and his facility in writing Latin verse, which could not be based on Beard. The statement that Marlowe's book involved arguments about the authorship of the Bible may well have some truth to it, for Marlowe's alleged remarks about the New Testament being "filthily written," and about the Old Testament's doubtful chronology, might conceivably have been part of an argument about the authorship of the Bible.

Aldrich's most entertaining recollection about Marlowe is his story of Mr. Fineaux of Dover, which Oxinden entered in both of his commonplace books, as well as jotting it in the margin of his copy of *Hero and Leander*. The first entry in the commonplace books is dated 12 February 1640, but the version in the Folger commonplace book is somewhat more pungently phrased:

> Mr Ald. sayd that Mr Fin[eau]x of Dover was an Atheist & that hee would go out at midnight into a wood, & fall downe uppon his knees & pray heartily that the devil would come, that he might see him (for hee did not believe that there was a devil) Mr Ald: sayd that hee was a verie good scholler, but would never have above one booke at a time, & when hee was perfect in it, hee would sell it away & buy another: he

[52] BL Addit. MS 28012, ff. 514–15. The texts of Oxinden's longer comments on Marlowe are included in the appendix. Mark Eccles discusses Oxinden and his commonplace books in detail in "Marlowe in Kentish Tradition," *Notes and Queries* 139 (1935).

learnd all *Marlo* by heart & divers other bookes: *Marlo* made him an *Atheist*. This Fineaux was faine to make a speech uppon *The foole hath said in his heart there is no God*, to get his degree. Fineaux wold say as Galen sayd that man was of a more excellent composition than a beast, & thereby could speake: but affirmed that his soule dyed with his body, & as we remember nothing before wee were borne, so we shall remember nothing after wee are dead.[53]

Marlowe biographers have generally accepted Eccles's suggestion that this Fineaux was Thomas Fineaux, the eldest son of Captain Thomas Fineaux of Hougham. A Thomas Fineaux, probably Captain Thomas's son, matriculated at Corpus Christi College in the Easter term of 1587, the same year that Marlowe took his M.A. However, since Marlowe's attendance was light during that term, he may have had little or no contact with Thomas Fineaux, and Thomas, as far as we know, never took a degree. Furthermore, if Marlowe made Thomas Fineaux an atheist by direct influence, which Oxinden's comments are often taken to mean, he must have developed his evangelical atheism even before he left Cambridge. Otherwise, we hear no direct imputation of such beliefs to Marlowe until the 1590s.

John Fineaux, possibly Thomas's younger brother, is arguably more likely to have been Marlowe's admiring disciple. A John Fineaux was a scholar at the King's School in Canterbury in 1590, and we know that Marlowe visited Canterbury in the fall of 1592, when John was still studying there. John proceeded to Cambridge in 1593, where he was an exact contemporary of Simon Aldrich, taking his two degrees in the same years, 1597 and 1600. It seems no accident that Aldrich knew a great deal more about "Mr Fineaux" (such as his habit of buying one book at a time and learning it by heart) than he would probably have known about Thomas Fineaux, who had attended Cambridge six years before Aldrich arrived. Most compelling of all, John Fineaux, unlike Thomas, got his degrees. It also seems significant that John, unlike Thomas, was at Cambridge between 1593 and 1600, an optimal time for him to buy Marlowe's books one at a time and learn them by heart, since most of them were published or reprinted between 1594 and 1604.

The dominant impression one gets from Oxinden's notes on Marlowe is that he and Aldrich admired Marlowe's gifts as a playwright and poet, were

[53] Henry Oxinden, Folger Commonplace Book, 54.

intrigued rather than appalled by his life, and thoroughly enjoyed gossiping about him. Although Oxinden had obviously read Beard, he nowhere condemns Marlowe, nor does he suggest that Aldrich condemned him. Like many individuals in the Renaissance, Oxinden seems to have had a high tolerance for contradictions. Extensive portions of his commonplace books are devoted to fervent religious meditation, yet often on the same or the next page he would jot down a love sonnet or a bawdy doggerel riddle for future reference: "A mayden head is / A Lamp which lasses beare about / Till putting in doth put it out."[54] Two of the several passages he copies out of Marlowe have to do with uncontrollable passion, such as a couplet from *Hero and Leander*, "Love is not full of pity (as men say) / But deaf and cruel where he meanes to prey," to which Oxinden sagely adds, "Love, & drunkenes, cannot be controled."[55] Oxinden also comments on Cicero's skepticism in the *Tusculian Disputations* and muses, "It is no damnable heresie to doubt of some of the bookes of the old & new Testament."[56] All in all, Oxinden's and his friend Aldrich's fascination with and genial tolerance of Marlowe's eccentricities, as well as their respect for his talent, are probably far more typical of sixteenth- and early-seventeenth-century attitudes than the censorious rant of Thomas Beard.

Oxinden's commonplace books were written during the twilight of Marlowe's fame among his contemporaries. The popularity of his plays peaked in the 1590s, and *Doctor Faustus* in particular continued to be performed profitably in the 1600s and 1610s. But by the time Heywood revived *The Jew of Malta* in 1633, cultural amnesia had set in to the extent that Heywood felt he needed to remind his audience in his prologue that Marlowe was the "best of poets" when the play was created "many yeares agone." Marlowe's plays, in short, were now historical relics, fondly or indulgently remembered, perhaps, by those old enough to have seen them performed during their heyday. Indeed, Heywood felt he needed to connect the play to the current vogue for character writing ("a sound Machiavel; / And that's his character") to make it more palatable to a Stuart audience. To Heywood, Marlowe's "lasting fame" rested on *Hero and Leander*, although he seemed to think that Edward Allen's performances as Tamburlaine might be remembered as well. We can see the same lapse of popular drama into cultural limbo today: few people under twenty have seen films made fifteen years ago, and even fewer people

---

[54] Ibid., 60.
[55] Ibid., 58; *Hero and Leander*, 771–72.
[56] Oxinden, Folger Commonplace Book, 40, 55.

under thirty know who Noël Coward was. Drama is kept alive only by being read and taught, performed and screened by successive generations.

It would be well over a century before Marlowe began to regain the admiration and respect his contemporaries had lavished on him, almost two centuries before his plays reappeared on stage. But in the interim, perhaps he would have preferred anonymity and neglect to mindless censure and lubricious gossip.

9

Marlowe Lost and Found

The living, not the dead, can envy bite,
For after death all men receive their right.
Then though death rakes my bones in funeral fire,
I'll live, and as he pulls me down mount higher.

Amores, book 1, elegy 15, 39–42

GIVEN THE EPHEMERAL nature of drama, and the lack of stature enjoyed by contemporary authors during and shortly after Marlowe's lifetime, Marlowe's sudden death at the age of twenty-nine virtually insured at least a temporary lapse into obscurity. Virtually all those who still remembered Marlowe's plays or the gossip that had circulated about him outlived him by only four or five decades, and since the number of plays he produced was small compared to the number written by Shakespeare or Jonson, there was no incentive to publish his collected works in folio. Jonson secured his own legacy by publishing his collected works himself, Shakespeare's fellow players published his plays, and Beaumont and Fletcher's plays were published in folio in 1647. As a result, those playwrights whose works were gathered and published in folio in the first half of the seventeenth century became the best known and most highly regarded of Elizabethan and Jacobean playwrights after the restoration of Charles II.

Hero and Leander continued to be read and admired in the middle to late seventeenth century, but one incomplete narrative poem, however brilliant, could not establish Marlowe as a major author. *Doctor Faustus* was still appearing in print in 1663, in a badly mangled version "with New Additions as it is now Acted." It continued to be performed into the eighteenth century in versions such as William Mountford's *The Life and Death of Doctor Faustus, Made into a Farce. With the Humours of Harlequin and Scaramouche. . . . With Songs and Dances between the Acts* (ca. 1688), or John Thurmond's and

John Rich's harlequinades of the early 1720s: *Harlequin Doctor Faustus: With the Masque of the Deities, The Comical History of Doctor Faustus*, and *The Necromancer: or, Harlequin Doctor Faustus*.[1] Of course Marlowe's name was no longer associated with these entertainments, and in them, the farce and spectacle that had once honed the tragic irony completely overwhelmed it. The *Faustus* Marlowe created was an inspired amalgam of popular narrative and performance traditions, medieval drama, and classical tragedy, but in the hands of showmen and craftsmen rather than artists this synthesis collapsed, and the popular elements became increasingly dominant. Marlowe scholars generally deplore Mountford's, Thurman's, and Rich's versions of *Faustus*, but they have more than a little to tell us about Marlowe's own flair for showmanship, and the inherent theatrical vitality of the material he chose to mold into a great play.

Tamburlaine and *The Jew of Malta* also continued to be performed in the early decades of the seventeenth century. Heywood revived *The Jew of Malta* in the early 1630s, which led to its subsequent publication in quarto in 1633. Also, Edmund Grayton mentions in *Festivous Notes on Don Quixote* (1654) that players at festivals were prepared, "notwithstanding their bills to the contrary, to act what the major part of the company had a mind to; sometimes *Tamburlaine*, sometimes *Jugurth*, sometimes *The Jew of Malta*, and sometimes parts of all these."[2] Apparently these plays, though no longer "in fashion,"[3] were still known and appreciated by playwrights, actors, and audiences in the first half of the century. However, after the interregnum they were much less well known. When Charles Saunders's *Tamburlaine the Great* was criticized as being "only an Old Play Transcrib'd" in 1681, he protested, "I never heard of any Play on the same Subject, untill my own was Acted," though he acknowledges "a Cock Pit Play going under the name of the *Scythian Shepherd*, or *Tamberlain the Great*, which how good it is, anyone may judge by its obscurity."[4] Obviously *Tamburlaine* was known to some as an "Old Play" in the 1680s and was still being performed occasionally, but it was no longer familiar to everyone.

For the most part, during the late seventeenth and early eighteenth centuries Marlowe was known as a playwright mainly to booksellers, who listed all of Marlowe's plays as available for purchase, and to a few others with a special interest in old plays. Milton's nephew Edward Phillips, in *Theatrum*

---

[1] M. Willson Disher, *Clowns and Pantomimes* (New York, 1925), 243–44.
[2] Quoted in Frederick S. Boas, *Christopher Marlowe: A Biographical and Critical Study* (Oxford, 1940), 296.
[3] Heywood's Prologue Spoken at Court, line 2.
[4] Quoted in C. F. Tucker Brooke, *The Reputation of Christopher Marlowe* (New Haven, 1922), 384.

Poetarum (1675), describes Marlowe as "a kind of second *Shakesphear,*" though he immediately dismisses him as "inferiour both in Fame and Merit." Phillips dimly recalls that Marlowe "in some riotous Fray came to an untimely and violent End," but he seems to be totally unaware of, or uninterested in, Marlowe's alleged atheism.[5] In addition to *Faustus,* "which hath made the greatest noise, with its Devils and such-like Tragical sport," Phillips mentions *Edward II, The Massacre at Paris, The Jew of Malta,* and *Dido.* He erroneously ascribes *Tamburlaine* to Thomas Newton, and Phillips was also the first to claim in print that Marlowe, like Shakespeare, "rose from an Actor to be a maker of Plays," a story which has never been confirmed. Perhaps by Phillips's time stories about Marlowe were confused with reports about Shakespeare and Ben Jonson, or perhaps Marlowe did perform in school or university productions. He may even have acted occasionally in professional productions, as playwrights and screenwriters sometimes do today, though he almost certainly never acted as a professional.

The publication of the first edition of Dodsley's *Old Plays* in 1744 is generally regarded as a turning point in the knowledge and reception of Marlowe and his works. This edition, which included *Edward II,* was symptomatic of a new interest in Renaissance plays other than Shakespeare's as important literary artifacts rather than mere rarities or curiosities. It was followed by a second edition of 1780, edited by Isaac Reed, which included *The Jew of Malta.* In the meantime, actors such as Garrick and Kemble, and the scholars Reed, Richard Heber, George Steevens, and Edmund Malone, began collecting early editions of plays and poems. Malone was curious enough about Marlowe to seek out some of his university records, thereby determining to his satisfaction that Marlowe was a graduate of Corpus Christi College, born around 1565, who was probably never a professional actor. Malone also gathered a number of early references to Marlowe in the works of his contemporaries, copying them into the collection of early editions of Marlowe's plays, which he acquired and had bound together.

At around the same time, Marlowe's moral character became an issue in an exchange between the scholars Thomas Wharton and Joseph Ritson. Wharton, a professor of poetry at Oxford, tried to overlook Marlowe's alleged vices in his *History of English Poetry* (1774–81) because of his merits as a poet. Ritson countered by publishing the complete text of the Baines Note in his *Observations on Wharton* (1782). To Malone, Wharton, and Ritson, Marlowe was no longer a forgotten scribbler of old plays but a vital intellectual interest, although one might wonder why they had so little to say about him

[5] Quoted in ibid., 387.

in print. Thomas Dabbs argues that the failure of these pioneering Marlowe scholars to engage in more extensive public praise of Marlowe may have been influenced by his tainted reputation,[6] and Marlowe's reputation undoubtedly did disturb Wharton, as indeed it had disturbed some of his acquaintances and admirers during and immediately after his lifetime. But the limited audience for such discussions in the late eighteenth century may have had more to do with the lack of printed commentary than squeamishness about Marlowe's unholy life. Malone, for example, seems completely neutral on the subject of Marlowe's character and beliefs. In his annotations on his collected works of Marlowe he simply mentions the Baines Note, points out its weaknesses as evidence, and also cites evidence that might support it.[7]

This new scholarly and antiquarian interest in Marlowe, which inspired the first (but hardly the last) forgery of a Marlowe-related document,[8] was a prelude to the flood of editions of Marlowe's work that began to appear in the early nineteenth century. The publication of Charles Lamb's *Specimens of English Dramatic Poets* in 1808, in which Lamb evinced enthusiasm for certain features of Marlowe's plays, particularly *Edward II*'s death scene, probably encouraged the trend. In 1810, *Edward II* and *The Jew of Malta* were reprinted in Scott's *The Ancient British Drama*. *Doctor Faustus* and *Edward II* appeared in the first volume of Dilke's *Old English Plays* (1814). *Dido, Queen of Carthage* followed in 1825, in volume 2 of the Hurst, Robinson and Company's *Old English Drama*. During the same time span, Marlowe's translation of Lucan, and of course *Hero and Leander*, were also being reprinted in editions of early English poetry. In 1818, William Oxberry began editing and publishing all of Marlowe's plays individually, along with *Lust's Dominion*, which he mistakenly believed to be Marlowe's. Later, in 1827, Oxberry gathered these plays in one volume, *The Dramatic Works of Christopher Marlowe, with prefatory remarks, notes, critical and explanatory. By W. Oxberry, comedian.* Publication of this volume followed almost immediately on the three-volume Pickering edition of the *Works of Christopher Marlowe* (1826).

This sudden surge of interest in Marlowe is not as puzzling as Boas thought.[9] The rise in literacy that made the novel increasingly popular and commercially viable in the late eighteenth and early nineteenth centuries also fostered a growing interest in early English literature and a renewed ambition to elevate English literature to the same status as the Greek and Latin

[6] Thomas Dabbs, *Reforming Marlowe* (Lewisburg, Pa., 1991), 30.
[7] Brooke, *The Reputation of Christopher Marlowe*, 393.
[8] Ibid., 391.
[9] Boas, *Christopher Marlowe: A Biographical and Critical Study*, 301.

classics. New magazines appeared that catered to this interest, and scholars and antiquaries further encouraged the trend by publishing articles and books in which they introduced novice readers to many Renaissance authors including Marlowe, particularly to works not readily available in print, which they quoted at length to demonstrate their fine points. Shakespeare attained his lofty status as the greatest of all English authors during this period, while Marlowe, as Dabbs observes, "is the only Elizabethan or Jacobean playwright whose status changed so greatly in such a short period of time."[10] This rapid ascent occurred partly because scholars rediscovered the great respect that Marlowe's contemporaries, including Shakespeare, had for his work, which validated and encouraged their own enthusiasm.

One of Marlowe's most enthusiastic advocates during the early nineteenth century was J. P. Collier, whose series of articles "On the Early English Dramatists" in *Edinburgh Magazine* (1819–21) was clearly intended to raise popular awareness of and appreciation for the work of Marlowe and his contemporaries. Significantly, Collier begins his first article dealing mainly with Marlowe by citing evidence that "perhaps no poet in the reign of Elizabeth was in greater repute among his contemporaries and more immediate successors" than Marlowe.[11] He mentions several of Shakespeare's references to Marlowe and in a later installment states that Shakespeare's indebtedness to *Edward II* in *Richard II* has already been observed. Though he never spells out his views fully, Collier sees Marlowe as "the first, or one of the first, to bring blank-verse into common use upon the stage in preference to rhime." Marlowe is a "master-poet" who both preceded and influenced Shakespeare, and a possible founder of what Collier, probably following Schlegel, calls "the *romantic drama*," of which Shakespeare was supposedly the principal practitioner.[12] In *The Poetical Decameron* (1820), a book explicitly intended to "treat an antiquarian subject in a popular way,"[13] Collier presents his ideas in the form of a discussion among three literate young men with an infectious enthusiasm for early English literature. They discuss both Marlowe's violent death and his alleged atheistic opinions with keen interest and even gusto rather than distaste. However, these matters are dismissed as finally unimportant, because "we cannot now come at the truth," and, most important, "nobody denies that he was a first rate poet."[14]

[10] Dabbs, *Reforming Marlowe*, 30.

[11] John Payne Collier, "On the Early English Dramatists Who Preceded Shakespeare," part 1, *Edinburgh Magazine* 6 (June 1820): 517.

[12] John Payne Collier, "On the Early English Dramatists Who Preceded Shakespeare," part 2, ibid. 7 (August 1820): 148.

[13] John Payne Collier, *The Poetical Decameron* (Edinburgh, 1820), 1:v.

[14] Ibid., 1:128, 2:273–74.

An anonymous article published the following year in *Retrospective Review, and Historical and Antiquarian Magazine* as part of a series on "The Early English Drama" is even more ebullient. The author immediately addresses the issue of Marlowe's religious opinions, pointing out that the allegations are weakly supported by evidence, and that "the moral tendency of his plays is always exemplary," in that "Marlowe does ample poetical justice on his criminal characters."[15] He then turns to Marlowe's works, remarking like Collier that "one cannot but be struck with the high reputation which he acquired in the age in which he lived. He is the greatest name on the theatrical roll before Shakespeare. He rose above all his predecessors and contemporaries in vigor of imagination and originality of conception."[16] After a number of lengthy quotations and observations on individual plays, among them the comment, following Lamb, that the scenes of *Edward II*'s abdication and death "leave an impression on the mind not easily to be erased," the author concludes, "To the genius of Marlowe, the English Drama is considerably indebted."[17] This is perhaps the first time the term "genius" was applied to Marlowe. It would certainly not be the last.

These articles were by no means the first to praise or promote Marlowe. A letter written by Alexander Blair to John Wilson on 29 April 1819 makes reference to quotations or excerpts from Marlowe that Blair encountered in Wilson's magazine—possibly Henry Maitland's article on *Doctor Faustus* in the *Blackwood's Magazine* of July 1817, in which Maitland supplied "extracts sufficiently copious to exhibit its peculiar spirit and character":[18]

Marlowe is the writer in whom (excepting Shakespeare) I have always conceived—with very little knowledge of him—*most* tragic might & imagination: & what I have since seen of him in your magazine still more exalts my conception of him. His spirit seems to me to have dwelt in the innermost motions of men's hearts. I do not mean that he draws an entire passion, still less character, well:—but he has got at some of the workings of passion in a way that is truly startling. In *Titus Andronicus* the few lines that are really good seem to me like Marlowe—unlike Shakespeare.—It seems to me like a spirit shaken with the trance of passion—not like genius painting. The beauty of his words & imagery is exceeding: it seems as if there had been in him

---

[15] "The Early English Drama, Art. X.," *Retrospective Review, and Historical and Antiquarian Magazine* 4 (1821): 145.

[16] Ibid., 146.

[17] Ibid., 144, 181.

[18] Quoted in Brooke, *The Reputation of Christopher Marlowe*, 396.

very impressible sense: which received the beautiful looks of things, with deep tender and unchangeable impression.—The darkness of Fate overshadowing human life, & the fearful energies of wickedness in men's hearts, strongly possess his imagination.—There are many of our tragic writers in whose pourtrayings of the scenes of existence there is a gloom that is quite oppressive to the soul. He is one of them.[19]

Blair's letter suggests that the sudden upsurge of interest in Marlowe in the early eighteenth century cannot be ascribed to a single cause. It was a spontaneous cultural event that seemingly began with the publication of Marlowe's plays, or of quotations and extracts from them, in books and magazines—apparently in an attempt by scholars and antiquaries to share their enthusiasm for Renaissance literature with a larger audience. These publications generated an unexpectedly intense positive response from readers like Blair, in whom they seem to have struck a powerful intellectual and emotional chord. This led to more publication of Marlowe's works, more articles reappraising him, and more research. Blair's letter also suggests that the darker strains of Romanticism—its emphasis on unbridled individualism, rebellion, violent passion, melancholy, and death—made readers in this period far more receptive to Marlowe's plays than were readers in the late seventeenth and early eighteenth centuries.

Collier thought so highly of Marlowe that he planned to do a scholarly edition of his plays, one which would supersede the Oxberry and Pickering editions. However, sometime in the late 1830s or early 1840s, Collier decided that he was too deeply involved in his numerous other projects, including his eight-volume edition of Shakespeare, to compete with Alexander Dyce, who was also contemplating an edition of Marlowe's plays. With seeming magnanimity, Collier gave some of his Marlowe material—including several forgeries of his own invention—to Dyce, who incorporated this information and misinformation in his landmark *Works of Christopher Marlowe, with Notes and Some Account of His Life and Writings* (1850). Dyce's edition set an unprecedented standard of scholarship in the study of Marlowe. He not only gave serious thought to textual issues and brought his formidable knowledge of Renaissance literature to bear on Marlowe, but also undertook his own biographical research. Dyce was the first to publish records of the Marlowe family in St. George's parish in Canterbury, as well as evidence of Marlowe's attendance at the King's School. This eminently respectable edition by the

[19] Folger Y.c.165 (1).

equally respectable Reverend Dyce secured Marlowe's place as a major author in the canon of English literature, although if Dyce had not performed this service for Marlowe, someone else surely would have. Dyce's edition was followed by many more.

In the twentieth century, Marlowe's reputation continued to rise, and he was regularly described as a genius. If his works and life appealed to Romantic sensibility, they appealed just as strongly, if not more strongly, to the twentieth-century intellectual's growing cynicism, distrust of authority and institutions, alienation, anomie, and acute interest in politics, class conflict, sexuality, and gender. Marlowe's works were now seen as quintessential expressions of intellectual, political, sexual, and personal rebellion, and at the same time, they were perceived as being much cooler in manner and tone than they appeared to Blair—ambiguous, ironic, and detached, rather than "shaken with the trance of passion" in high Romantic style. As new dramatic forms arose in reaction to melodrama and realism, Marlowe's sound dramatic and theatrical instincts (as distinct from his poetic skill) were rediscovered and admired. What we know of Marlowe himself was tweaked to fit new iconic molds and political agendas: he was now the intellectual and social revolutionary; the jaded spy; the openly gay man; the anarchistic bad boy; and ultimately, the victim of corrupt, oppressive authority or political machination.

Even some of the more bizarre twentieth-century theories about Marlowe, such as those that champion him as the author of Shakespeare's plays, seem to derive remotely from the radical elevation of Marlowe's status in the early nineteenth century. The idea that Marlowe was Shakespeare was first suggested, not surprisingly, in the *Monthly Review* of 1819: "Can Christopher Marlowe have been a *nom de guerre* assumed for a time by Shakespeare? . . . This much is certain, that, during the five years of the nominal existence of Marlowe, Shakespeare did not produce a single play."[20] In 1819 this theory could be excused because its creator had limited information. But it persisted in inverse form in the twentieth century, like Oxfordian theories about the authorship of Shakespeare's plays, through deliberate selection and distortion of evidence and unrestrained fanciful speculation. Like Oxfordianism, theories that Marlowe was Shakespeare seem to satisfy some deep psychological need to dethrone an authority figure, and who better than Marlowe, the anti-authoritarian poster boy, to meet that need?

Since Marlowe and his work have now survived over four centuries of change in taste and critical theory, the shoemaker's son of Canterbury, who

[20] Brooke, *The Reputation of Christopher Marlowe*, 397–98.

defined himself as a scholar and poet, has apparently achieved his coveted secular immortality through verse. But it is a strange immortality, continually shifting with time and with the perceiver, not at all the triumphant apotheosis of self that Marlowe seems to anticipate in the lines of book 1, elegy 15 of the *Amores* quoted in the epigraph. One suspects that Marlowe would barely recognize many of the images that scholars and admirers have imposed on him in kaleidoscopic succession. He would probably be at least as disappointed as we are by how little we know about his life, while many of our interpretations of his works, however well founded they seem to us, might seem bizarre and incomprehensible to him. And it was his poems and plays, of course, that he relied on most: "Verse is immortal, and shall ne'er decay" (*Amores*, 1.15.32).

Still, if personal immortality has proven more elusive than Marlowe expected, simple fame has its compensations. We will never know exactly who Marlowe was, but Marlowe is a name to conjure with in select circles. Literate people recognize and respond to it. They know it signifies an exceptionally talented poet, a daring innovator who died young and violently, from whom Shakespeare learned part of his trade. Beyond that bare outline, we invent our own Marlowe. But perhaps it is better to exist merely as a figment of others' imaginations—especially such an alluring, seductive, glittering figment—than not to exist at all.

Appendix

INTRODUCTION

The Marlowe documents were published piecemeal as scholars discovered them and incorporated them into arguments about Marlowe, beginning in the eighteenth century. For some reason, no one assembled complete texts of the most crucial documents in one volume—to the serious inconvenience of anyone who wanted to study Marlowe's life in detail. What follows is a gathering of the most important documents on which our knowledge of Marlowe is based, arranged in chronological order or a close approximation thereof. Reading through them provides a necessarily fragmentary but vivid impression of significant moments in Marlowe's life.

The location and classification of each document is indicated in its heading, using the abbreviations found at the beginning of this book. I have studied all these documents (and many others) firsthand and have freshly transcribed and translated them as accurately as possible. I have also provided comments on significant features of the documents, their context, and the interconnections among them. Some of these texts have never been printed before. For example, Thomas Walsingham's pardon for outlawry (debt) is a new discovery and appears here for the first time. The coroner's account of the death of William Bradley is translated in its entirety for the first time, rather than being transcribed in Latin and paraphrased or selectively quoted in English.

In transcribing and editing these documents I have preserved individual idiosyncrasies of spelling and punctuation, including the common use of slashes instead of, or in conjunction with, periods. However, I have modernized the conventional Elizabethan usage of *j* and *i*, *u* and *v*, *ff* for *F*, and *ye* for *the*, which have no interpretive significance. In editing legal documents I have silently expanded Latin abbreviations, since these had no meaning in themselves but were simply a convenient form of shorthand. Conventional abbreviations in English are treated similarly; less familiar ones are expanded in square brackets. Angle brackets indicate words and phrases deleted by the person writing the document. Wavy brackets enclose material added by the scribe.

As I discovered when I was able to examine the Marlowe documents directly, some minor variations in different scholars' transcriptions of these texts are inevitable. Deciding whether a letter is capitalized or not, which punctuation mark the scribe intended, and sometimes even what word the writer meant can be subjective. Many sixteenth-century documents are now faded, damaged, or dirty, and bad handwriting is difficult to read in any script.

The principles I have followed in deciding which documents to include require some explanation. Most records of Marlowe's schooling are lists including his name, which obviously do not require transcription or lend themselves to it, and present no difficulties in interpretation. These are therefore omitted. The Buttery Books of Corpus Christi College, on the other hand, might constitute a book in themselves, and would be most useful in that form, but it would be impractical to reprint all the possibly significant portions of them here. I therefore chose to discuss significant features of the Buttery Books in the narrative. I have included several documents containing information about people of significance and probable significance in Marlowe's life such as John Gresshop, John Benchkin, Richard Baines, and Thomas Walsingham. I have also included a second letter of Robert Sidney to Lord Burghley, which appears in print for the first time, since it illuminates Sidney's first letter concerning Marlowe and Baines, and may clarify the career of Baines as well. I chose not to include a letter by Thomas Drury to Anthony Bacon dated 1 August 1593 because it does not mention Marlowe, though it obviously is somehow related to events unfolding around the time of his death. It seemed more appropriate to discuss Drury's letter, including its many ambiguous and disturbing features, in the narrative.

MARLOWE FAMILY PARISH REGISTER ENTRIES, CCA

According to a prefatory note, the surviving Parish Register of St. George is a copy of records kept on loose sheets of paper that were in serious disorder. The first sheet of the original record of christenings, marriages, and burials was dated, but if a second sheet was required to continue the entries later in the year, the date was not repeated on the second sheet. These second sheets could easily be shuffled out of order. Therefore the copyists incorrectly entered Margaret Marlowe's christening date, which was written on a loose second sheet in 1566, as 28 December 1548. Someone—probably a forger who wanted to clarify Marlowe's family history— later entered Margaret's birth in the parish register as ii December 1565, erasing and writing over a legitimate entry for "An the daughter of William Man," who was buried on 18 December 1565. The Archdeacon's Transcript of the register records Margaret's birth as 18 December 1566. However, xviii may be an error for xxviii, or vice versa. Such errors in copying Roman numerals were common.

St. George's Parish
Marriage

1561   The 22th of May were maried John Marlowe and Catherine Arthur./

Christenings

1562   The xxith of May was christened Mary the daughter of John Marlowe.

1563/4 The 26th day of February was christened Christofer the sonne of John Marlow.

1566 [Archdeacon's Transcript] The xviii day off desember was crystenyd Marget the daghter off John Marle

1568 The last day of October was christened the sonne of John Marlowe.

1569 The 20th day of August was christened John the sonne of John Marlow. [This is actually Joan or Jayne, a daughter.]

1570 The 26th day of July was christened Thomas the sonne of John Marle.

1571 The 14th day of July was christened An the daughter of John Marle/

1573 [Archdeacon's Transcript] the same daye [18 October] was crissoned Darety the daugter of John Marly.

Burials

1568 The 28th day of August was buried the daughter of John Marlowe./
The 5th day of November was buried the sonne of John Marlow./

1570 The 7th day of August was buried Thomas the sonne of John Marlow./

1604/5 John Marloe clarke of St: Maries was buried the 25th of January./

Parish of St. Andrew
Christening

1576 Thomas Marley the son of John—viii Apell

Marriage

1582 John More & Jayne Marley—xxii Apell

Parish of St. Mary Bredman
Marriages

1590 The xvth day of June were maryed John Jorden & Margaret Marlowe./

1593 The xth day of June were maried John Cranforde & An Marlowe./

1594 The xxxtith day of June were maried Thomas Graddell & Dorithie Marle./

All Saints Parish
Burial

1604/5 Catheren Marlowe was buryed the xviiii daie of Marche anno predicto [in the foresaid year]

ASSORTED PARISH REGISTER ENTRIES IN CANTERBURY, 1582–1605, CCA

A number of entries in the Canterbury parish registers, in addition to those of the Marlowe family, have relevance or possible relevance to Marlowe's life. The St. Mildred's parish register notes the burial of Katherine Benchkin, as well as the

burial of her husband, James, and the christenings of some of their son John Benchkin's children. It also records the burial of Thomas Greenleaf, the husband of Mrs. Benchkin's kinswoman whom she named overseer of her will, and an associate of Marlowe's father in the shoemaker's company. A Thomas Fineaux, gentleman, of Canterbury, possibly a kinsman of the Mr. Fineaux who was allegedly acquainted with Marlowe and converted by him to atheism, was issued a license to marry Susanna Alcock, also of Canterbury, on 2 June 1592. He was killed by Henry Simpson in a tavern brawl (William Urry, City Archivist's Report, 19 February 1958) and buried at All Saints in 1597. John Marlowe's old acquaintance Lawrence Applegate, who was tried in ecclesiastical court for slandering Mrs. Chapman's daughter Godelif Hurte, was buried at St. George's in 1612.

All Saints Parish
Burials

Anno Domini 1597.Thomas Fenyuxe gent was buryed the, 25. of September.

A "Christopher Feneuxe gent," probably a relative of Thomas, was buried at All Saints on 5 September 1605.

St. George's Parish
Burial

Larrance Applegate buried the iiii day of January 1612.

St. Mildred's Parish
Christenings

1596:	Thomasyn Benchkyn daughter of John ii July
1598:	Thomas Benchkyn sonne of John 16 July
1605:	Katherine the daughter of John Benchkin Jan. 3

Burials

1582:	James Benchkyn buried 18 Apryll
1586:	Katherine Benchkyn widow buryed 25 July
1604:	Thomas Greeneleafe householder Septemb. 10

INVENTORY OF JOHN GRESSHOP'S ESTATE, 23 FEBRUARY 1580, CKS PRC21/4, FF. 169–75

This document reveals a great deal about Marlowe's schoolmaster at the King's School, John Gresshop, especially about his education at Oxford, his teaching methods, and his living conditions. The Gresshop inventory is also printed in William Urry, Christopher Marlowe and Canterbury (London, 1988), 108–22. While the printed text in Urry is substantially accurate, it contains a number of minor errors and several omissions. I have corrected most of these. However, because a few items in the manuscript are not clearly legible, some guesswork has been inevitable.

Gresshop had extensive holdings in reformist/humanist writings; his library included, among many others, works by Luther, Sturm, Bucer, Oeculampadius, Melanchthon, Agricola, Beza, Brugenhagen (Pomeranus), Calvin, Knox, Vives, Erasmus, Pietro Martire (Peter Martyr), Valla, Fabricius, Dolet, and Zwingli. This wide range of material reflects not only Gresshop's thorough familiarity with theological issues but also his knowledge of the most advanced humanist pedagogical literature.

Certainly one of the most recent additions to Gresshop's library was his copy of Stephen Gosson's The Ephemerides of Phialo, *a work modeled closely on Lyly's* Euphues *and published in 1579. Gosson, a Canterbury native, was baptized in the same parish church as Marlowe and came from a similar family background. After studying under Gresshop at the King's School he proceeded to Oxford, tried his hand as a playwright in London, repented, and attacked the theater in* The School of Abuse, *published earlier in 1579. Gosson's early career path may well have been a model for Marlowe's, just as Lyly's had been a model for Gosson's.*

Greshop

The apprisement of suche goodes as were late Mr John Greshops schoolemaister at Caunterburie deceased made the xxiii^th of february 1579 R. R. Eliz. 22 [1580]. By Mr. Thomas Swifte Mr Will. Browne ministers of the saide churche, Mr John Marden singinge man, and [blank] Faunt singing man.

Goodes in the great chamber where he died.

A joined bedstedell wth head and tester of wainescot wth a rope and a mat—xii s.
A fetherbed, a Boulster, and a pillowe—xxx s.
An olde matteris there prised at—ii s vi d.
A paire of old blankets—iii s. iiii d.
A coverlet of greene dornix—viii s.
A white rug blanket—vi s viii d.
Three olde curtins of say Red and greene wth iii curtin Rods—iiii s.
An olde presse cubberd wise of wainscot—xvi s.
A joyned cheste—v s.
A plated cofer—x s.
An olde cubberd—ii s. vi d.
A table upon a frame and a forme—ii s. vi d.
An olde courte cubberd—xii d.
A paire of Andirons, fireshovell, tounges, and gridiron—v s.
A paire of olde bellowes—ii d.
Two olde turned chaires—xii d.
An ould Curtin in the window wth a rod—viii d.
A hoope for a Basan, and a hooke for a towell—viii d.

The painted clothes there—xvi s.
apparell
Two paire of olde carsey hose—iii s. iiii d.
His best dublet of rashe, and best hose of the same—xiii s. iiii d.
Two old dublets one of rashe, and thother of mockadow—iii s. iiii d.
An olde spanishe lether Jerkin—ii s.
A cap, and a hat—ii s.
An olde peese of course serge—xii d.
An olde mockadowe cassok—xii d.
A black cloth cote—viii s.
A cloake w^t sleeves—xiii s. iiii d.
A rounde cloke with silver clapses—xxxx s.
An olde gowne of buffin faced w^t budge—x s.
The beste gowne—liii s iiii d.
An olde cloth gowne faced w^t budge—x s.

In the plated chest
A surplace and a hood—vi s. viii d.
Five olde shirtes—xii s.
Five iii cornerd kirchers—ii s. vi d.
Three handetowells—xii d.
Three short table clothes—iii s.
Foure olde pillowberes—iii s.
xi table napkins—iiii s.
An olde wallet—iii d.
Certaine new cloth and Remnantes—iii s. iiii d.
vi paire of sheetes—xxx s.
iii course sheetes for boyes—v s.
v sheetes in a bag—xx s.
ii good shirtes wth ii peeses of shirtes in a bag—x s.
v pillowe cotes—vi s. viii d.
An olde corner kircher and vi handkerchers—xx d.
foure tynne spoones—ii d.
A pot, and a glasse—xii d.
A dagger—vi d.
A girdle—i d.
A girdle of chaungeable silke—xii d.
And olde crowne of a velvet hat—ii d.
A Jacket of olde damaske—iii s. iiii d.
Sixe bookes in the cofer—ii s.

In the paved Chamber
A foldbedsteedell, coorde, and mat—xiii s. iiii d.
The tester of the same bed w^t iii curtins of unfrised cotton all greene—vi s. viii d.

A little fether bed, a boulster, a pillowe, and a mattrice—xxvi s. viii d.

A course paire of blankets, whereof one is linse wolse—iii s. iiii d.

A coverlet of tapistrie course—xiii s. iiii d.

iii curtyn roddes—xii d.

5 olde joinde stooles and a courte cubberd—iiii s.

A square table, and a joined foorme—iiii s.

A little old cubberd, and an olde chaire—ii s.

Two pewter Basons, and one pewter dishe—ii s.

A glasse lanterne—xii d.

Two tyn candlestickes and a pewter pot—xvi d.

A rapiar, and a skene—iiii s.

Two stone pots—iiii d.

A table of praedestination—iiii d.

The hanginges—x s.

A curtin rod in the windowe—vi d.

viii cushins—viii s

A longe cushin—xvi d.

A cubberd clothe partie coloured w^t rowse—ii s

A peece of penniston greene—vi d.

A deske—iiii d

ii chaires—xii d.

A lattin candelsticke—viii d.

An olde ches boarde and men-xii d.

A cofer w^t a locke upon it for Wilder—xx d.

A covering of rowed worke and coloures much like to churche worke—x s.

A flocke bed and a strawe bed, and a flocke boulster—v s.

An olde fethered boulster—ii s.

A matterice, a mat, and a flocke boulster in the chamber underneath Mr Dorrels chamber ad lavam—xvi d.

In the chamber of W. D.

A bedsteedell—xx s.

A rounde table wt a seat very olde—xii d.

A joyned stoole—vi d.

Two olde courte cubberds—ii s.

Two olde peweter chamber pots—xvi d.

An old lattin candlestick—

In Buls chamber

A little olde fetherbed and an olde flocke boulster—x s.

A truckle bed and a mat—ii s. vi d.

A table wt trestells—vi d.

An olde foorme—iiii d.

Summa totalis xxviii^li iiii s. v

Thomas Swyfte
William Browne

In the upper study by the schoole doore
(In primis in the windowe bookes—xxxvi
Item upon the east shelve bookes—Cxiiii
Item upon a hie shelve westward bookes—xxviii
Item upon a shelfe under that bookes—xxxvi)

Viz. Libri in folio
Brentius in Osea, una cum Buceri libro de regno christi—iii s. iiii d.
Concordantiae Zisti Graeca—ii s.
Hofman de paenitentia—iiii s.
Tabulae locorum Philippi Melancthonis—ii s. vi d.
Roffensis [John Fisher] contra Lutherum—ii s.
Philippus presbiter in Jobu—xii d.
Biblia pagnini—ii s. vi d.
Liber Charlaceus—
Tomus tertius et 4^tus et v^tus operus Melancthonis—iii s. iiii d.
Commentarius in rhetorica Ciceronis—iii s. iiii d.
Commentarii Doleti vol 2 libri due—x s.
Urbani grammatica graeca—viii d.

quarto
Institutiones Juris Civilis graecae—xii d.
Demosthenis Epistolae, pars thucididis, Comaediae Aristophanis uno vol
    graeca—postilla pervetus—
Opuscula quaedam Lutheri, Calvini, Bullingeri, Gualteri uno volumine in
    quarto—x
Claudius Sissellus de providentia—vi d.
Martir [Peter Martyr] de Eucharistia—iiii d.
Martir in Epistolam ad Corinthios—iii s.
Casninus in Galatas—viii d.
Victoria papatus—xii d.
Calvinus in psalmos—xx d
Oecolampadius in Danielem—x d.
Retmanius de Justificatione—iii d
An Answere to the Crosse Anglice—x d.
And Englishe booke for the government of women alias the harborow etc.
    —iiii d.
Lanaeterus in Josnan—xii d.

octavo

Petrus Lombardus—vi d.

Liber Digestorum—viii d.

Opera quaedam minuta Augustini—iiii d.

Zodiacus vitae Anglice—vi d.

Bezae Epistolae—

Liber vetus hieromini vidae de poetica—1 d.

Martir de Caelibatu et voti—12 d.

Lutherus in Ecclesiasten—4 d.

Wolfgangus Capito de Missa et iure magistratus—6 d.

Ecclesiasticae disciplinae liber—4 d.

Sturmii prolegomena—4 d.

Pii poetae uno volumine—6 d.

Lutherus in 7 caput prioris ad Corinthios—4 d.

Carmina phocilidis graecco latina—2 d.

An English booke of divinity Commen places—4 d.

Catechesis Christiana—2 d.

De linguae graecae pronunciatione liber—3 d.

Ars loquendi et tacendi Knanstino Autore—2 d.

A viewe of mans estate englishe—2 d.

A Catechisme Englishe—1 d.

Nowels Catechismes two in Latin, one in Englishe—

Portius de ponderibus et mensuris—1 d.

the Sickmans salve—6 d.

Melancthon de renovatione Ecclesiasticae disciplinae cum caeteris—6 d.

Liber de vitae et obitu Buceri Carro authore—6 d.

Prima pars Biblioni graece et Secunda graece, item at tertia—3 s. 4 d.

A faithfulll admonicion made by Knokes—2 d.

Varia poemata quorundam veteris de corrupto Ecclesiae statu—6 d.

Liber psalmorum Davidis cum Annotationibus Stephani—

Gregorius Nissenus de opificio hominis, cum opellis Ignatii—12 d.

Boetii Consolatio—14 d.

Epistolae Calvini duae—6 d.

Catechismus Calvini—2 d.

Beconus et Bertramus de Caena domini uno volumine—8 d.

The Anatomie of the Masse—4 d.

De religionis Conservatione, et de primatu magistratuum Laurentio humfredo autore—

Pandectae Scripturarum—6 d.

Oecolampadius in Mathaeu—6 d.

Oecolampadius in Joanni—6 d.

De compescendis animi affectibus Aloisius Luisinus—3 d.

Oecolampadius in Genesiu—5 d.

Opera Erasmi quadam uno volumine—4 d.

Dionisius Carthusianus in Luca—5 d.

Ecclesiastes Erasmi—

Sententia prosperi—8 d.

Virelus upon the Lordes Praier in Englishe—6 d.

Liber de differentia Ecclesiasticae et regalis potestatis—4 d.

Apologia Erasmi adversus quosdam Monachos—

Herman Archbishop of Colenia in Englishe—6 d.

Peregrinatio Belgica—6 d

Oecolampadius in 4 minores prophetas—6 d.

historia ecclesiastica Eusebii Latine—3 d.

Silva Bibliorum Hominis—6 d.

Oecolampadius in haebraeos—4 d.

Trahern Upon the Apocalipse Englishe—

fabritius in Abacuc [?] et prophetas minores—12 d.

Artopaeus in Genesiu—4 d.

Opera Cypriani aliquot 2 vol—16 d.

Ratio perveniendi at veram theol. Erasmo autore—6 d.

Lutherus de servo arbitrio cum aliis—6 d.

Pomeranus in Epistolas Pauli—4 d.

The reliques of Rome—

Pandectes of the evangelical Law made by pannel English—6 d.

Colonienses adversus Melancthonem et aliorum—5 d.

Anthologicon, id est florilegium graecorum aliquot—6 d.

Synesii Epistolae—6 d.

Bezae poemata—6 d.

Lavaterus de spectris—6 d.

Olaus magnus de gentibus Septentrionalibus—8 d.

Catechismus ex decreto Concilii Tridentii—6 d.

hemmingius de superstitionibus vitandis—4 d.

Sermones aliquot Oecolampadii—-3 d.

Catechismus Carnuti—

A sermon of Porders Englishe—3 d

Jewel against Cole—

Peter Viret Englished by Shute—

Nowels Catechisme in Englishe 2 of them—

Doctor Smithes unwritten verities—2 d.

Stephen Gardiners devels sophistry—0

Perrins sermons Englishe—2 d.

Aliquot orationes demosthenis conversae a Carro Anglo—6 d.

Wittingham of obedience to superior powers—2 d.

A treatise for ministers apparrel Englishe—4 d.

Marsilius ficinus de Christiana religione—6 d.

Methodus Confessionis—3 d.

Danaeus de beneficis—

Knoxe upon praedestinacion—4 d.
Confessio Saxonicarum Ecclesiarum—2 d.
Quaestiones pueriles Joannis Agricolae—2 d.
Catechismus Anglicus autore Anonumo—2 d.
Liber de Commuratione Scoticae reginae—
Cranmers Confutacion of unwritten verities—4 d.
Sillogisticon foxii—3 d.
The Christian state of matrimonie Englishe—1 d.
of obedience of Subjectes Englishe—2 d.
An Englishe booke of the disclosing of the great bull—1 d.
A booke of Songes and Sonnettes Englishe—1 d. [Tottel's Miscellany]
The philosopher of the Court in Englishe—2 d.
Confessio Ecclesiarum helveticarum—4 d.
An Invective ageinst treason in Englishe—1 d.
Epistola Lutheri contra Sabbatharios—1 d.
The benefit of Christes death in Englishe—1 d. ob
Goughes answere ageinst fecknam—
Norton's admonicion to the Queenes subjectes—1 d.
An Admonicion in Scottishe—
Against the use of Popishe garments in the Church—1 d.
A politicke discourse—
An Informacion to the parliament englishe—ob
Luciani dialogi aliquot—viii d.
Fentons discourse of the Warres in France—2 d.
An Englishe Catechisme—
Bonners Dirige—i d.
A sermon of Deringes—1 d.
An Englishe Catechisme—2 d.
Quaestiones Bezae—3 d.
A Sermon D fulcke—
A warning ageinst papists—1 d.
Calvinus de Praedestinatione—3 d.
A Sermon of Bradfordes—1 d.
Tragical discourses by the L Buckhurst— [Sackville's *Mirror for Magistrates*]
The fall of the Late Arrian—2 d. [by John Proctour]
Vincentius Livinensis de Antiquitate fidei Cath.—2 d.
Vives de Anima Libri tres—16 d.
Macrobii opera—8 d.
Aristoteles de mundo—4 d.
Lexicon graecolatinum Ciceronianum—8 d.
Institutiones fricksii Medicinales—10 d.
Gazae Grammatica Graeca—4 d.
Syntaxis linguae graecae Varennio authore—4 d.
Demosthenis et Aeschinis orationes contrariae—8 d.

Marcellus de proprietate linguae latinae—12 d.
Marsilii ficini opuscula—vi d.
Albertus magnus de formatione hominis—1 d.
Luciani dialogi Latini facti—8 d.
Digestorum liber secundus—8 d.
Hesiodus Graecolatinus—6 d.
Budaei Annotationes in Pandectas—6 d.
Lingua Erasmi—6 d.
Adrianus Cardinalis de Sermone Latino—3 d.
Platinae dialogus de falso et vero bono—2 d.
Some of Zenophon translated into Englishe—4 d.
Vives de Lingua Latina—2 d.
Polibius in Englishe—4 d.
Vives de disciplinis—12 d.
De ratione studii puerilis—6 d. [also by Vives]
Erotemata rhetorica Jodoci—8 d.
Sabellicus de moribus gentium—
Poema Alcimi—2 d.
Balduinus de Constantino Magno—20 d.
Caelius Secundus de Artificio Disserendi—4 d.
Sebastianus forius de historiae institutione—4 d.
Aristoteles de arte rhetorica graece—2 d.
Histora Sacramentaria de Caena—8 d.
Phocilidis Poema ἑλληνικον—2 d.
Nominis in Evangelium Joannis—3 d.
Alciattus de quinque pedum praescriptione—3 d.
Aristophanis εἰρηνή graece—2 d. [*Peace*]
Item thre Paper bookes—
Demosthenes πρὸς Λεπτίνην—1 d.

bookes in decimo sexto
herodianus graece—4 d
Cominei historia—8 d.
Bellum grammaticale—1 d.
Galeni de Compositione pharmacorum—8 d.
Ilias homerii graece—6 d.
Petrus Crinitus—12 d.
Methodus medendi Galeno authore—10 d.
Biel de Canone Missae—3 d.
Pentateuchus Moisis—4 d.
Catechismus Calvini Graecolatinus—4 d.
Gribaldus de ratione studendi—6 d
Contemplationes Idiotae—2 d.
Problemata Arist.—4 d.

Fenestella de Magistratibus—8 d.
Knoxes Epistles—1 d.
Compendium theologicae veritatis—0
Ovid de tristibus Englishe—2 d
Nowel's Catechismes in numbr v—12 d.

Plate and other things of the said Mr Greshops

Inprimus a pot of silver and gilt with a covir waying ix ounz one quarter at iii s
ix d the ounce—xliiii s viii d
Item iii silver spones waying iiii ounces and a quarter—xx s. vi d.
Item a bosse of a gyrdle and a whistle ii ounces almos—ix s. vi d.
Item two gold Rings half an ounce—i s.
Sum of the plat—vi li. iiii s. viii d.

In the lower study

in folio
Imprimis Plato Latine—ii s.
Opera Petrarchi—vi s.
Scotus in 4um Sententiarum—viii d.
Officia Ciceronis cum Commentario—
Munsteri Cosmographia—iiii s.
Thesaurus Ciceronis—vi s viii d.
Annotationes Erasmi in novum testa[mentum]—iiii s.
Fabians Chronicle—iii s.
Biblia Latine—iii s. iiii d.
Biblia Castalionis—iiii s.
Martir in Judicum, et Samuelem—vi s. viii d.
Concordantiae Bibliorum—xii d.
Martir in Rom. Anglici—iii s iiii d.
Flores historiarum—iiii s.
Familiares Epistolae Ciceronis cum Comment[ario]—ii s. vi d.
Chaucer—ii s.
Boccatius de genealogia Deorum—ii s.
Loci Communes Martiris—v s.
Galenus de temperamentis cum aliis—ii s.
A Geneva Bible—v s.
Virgilius cum Commentario—ii s.
Jewesl [*sic*—slip for Jewels] Defence of the Apologie—iiii s.
Ovidii Metamorphosis cum Comment[ario]—viii d.

In quarto
Grammatica Clenardi cum annnot. Antesignani—xii d.
Lavaterus in proverbia—xx d.

Foxius in Osorium—
Aschams Schoolemaster—iiii d
Camerarius et Alii in tusculanas quaest[ionibus]—xii d.
Dictionarium poeticum—xvi d.
Officia Ciceronis, cum diversorum Commentariis—xvi d.
Philo Judaeus in Decalogum—vi d.
Martir in Ethicam Arist.—ii s.
Valla de summo bono—viii d.
Langnettes Chronicles—xvi d.
The Image of both Churches—iiii d.
Psalterium Latinium—iiii d.
Dionisius Carthusianus de orthodoxa fide—iiii d
Bibliand. de fatis Monarchiae Romanae—
Alworthus [?] contra de visibilim Monarchiam Saunderi—iii d
Cartwrightes replie ageinst Whitegift—ii d
Higini historia—iiii d.
Aristophanes Graec.—vi d
Arist. Politica Strabaeo tralatore—iiii d
Wilsons logick English—viii d
Some bookes of Ovides Metam. English—ii d.
the praise of foly Englishe—ii d.
Haddoni Opellae—iiii d.
A discourse of the affaires in Germany by Ascham—ii d.
Liber Juris Canonici prima pars—xii d.

In octavo
Institutiones Calvini—ii s. vi d.
Plautus—xii d.
Grammatica Graeca Crusii—xx d.
Pii quidam poetae uno vol.—x d.
Pars quarta Livii—vi d.
Diallacticon Sacramentarium Boqnino [?] autore—vi d.
Plutarchi quadam opuscula—viii d.
Terentius Cum Commentario—xii d.
Sophiclis Tragaediae Latine—viii d.
Confessio Bezae, cum aliis—xii d.
Claudinaus poeta—xii d.
Locii Communes Joannis Manlii—xii d.
Facetia Bebetii cum aliis—viii d.
Facetia Brusonii—viii d.
A praesident for a prince—ii d.
Valnetinus Erithraeus de Conscribendis Epistolis—viii d.
Agrippa de vanitate Scientarium—vi d.
Apollinarius graecus in psalmos—vi d

Tusculanes Quaestions Englishe, wth the offices—vi d
Ovides Metamorphosis wth the pictures—viii d.
Syntaxis Languae graecae—iiii d
Linacri Grammatica—viii d
Sophoclis Tragaediae graece—viii d.
Solinus polyhistor.—viii d.
A pretious perle, id est, an englishe booke so called—iii d.
Eliottes governor—vi d
Erasmus Enchiridion englishe—iii d.
Castalionis Dialogi Sacri—xii d.
Catechismus Chytraei—iii d.
Physica, et Ethica valerii—iiii d.
De ratione discendae linguae Graecae—vi d.
Sadoletus de pueris instituendis—iiii d.
The new testament in Englishe—xii d.
Erotemata de Copia rerum et verborum, cum aliis—vi d.
Arithmetica Gemmae frisii—iiii d.
Processus Judiciarius Panormitani—ii d.
Aesopii fabulae—ii d.
Juvenalis—iii d.
Orationes. 6. Isocratis sex exiguis sed distinctis vol—ii s.
Utopia Mori Latine—ii d.
Theophil in evangelica—xii d.
Theoph. in Epistolas—xii d.
Homilae Bedae—viii d.
Cranmerus de Transubstantiatione—iiii d.
Claris theologiae—iiii d.
Sermones de tempore—iiii d.

In decimo sexto
Fabritius de poetica—vi d
Flaminius in psalmos—viii d.
Novum testam. graece—viii d.
Epistolae ad Atticus—xii d. [Cicero]
Epistolae familiares—vi d [Cicero]
Commentarii Caesaris—vi d.
Flaminii paraph. in 30 psalmos cum aliis—iiii d.
tres lib. de vitis Imperatorium Romanorum—ii s. [Suetonius]
Preces Sacrae—iiii d.
Officia Ciceronis et Terentius uno vol—xii d.
Testamentum graecis in duabus partibus—x d.
Frutisius de medendi—viii d.
Sibillina Oracula cum aliis—vi d. [supposedly by Phocylides]

Virgilius—viii d.

Manutii Epistolae—viii d.

Libri proph. omnium—vi d.

Palingenius—vi d.

Aulus Gellius—xii d.

Concordantiae biblioni et Canonum perexignae—ii d.

Ephemerides Phialo—ii d. [by Stephen Gossen, Gresshop's former pupil; published 1579]

A Dispraise of the Courtiers Life—ii d.

A praeparacion to the Lordes Supper—i d.

A touche stone for this praesent time—i d.

Symbola Joannis Laezii—i d.

Vassaeus de Judicio Trinarum—i d.

Summa totalis Inv^m—xlvi^{li} xii s. x d.

Priced by Mr John Hill Prebendarye in ch[r]ists churche in Canterbury
Frauncis Aldriche and [blank] Rose the ii Martii 1579

Besides the bookes above named there are of old rustie bookes about xviii

Monye found after his deathe

Inprimis a spurre royall and a frenshe crowne of the value of—xxi s.

Item in mylle sixepences and Edward twelvepenns—xix s. vi d.

Item in pence and thre halfe pence—xl s.

Item in ready sylver in the tawnye purse—iiii^{li} ii s. xi d.

Item in an other purse—ii s. x d.

Summa Totalis viii li. vi s. iii d.

INVENTORY OF JAMES BENCHKIN'S GOODS, 30 NOVEMBER 1582,
CKS PRC 10/10 FF. 740–50

After John Benchkin's father, James Benchkin, died in April 1582, an inventory of his property was prepared under the supervision of Mrs. Benchkin's kinsman Thomas Greenleaf. Like the inventory of John Marlowe's property, this document gives a clear indication of the relative wealth and social status of the Benchkin family, which was definitely superior to that of the Marlowes. However, it differs from John Marlowe's inventory in that it was prepared during Christopher Marlowe's lifetime, not long before Mrs. Benchkin changed her will, and therefore it records much of what Christopher and his kinsmen saw when they came to her house to serve as witnesses. The fireplace equipment adorned the fireplace in the parlor where Mrs. Benchkin burned her old will in their presence. In all probability the virginals, armor and weapons, map, painted cloths, and the table bearing the queen's coat of arms were also there when the will was signed and witnessed.

The inventory reveals that the Benchkins were engaged in manufacturing wool cloth, which explains why Mrs. Benchkin made provision in her will for loans to assist others in the same trade.

The inventory of all such goodes, debtes, mony & householde stuff, as were late James Benskyns, of the parish of Saint Mildred in the Cittye of Canterbury deceassed. Prised by Thomas Greeneleafe, and Marck Clarcke, the xxx day of November Anno 1582; Anno Regina Nostro Elizabeth xxv.

In the hall   viz

In primus one joyned cubbard, with a lofte...xiii^s iiii^d

Item one table with a frame, iiii stooles, & ii formes ....x^s

Itm v great Cushens & iiii small & ii old Carpetes...........................xiii^s iiii^d

Itm one payre of cobirons & a cradle of iron ....v^s viii^d

Itm one barrell of Tarrys..iiii^s

Itm two old Chayres...ii^s

Itm a payre of old virginalls...xx^d

Itm all the paynted clothes & a cubbard clothe...v^s

Itm one woolen wheele & ii payre of cardes...xii^d

Chamber over the hall

Item one joyned Bedstedell...xiii^s iiii^d

Itm iii fether Beddes ....iiii^{li}

Itm I coverlyt & iiii blancketes ....xxx^s

Itm xvi pyllowes of fethers...xxxiii^s

Itm xii chestes great & small ....xxiii^s

Itm iiii small coffers ....iiii^s

Itm one lyttle table...xii^d

Itm one Bassen & a Ewer of pewter ....v^s

Itm v chaffing dishes of lattyn ....xiii^s iii^d

Itm xxvi pottes of pewter great & small ....xx^s

Itm v saltes of pewter & one goblet ....ii^s

Itm xxii saucers of pewter ....vi^s viiii^d

Itm one dossen of poringers of pewter...v^s

Itm xxv pewter dishes & ii frutes dishes..xiii^s iiii^d

Itm two tasters of pewter ....vi^d

Itm iiii chamber pottes of pewter..vi^d

Many other metal utensils are listed, including a large number of platters, a colander of pewter, five basins, a charger, and a mortar and pestle of brass.

Itm ii old Lutes..v^s

Itm one dagg with a case and 2 old capcases ....2^s 6^d

Itm iiii swordes & ii daggers ....vi^s ii^d
Itm ii old Deskes ....xvi^d
Itm III old hampres & a basket ....viii^d
Itm one gowne of grograyme..xxx^s
Itm one gowne of broad cloth furred ....xxx^s
Itm one Cloake cowller browne [?] blewe ....xxxvi^s vii^d
Itm iii Cloakes newe & old..xx^s

Many items of men's clothing are listed, including a buff leather jerkin, a leather doublet, hose, jackets, a satin doublet valued at twenty shillings, and gaskins. The household linen includes thirty pair of sheets, a dozen tablecloths, damask napkins worth thirty shillings, thirteen silver spoons, a carpet, more painted cloths, and "9 stone pottes covered."

In the parler

[the room where Mrs. Benchkyn's will was signed]

Item one joyned press...xx^s
Item one payre of vyrgynalls..xx^s
Itm ii lyttle cubbards ....x^s
Itm two Callyvaes a Curryss & ii head peeces ....xx^s
Itm one bible & a Testament & a booke of comon prayer ....xiii^s iiii^d
Itm iiii payre of Tonges, ii fire panns & a pothangers...............vi^s viii^d
Itm one payre of Andyrones of Iron..v^s
Itm one rownd Table & ix stooles..x^s
Itm vi old Cushions...xx^d
Itm one Cubbard cloth & a cushen ....iii^s iiii^d
Itm all the paynted clothes, a mapp & a table with the queenes Armes: an old
    curtayne ....iii^s iiii^d
Itm one little casket of bone ....xii^d
Itm ii olde matted chayres...iiii^d
Itm iii dossen of trenchers ....vi^d
Itm one payre of bellowes ....iii^d

The Second Chamber

Itm xii quarters of wooll ....xxiii^s
Itm one long chest & a wadding [?] trowgh.......................................iii^s
Itm one bushell & a basket & ii old boxes..ii^s

The Third Chamber

Itm one chest with sertayne bookes in it ....xxv^s
Itm ii long settles ....iii^s iiii^d
Itm xii quarters of corse wooll...xiii^s iiii^d
Itm iii lyttle Tables..vi^s

Itm iii old chest ....xviii^d

Itm ii old formes & a fann ....xx^d

Itm one stone mortar & a wayght of lead ....xx^d

Itm one old presse & iii baskettes ....xx^d

Itm all the very old clothes in the sayd chamber ....ii^s vi^d

Itm one olde chayre ....vi^d

The Chamber over the parler

Item one joyned Bedstedell..xiii^s iiii^d

Itm one truckle Bedd...xii^d

Itm ii fether beddes iiii bolsters, & iii coverlittes.............................iii^li

Itm two coverlittes of Tapistrye...xxvi^s viii^d

Itm an old coverlyt..ii^s vi^d

Itm iii old carpettes & a vallannse..v^s

Itm iii corstettes & ii allmayne Ryvettes ....l^s

Itm ii old chestes ....v^s

Itm one halbart a pollax & a bedsine [?] byll....................................ii^s

Itm iii Javelyns & a forrest byll...ii^s

Itm vi quarters of corse wool ....vi^s

Itm v baskettes & iii payre stock cardes...iiii^s iiii^d

Itm one close chayre of stringe...xx^d

Itm a payre of scales..xi^d

Itm ii t[illegible] & a plumbe ....xii^d

Itm xxx^li of leden waytes...xx^d

In the woll lofte

Item one hundreth quarters of wool...vii^li x^s

Itm ii old sarplats & a quill ii

In the kichin

This part of the manuscript is badly faded and mostly illegible. However, among the items listed are eleven brass pots great and small, valued at three pounds, two old swords, three iron trivets, a tin bottle and other old bottles, two grates and two old lanterns, mattocks, shovels, augurs and wimbles.

In the house next adjoyninge

Item one great chest..vi^s viii^d

Itm one folding table & a forme...iiii^s

Itm one old cubbard & a little table ....ii^s

Itm old paynted clothes...ii^s

Item in cloth redy made in the house russett & white ....xl^li

Item in his purse in redy monye...xl^li

Item debtes owing at his dissease ....xxxvi[li]
Item owing him in desperate debttes ....xxxv[li]

xvii[li] iiii[s] xi[d]
Summa totallis—Ciiiixx <xi[li] x[s] vi[d]>

WILL OF KATHERINE BENCHKIN, 19 AUGUST 1585, CKS PRC 16/36

The will of Katherine Benchkin is remarkable if only because it preserves the only undisputed sample of Marlowe's handwriting, his signature as a witness. The note "this is Katherine Benchkin's mark" also resembles the hand of Marlowe's signature far more than it resembles the other hands on the will, and we know from later depositions by the other witnesses that Marlowe read the will aloud before Mrs. Benchkin signed it. However, we cannot be certain he added the note.

The will is dated 19 August 1585 and was undoubtedly signed at this time, during one of Marlowe's long absences from Cambridge. John Benchkin made his first appearance at Corpus Christi College that summer, just before Marlowe left, and it seems likely that the two of them returned to Canterbury together. John Benchkin apparently was, or soon became, a close friend of Marlowe's.

It is possible that John Benchkin wrote the will for his mother, since the scribe does not identify himself and sign as a witness, as the scribes did on both of Marlowe's parents' wills. In September 1617, John Benchkin wrote out a will at the request of a neighbor, Sir Thomas Harflete, who was on his deathbed, as John later swore in a deposition (CCA X.11.15, 245b–247b). And if John did write Mrs. Benchkin's will, which named him as chief beneficiary and executor, it was prudent to have several witnesses who could later testify to its legitimacy. Perhaps this is why John Marlowe and Thomas Arthur were asked to join the younger men, John Moore and Christopher Marlowe, as witnesses.

Thomas Greenleaf, who is named overseer of the will, belonged to the same shoemaker's guild as Marlowe's father, so the two undoubtedly knew each other well. Although it is obvious from Mrs. Benchkin's will that John Benchkin's family was far wealthier than the Marlowes, this does not seem to have prevented amicable relations between the two families.

Words in wavy brackets are later additions by the scribe.

In the name of God Amen. The xix[th] day of August in the xxvii[th] year of the raigne of our Sovereigne Lady Elizabeth by the grace of god of England France and Ireland Quene Defender of the feith &c/ I Katherine Benchkyn of the parishe of St Myldred of the citie of Canterbury widowe being in good and perfect remembrance (god be praysed therfore) considering with my self that all peop[l]e are mortall and uncertaine of the hower of their deathe, I do therfore make my last will and Testament in manner and forme following That is to say.

First I commend my sowle to almightie god my maker redemer and comforter most stedfastly trusting to be saved and inherite eternall life only by the deathe and passion of my Lord and savior Jesus Christ, And my will is that after my discease my body be decently buried in the churchyard of the parishe of St Mildredes aforesayd As nere to the grave of my late husband Jeames Benchkyn as may be. Item I will, there be made att my buriall a sermon by some learned preacher, Item I give to the poore peop[l]e of the parishe of St Mildred aforesayd xx^s, to be distributed amongest them within one weeke next after my buryall. Item I give to the poore people of the parishe of St Marie of Northgate of the same cittie, xx^s, to be distributed amongest them within one weeke next after my buryall. Item I will that my executor shall pay to the mayor and cominaltie of the said citie of Canterbury for the time being xx^{li} of good and lawfull monie of England within one {yere} next after my discease. And my will is that the sayd Mayor and cominaltie of the same citie for the time being shall with the said monye within one yere next after the receit thereof buy one Tenement within the sayd citie of Canterbury or within the liberties of the same And that the yearlie proffittes and revenewes of the said Tenement shalbe and remaine to the use of the brothers and sisters of the Hospitall commonly called Maynardes spittle Sett and being within the said parishe of St Myldred forever, And my will is that the said Mayor and cominaltie of the said citie of Canterbury for the time being shall uppon the receipt of the sayd xx^{li} be bounden in writing obligatory to my executor his heires or assignes in dowble the value thereof, either to bestowe the same xx^{li} in manner and forme as is aforesaid and to the use as is aforesaid, or ells to repay the same xx^{li} to my executor or to his assignes To the use of my {said} executor his heires & assignes within one yeare and a quarter next after the said receipt thereof. Item I give and bequethe to Jehan Ansted my mayd servant v^{li} of good and lawfull mony of England, A fetherbed A bolster a blanckett a coverlet iiii^{or} payer of Sheetes ii^o pillowes two fine pillowe coates a spitt a dripping pan a brasse pott of ii^o Gallons or thereaboutes, a cobyron a Stupnett a chafing dishe & a chest To be payd and delivered her within one yere next after my discease, Item I constitute and appoint John Benchkyn the sonne of my late disceased husband Jeames Benchkyn to be the sole executor of this my last will and testament and I desyer my kinsman <Robert> Thomas Greneleafe to be the overseer of the same. Also I will that the ccc^{li} that is now in my cosen Greneleafes handes, to the use of the said John Benchkyn yf he dye before he comme to the age of xxi^{ty} yeares shalbe payd to the mayor and cominaltie of the citie of Canterbury for the time being to the uses and intentes herafter following That is to say I will that the sayd ccc^{li} shall from time to time herafter forever, by the major and cominaltie of the sayd citie of Canterburie or the more part of them for the time being be freely lent to suche persons as shall inhabite & dwell within the sayd citie of Canterbury and liberties of the same, using the trade of clothe making, that is to say in making of wollen clothe And my will is that noe man shall have above l^{li} thereof att one time. But a lesse portion thereof as yt shall seme meete to the sayd mayor and cominaltie of the sayd citie of

Canterbury or the more part of them for the time being during the space of fower yeres without paying anie thing for the use and occupieng thereof, And that every {suche} person which shall receive suche summe of mony or lesse (as to the {sayd} mayor and cominaltie or the more part of them for the tyme being shall seme good as aforesaid) shalbe bound with two sufficient suerties to the mayor and cominaltie of the said citie of Canterbury or the more part of them in dowble the value thereof for the repayment of the same to them, att every suche iiii yeares end, and so from iiii yeares to fower yeares in manner and forme as is aforesaid forever, Item I give and bequethe to Julyan Bonham of Stalesfeld iii^{li} of good and lawfull monie of England to be payd unto her Immediately after my discease, Item I give and bequethe unto the ii^o children of my sayd sister Julian Bonham xl^s apeese to be payd unto them within one yere next after my discease. Item I give and bequeth to the iii children of my sister Johan Wells xl^s a peese to be payd to them within one yeare next after my discease Item I Give and bequethe unto Stephen Glover Josua Glover Richard Glover Nicholas Greneleafe and John Greneleafe the childeren of Margaret Greneleafe my kynswoman now wife of the sayd Thomas Greneleafe xl^s a peese of good and lawfull mony of England to be payd unto them within one yere next after my sayd decease, Provided alweis and my will is that if anie of the said childeren shall chaunce to die before his or their portion shalbe due to be payd, then my meaning is that my said executor shall have his and their portions so dyeing to his owne use for ever, Item I give and bequethe to the sayd Margaret Greneleaf my kinswoman xl^s of good and lawfull monie of England to be payd her within one yeare next after my sayd decease. Item I give and bequethe to Margery Drawnam my kinswoman xl^s of good and lawfull mony of England to be payd her within one yere next after my sayd decease. Item I give to John Benchkyn my late husband Jeames Benchkyns brothers sonne xl^s to be payd unto him imediatlie after my decease, Item I give unto Margaret Fusser my daughter in lawe xl^s to be payd unto her imediatlie after my discease, Item I give unto Haywardes wief my late husband Jeames Benchkins kynswoman xl^s of good and lawfull monie of England, Item I give to the five childeren of John Fusser vi^s viii^d a peese, Item I give to my daughter in lawe John Wevells wief xl^s Item I give to her ii^o childeren vi^s viii^d a peese, Item I give to my sonne in lawe John Hart xl^s, and I give to his sonne George Hart vi^s viii^d, Item I give to Agnes Post widowe my kinswoman xx^s, Item I give to my cosen Harris wife of Pluckley xx^s Item I give to Fordes widowe of the parishe of St Mary of Northgate xx^s to be payd imediatelie after my decease, Item I give to Aunsells widowe of St Mildredes aforesayd xx^s, Item I give to Crowder of the same parishe xx^s Item I give to Joane Ys of the same Parishe xx^s Item I give to Adams widowe xx^s Item I give to Drables widowe xx^s. Item I give to my cosen Agnes Poyser xx^s, Item I give to Agnes Aunsell the daughter of the foresayd widowe Aunsell xx^s, Item I give to Johan Aunsell her sister xx^s. And my will and meaning is that all those above named whene noe time of payment is expressed shalbe payd presentlie after my descease. Item I give to Mr Hills parson of St Mildredes aforesayd xx^s to be payd him within one yere next after my said

decease. Provided that if anie here mencioned in this my will shall fortune to dye
before the payment of the monie above bequethed, Then I will that the legacie of
him her or them so dyeing shalbe and remaine unto the aforenamed John
Benchkyn my executor his heyres and assignes. The resydewe of all my goods
chattells and moveables whatsoever not bequethed my debtes and legaces payd
and all ordenarie charges satisfied I give and bequethe unto the aforenamed
John Benchkyn my sayd executor and his assignes for ever. Provided alweis and
my will and minde is, that if the sayd John Benchkyn shall dye beofre the age of
xxi^{ty} yeres that then the foresayd John Benchkyn my late husband Jeames
Benchkins brothers sonne shall have v^{li} of lawfull monie of England and of the
resydewe of my goodes given as aforesayd to the sayd John Benchkyn my
executor. And also I will that if my executor shall dye, (as aforesayd) Then I will
that Richard Glover my godsonne shall have out of the same resydewe of goodes,
given as aforesayd to the sayd John Benchkyn my executor. A fetherbed and a
dozen of damaske napkins, And the resydewe of that goodes to be sold to the
value thereof And my cosen Thomas Greneleafe (if he shalbe then living) to have
the buying thereof before another. And the monye thereof coming to be payd to
the mayor and cominaltie for the time being of the citie aforesayd by them to be
imployed towardes the maintenance and bringing up of poore childeren within
the same citie. Provided also and my will and intent is, that yf my executor John
Benchkyn dye (as is aforesayd) That then the sayd Thomas Grenelefe shall have
to him and his assignes the ii leases whereof thone is of ii gardens in the parishe
of St Mary of Northgate aforesayd and now in the occupacon of one George
Jeffrey, and the other is of ii howses within the parishe of St Mildred aforesayd./
In witnes whereof I the sayd Katherine Benchkyn to this my present will have
sett my marke and seale in the presence of

Jhan Marley   this is Katherine Benchkins mark
Thomas Arthur   [cross drawn] [Remnants of seal]
Christofer Marley
John Moore

DEPOSITION OF JOHN MOORE CONCERNING KATHERINE
BENCHKIN'S WILL, 30 SEPTEMBER 1586, CKS PRC 39/11, F. 234

*After Katherine Benchkin died in July 1586, her will was contested. When the case
came to court in September 1586, Marlowe had returned to Cambridge to complete
his M.A., but the three witnesses living in Canterbury, John Marlowe, Thomas
Arthur, and John Moore, all testified to the validity of the will. John Moore's
deposition is preceded by a paragraph in Latin identifying him as a shoemaker
who has lived in Canterbury for six years. Before that he lived in Feversham for
seven years, and in Ulcombe, where he was born, for fifteen years. His age is given
as approximately twenty-six.*

super testamentum Benchkin [on the Benchkin Will] examinatus ultime Septembris 1586 [examined 30 September 1586]

... somewhat more then a twelvmonthes agon as this deponent now
remembreth aliter certum diem et tempus non recolit ut dicit [otherwise the
exact day and time he does not recall as he says] hee this deponent together
with Thomas Arthur John Marly and Christofer Marley beeing requested by
John Benchin the testatrix her sonne came all unto the house of the saide
testatrix scituat in St Mildreds parishe in Canterburye which at their coming
they founde the said testatrix in a lower parlor of her saide howse in very good
healthe to this deponentes judgment and ymedyatly the saide testatrix went
upp into a chamber of her saide howse and brought downe her will written in
such forme as is exhibited and alsoe an other will which was made beefore the
will now exhibited and towlde this deponent and the rest that shee had sente
for them to be witnesses unto her will, and to see her owlde will burned
wheruppon she cast her saide owlde will into the fire and burned the same in
the presence of this deponent and the other parties afforenamed and then shee
gave her saide will now exhibited unto Christofer marley to bee redd, which hee
redd plainely and distinctly and being so red the saide testatrix acknowledgd
the same to bee her laste will and testament, revoking and disannulling all other
wills and testamentes by her before made and in witnes of the same she put
thereunto her hande and seale in the presence of this deponent and the partyes
afforesaide, and requested this deponent and the saide partyes to sett to their
handes wheruppon this deponent and the saide partyes subscribed their names
with their owne handes to the said will as witnesses to the same, and this
deponent saith that the saide testatrix was by all the tyme afforesaide not onely
in good remembrawnce but in perfect health to this deponentes judgment and
this deponent very well knoweth that the will whereuppon hee is now examined
beeing viewed and red by him at his examinacion is the self same will soe
acknowledged by the testatrix as is afforesaide as well for that hee seeth his
name subscribed to the saide will with his owne hand as also for that hee
remembreth divers legacies given in the saide will and amongest the rest that
she named and appointed John Benchkin her sonne executor of the same and
one Greenleafe of Cant her overseer and further willed as in the saide will
executed is deduced et aliter nescit deponere [and otherwise he knows nothing
to depose].

DEPOSITION OF JOHN MARLOWE CONCERNING KATHERINE
BENCHKIN'S WILL, 5 OCTOBER 1586, CKS PRC 39/11, F. 237

*John Marlowe's deposition supports that of his son-in-law John Moore regarding
the signing of Mrs. Benchkin's will. However, he recalls that Christopher Marlowe
and John Moore were already at the house when he and Thomas Arthur arrived,*

stopher Marley prays your honors that, having completed nine terms
his final disputation), in which he heard the regular lectures (not all of
as permitted according to the statute), together with all the opponencies,
nsions, and other exercises required by the royal statutes, they may suffice
m to commence in arts.

Robert Norgate
Henry Ruse, tutor]

OWE'S GOVERNMENT SERVICE, 29 JUNE 1587, PRO ACTS OF
PRIVY COUNCIL

*ecord of Privy Council proceedings indicates that Marlowe was reportedly
ing to go to the English seminary at Rheims and remain there. As a result of
umor, Marlowe was threatened with denial of his M.A. degree, so the council
ened on his behalf.*

*fortunately, the record is tantalizingly vague. It states that Marlowe was
oyed . . . in matters touching the benefit of his country," which apparently
ise to the rumors, but it does not indicate their nature. Perhaps Marlowe
lly went to Rheims, or perhaps he had no intention of going there. Since no
l exists indicating Marlowe's presence at the English seminary, it is virtually
n that he never presented himself there as a student. Perhaps he went
where overseas on official business, or perhaps not. Without more
mation, we cannot fully recover the meaning of this document.*

*e individuals listed at the left of the note are those privy councilors who were
at when this action was taken, notably including Lord Treasurer Burghley, the
ancellor of Cambridge. Mr. Secretary Francis Walsingham, who is often
ied to have employed Marlowe in intelligence work, was absent, yet the other
bers of the council were sufficiently familiar with Marlowe's service to the
t that they were prepared to vouch for him. It therefore seems plausible that
the very beginning of his government service, Marlowe did not work
ively for Walsingham.*

*plate of this document in manuscript form can be found in A. D. Wraight, In
h of Christopher Marlowe; A Pictorial Biography, photography by Virginia
rn (New York, 1965), 88.*

unii 1587

Archbishop:	Whereas it was reported that Christopher Morley was
Chancelor:	determined to have gone beyond the seas to Reames and
Treasurer:	there to remaine their Lordships thought good to certefie
Chamberlaine	that he had no such intent, but that in all his acions he
omptroler.	had behaved him selfe orderlie and discreetelie wherebie
	he had done her Majestie good service, and deserved to

*suggesting that the Benchkins had decided it would be prudent to recruit two
additional witnesses. Probably they anticipated that the will would be contested.*

v Octobris 1586

dixit [he says] that abowte a twelmonethes agon or moe as this deponent
remembreth and uppon a Sonday abowte the same daye as this deponent
remembreth aliter certum diem et temporis non recolit ut dixit [otherwise the
exact day and time he does not recall as he says] he this deponent beeing
requested by John Benchkin to come to the house of his mother Catherine
Benchkin scituat in St Mildreds parishe in Canterburye went thether
accompanied with <Joh> Thomas Arthur his prontese and coming thether they
founde there this deponentes Sonne Christofer Marley and John Moore, this
deponents sonne-in-lawe and prontesse, and beeing there altogether the
testatrix Catherine Benchkin towlde them that she had sent for them to bee
witnesses to her will and theruppon she tooke the will whereupon this
deponent is now examined unto Christofer Marly this deponents Sonne &
requested him to reade the same which beeing by him soe read the saide
testatrix acknowledged the same to bee her laste will and testament, and alsoe
caste into the ffire one other owlde will which she had before tyme made and
Burnt the same, and she utterlie disanulled all other wills and testaments by her
beefore made and subscribed her hand and mark and set her seale unto the
saide will whereuppon this deponent is now examined and also requested this
deponent and other the parties afforenamed to subscribe their names to the
same as witnesses unto yt which they did accordinglie. . . .

WILLIAM CLITHEROWE TO RICHARD BAINES, 21 SEPTEMBER 1586,
PRO SP 53/19

*While Richard Baines was studying in the Catholic seminary at Rheims, he would
have known his fellow student William Clitherowe. Clitherowe may well have been
the friend Baines tried to persuade to return to England with him. However,
Clitherowe remained a staunch Catholic who, after his ordination, continued to
live in exile on the Continent.*

*It appears that after Baines returned to England he did indeed, as he had hoped,
find employment supplying intelligence regarding Catholic activities on the
Continent. For that purpose he established a correspondence with Clitherowe using
the pseudonym Gerard Burghet, an alias later assumed by the agent Thomas
Barnes. However, it is evident from the note that Clitherowe knew the identity of his
correspondent, as well as the purpose of the correspondence. His communication
with Baines is guarded, but congenial.*

*The first half of the manuscript is written entirely in cipher, which is
transcribed in a text written between the lines. The transcription is in the hand of
Thomas Phelippes, who oversaw all coded correspondence for Walsingham. The*

remainder is in Latin. For some reason Phelippes failed to transcribe a name that appears in cipher in the Latin portion of the note.

The lieutenant colonel referred to in the last sentence of the ciphered section is presumably Iacomo Francisci or "Captain Jacques," who held that rank in Sir William Stanley's renegade Catholic regiment in the Low Countries. Mr. Owen, whose head was broken, may be Hugh Owen, one of the Welsh faction of exiled Catholics whose specialty was intelligence. The letter gives no clue regarding the matter of the lieutenant colonel, but Clitherowe's glancing reference to it suggests that he had mentioned it in an earlier letter, or that the incident was well known.

As Clitherowe indicates, he is using the new Gregorian calendar, so his date differs from the date assigned to the document in the Calendar of State Papers.

The following transcription omits the ciphers, which cannot be reproduced typographically—except for the one Clitherowe uses for his last name.

Addressed: A Monsieur

Monsieur [*sic*] Gerarde Burghet gentilhome Francois

A Londres

Payez le port

[To Mr. Gerard Burghet, a French gentleman in London. Pay the bearer.]

Endorsed: From Clitherow to Baynes [in Phelippes hand]

You are sayde to practise a mariage for the sonne of the D. of Parma with Arbella and hit is writen so in to Hage & Spain. For to disgrace and plage you, and one of the Counsell of England gave out this mattere of you as hit is sayd. The Brother of Sr Wm Stanley hath broken the heade of Mr. Owen and is in the sanctuary for hit. For the D. taketh hit done in despite for the matter of the Lieutenat Co: Conell

Ego cupio librum ultimae editionis/ petitus ille de quo quaeris, vivit, et valet. Erat abhinc 20s menses semel in periculo praedonum, sed evasit beneficio pedum/

Vestrum nuper per perditionem tradebatur, sed brevi per dei gratiam expugnibatur. Sunt nunc in obsidione eius nostri milites. Alioquin magna fortasse hic caritas victualium. Rem gratium facies si poteris vel per te ipsum vel per omnia significare uxor domini [ciphers] quod soror eius est in manga egestate necessariarum/ bene vale A Leo/ prima Octobris stylo novo

Wm [•]

[I would like a book of the latest edition. The one whom you seek and ask about lives, and thrives. He was away once for two months in danger of thieves, but he escaped by fleetness of foot.

To yours {your army} recently it {a town—reference uncertain; possibly Doesburg, which fell in early September 1586} was surrendered by treachery, but soon by God's grace it will be conquered. Our soldiers are now besieging it. Otherwise, perhaps, the price of victuals will be very high. You will do a kind-

ness if you are able, either yourself or by other means, to

Lord {ciphers} that her sister is in great want of necessiti

Gently farewell from Leo {?} the first of October new

MARLOWE'S SUPPLICATS FOR ADVANCEMENT TO

AND 1587, UNIVERSITY REGISTRY, CAMBRIDGE U

Part of Marlowe's formal request to the Senate to permit hi
B.A. is torn off, but since these petitions followed a set form
can be supplied. I have enclosed them in square brackets.

The "question" referred to in the supplicat is a ritual per
in which an official called "the Father" posed a question th
were required to answer. The exchange was ceremonial rat
of knowledge. Having completed this ceremony, the student
in the Lenten disputations—the final requirement for the a

Coll.   Supplicat reverentiis vestris Christopherus Ma
Corp.   termini completi, in quibus ordinarias lection
Christi.   omnino] secundum formam statuti) una cum
          ibus, r[esponsionibus,] caeterisque exercitiis, p
          sitis, sufficiant ei [ad respon]dendem quaestio
                                        Thomas

[Christopher Marlowe prays your honors that, having co
in which he heard the regular lectures (not all of them, as
the statute), together with all the opponencies, responsion
required by the royal statutes, they may suffice for him to
question.

                                        Th

Marlowe's supplicat for the M.A. follows a similar formula,
to the "question" and making other changes appropriate to
degree. This time the Master of Corpus Christi College, Rob
petition.

Coll.   Supplicat reverentiis vestris Christophorus Marl
Corp.   completi Corp. (post finalem eius determination
Chri.   tiones ordinarias audivit (licet non omnino secu
          statuti) una cum omnibus oppositionibus respor
          exercitiis per statuta regia requisitis sufficiant ei a
          artibus.

                                        Robertus N
                                        Henri

be rewarded for his faithfull dealinge: Their Lordships request was that the rumor thereof should be allaied by all possible meanes, and that he should be furthered in the degree he was to take this next commencement: Because it was not her Majesties pleasure that anie one emploied as he had been in matters touching the benefitt of his countrie should be defamed by those that are ignorant in th'affaires he went about/

MARLOWE AND THOMAS WATSON COMMITTED TO NEWGATE PRISON, 18 SEPTEMBER 1589, GLRO MJ/SR 284, NO. 12 NEWGATE CALENDAR

This document records the confinement of Watson and Marlowe in Newgate on suspicion of murder in the death of William Bradley. Apart from providing the correct date of the fight in Hog Lane (which is confirmed by the record of Bradley's burial), it also indicates where Watson and Marlowe lived at the time of the incident and reveals that Watson was recognized by Sir Owen Hopton as a gentleman, whereas Marlowe was not. Perhaps Watson was already known to Hopton, or perhaps he simply dressed and behaved more like a gentleman than Marlowe.

The fact that the name of the deceased is left blank is worth noting, since Watson and Bradley certainly knew each other. As Mark Eccles reveals in Christopher Marlowe in London *(Cambridge, Mass., 1934), 57–59, Bradley had bound Watson, Hugo Swift, and John Allen to keep the peace toward him not long before his fatal encounter with Watson in Hog Lane. Since Watson was pleading self-defense, perhaps he deemed it wise not to mention his previous differences with Bradley.*

Beside Watson's name is the notation "balliatus" (bailed); Marlowe's bears the notation "deliberatus per proclamationem" (released by proclamation). Latin abbreviations are silently expanded.

Thomas Watson nuper de Norton Fowlgate in Comitatu Middlesex generosus & xpoferus Marlowe nuper de eadem yoman

qui ducti fuerunt Gaole xviii° die Septembris per Stephanum Wyld Constabularium ibidem pro Suspicione Murdri viz pro morte [blank] et commissi fuerunt per Owinum Hopton Militem

[Thomas Watson late of Norton Folgate in the County of Middlesex gentleman and Christopher Marlowe late of the same, yeoman.]

who were led to jail the 18th day of September by Stephen Wild Constable of the same on suspicion of murder namely in the death of [blank] and were committed by Owen Hopton, Knight.]

*After the coroner's finding on 19 September 1589 that Thomas Watson had killed
William Bradley in self-defense, Marlowe, who had been imprisoned with Watson
in Newgate as a possible accessory, became eligible for bail. This document reveals
that Marlowe raised the needed sum with the help of two sureties. He was then
released pending trial, and on his appearance at the trial on 3 December was
cleared of any wrongdoing. Latin abbreviations are silently expanded.*

Marginal note: venit & deliberatur per proclamacionem [He appeared and was
released by proclamation.]

The first abbreviated word was previously read as revertitur *(he returned), but
similar documents in the sessions rolls indicate that the word used was* venire.

Middlesex sessionis [?] Memorandum quod primo die octobris Anno regni
domine nostre Elizabethe Regine nunc Etc. Tricesimo primo Richardus Kyt-
chine de Clyffordes Inne generosus et Humfridus Rowland de East Smythfeilde
in Comitatu predicto horner venerunt coram me Williamo Fletewoode Servi-
enti ad Legem et Recordatore Civitatis London uno Justiciarium domine nostre
Regine in Comitatu predicto assignatorum Etc et manuceperunt pro xpoforo
Marley de London generoso: vizt uterque manucaptorum predictorum sub
pena viginti librarum et ipse predictus xpoforus Marley assumpsit pro seipso
sub pena quadriginta librarum de bonis Catallis terris et tenementis suis et
eorum cuiuslibet ad opus et usum dicte Domine Regine levandarum sub Condicione quod si ipse predictus xpoforus personalliter comparebit ad proximam
Sessionem de Newgate ad respondendum ad omnia ea que ex parte dicte
Domine Regine versus eum objecientur et non discedet absque Licencia Curie
Quod tunc Etc. Aut alioquin Etc.

[Middlesex session memorandum that on the first of October in the thirty first
year of the reign of our lady Queen Elizabeth now Etc. Richard Kytchin of Clifford's
Inn, gentleman, and Humphrey Rowland of East Smithfield in the aforesaid
county, horner, came before me, William Fleetwood, Serjeant at Law and Recorder
of the City of London, one of the justices appointed by our lady the Queen in the
county aforesaid, etc., and put up bail for Christopher Marley of London, gentleman: that is to say, each of the sureties aforesaid under penalty of twenty pounds,
and the same aforesaid Christopher Marley undertook for himself, under penalty
of forty pounds to be levied of his goods and chattel lands and tenements by the
said Lady the Queen for her business and use, on condition that the same aforesaid
Christopher personally appear at the next Newgate Session to answer to all things
that may be objected against him on the part of the said Lady the Queen, and not
depart without the permission of the court Because then etc. Or otherwise etc.]

*The text of the coroner's inquest on the death of Bradley has been preserved in
several documents: the inquest itself, the gaol delivery roll, Watson's pardon, and a
copy in Originalia. All of these records are cited by Eccles (Christopher Marlowe
in London, 8–9) except the inquest, which seems to have been located later by
Bakeless. All of them also erroneously record the dates of Bradley's death and of the
inquest as the twenty-eighth and twenty-ninth of September, rather than the
eighteenth and nineteenth. Eccles confirmed the earlier dates by finding the record
of Bradley's burial on the nineteenth.*

*The text below, translated completely for the first time, is excerpted from
Watson's pardon. Latin abbreviations are silently expanded.*

perdona se defendendo pro Tho. Watson

Inquisicionis indentate capte apud Fynesburye in Comitatu middlesex vicesimo
nono die Septembris Anno regni nostri tricesimo primo coram Iuone
Chalkehill Generoso uno Coronatorum dicti Comitatus middlesex super visum
corporis Willelmi Bradley ibidem iacentis mortui & interfecti Quod ubi
prefatus Willelmus Bradley & quidam Cristoferus morley nuper de london
Generosus vicesimo octavo die Septembris Anno regni nostri tricesimo primo
supradicto fuerunt insimul pugnantes in quadam venella vocata hoggelane in
parochia sancti Egidii extra Crepulgate in predicto Comitatu middlesex inter
horas secundam & terciam post meridiem eiusdem diei ibi intervenit eisdem
die & Anno & infra horas predictas quidam Thomas Watson nuper de london
Generosus super clamorem populi ibidem adstantis ad separandum prefatos
Willelmum Bradley & Cristoferum morley sic pugnantes ad pacem nostram
conservandam Et gladium suum eam ob causam tunc & ibidem extraxit Super
quo prefatus Willelmus [*sic*—a slip for Christopher] morley seipsum retraxit &
a pugnando desistit Et super hoc predictus Willelmus Bradley videns eundem
Thomam Watson sic intervenientem ibidem cum gladio suo extracto dixit ei in
hiis anglicanis verbis sequentibus videlicet Art thowe nowe come Then I will
have a boute with the Et instanter idem willelmus Bradley in prefatum
Thomam Watsun tunc & ibidem insultum fecit & cum uno gladio & uno
pugione de ferro & Calibe predictum Thomam Watson tunc & ibidem
verberavit vulneravit & male tractavit Ita quod de vita eius desperabatur
racione cuius prefatus Thomas Watson cum gladio suo predicto de ferro &
chalibe precii trium solidorum quatour denariorum quem in manu sua dextra
tunc & ibidem habuit & tenuit seipsum contra predictum Willelmum Bradley
tunc & ibidem defendidit & a predicto Willelmo Bradley pro salvacione vite sue
usque ad quoddam fossatum in venella predicta fugiit ultra quodquidem
fossatum idem Thomas Watson absque periculo vite sue fugere not potuit. Et
predictus Willelmus Bradley insultum suum predictum continuando prefatum

Thomam Watson tunc & ibidem recenter insecutus fuit Super quo predictus
Thomas Watson pro salvacione vite sue predictum Willelmum Bradley cum
gladio suo predicto tunc & ibidem percussit dans ei unam plagam mortalem
sive vulnus in & super dextram partem pectoris ipsius Willelmi Bradley prope
mamillam profunditatis sex pollicum & latitudinis unius pollicis de qua
quidem plaga mortali idem Willelmus Bradley apud Fynesburie predictam in
predicto Comitatu middlesex instanter obiit. . . .

[Pardon of Thomas Watson for self-defense

Inquisition in duplicate taken at Finsbury in Middlesex County, the twenty-
ninth day of September in the thirty-first year of our queen before Ion
Chalkehill, gentleman, a coroner of the said Middlesex County, upon view of
the body of William Bradley, there lying dead and slain. Because in that place
the aforesaid William Bradley and a certain Christopher Morley, late of
London, gentleman, on the twenty-eighth day of September in the thirty-first
year of our queen above mentioned were fighting one another in a certain lane
called Hog Lane in the parish of St. Giles Cripplegate in the aforesaid Middlesex
County between the second and third hour of the afternoon of the same day, a
certain Thomas Watson, late of London, gentleman, arrived on the scene, in the
same day and year and between the hours aforesaid, upon the noise of the
crowd standing there, in order to separate the aforesaid William Bradley and
Christopher Morley who were thus fighting, to preserve our peace. And for this
reason he then and there drew his sword. Whereupon the aforementioned
Christopher Morley withdrew and stopped fighting. And whereupon the
aforesaid William Bradley, seeing the same Thomas Watson intervening with
his sword drawn spoke to him in these English words, as follows, "Art thou now
come? Then I will have a bout with thee." And immediately the same William
Bradley then and there assaulted the aforementioned Thomas Watson, and,
with sword and dagger of iron and steel, then and there beat, wounded, and
maltreated the same Thomas Watson. So that, despairing of his life, the
aforementioned Thomas Watson then and there defended himself against the
aforesaid William Bradley with his aforesaid sword of iron and steel of the value
of three shillings, four pence, which he then and there had and held in his right
hand, and for the saving of his life he fled from the aforesaid William Bradley
all the way to a certain ditch in the aforesaid lane to the point where, on peril of
his life, he could flee no further. And the aforesaid William Bradley continuing
his attack, the aforementioned Thomas Watson was then and there newly cut.
Therefore the aforesaid Thomas Watson, for the saving of his life, then and
there struck the aforesaid William Bradley with his aforesaid sword a mortal
blow or wound in and on the right side of the chest near the nipple of the same
William Bradley, of the depth of six inches and of the width of one inch, of
which same mortal stroke the same William Bradley, at Finsbury aforesaid in
the aforesaid Middlesex County, instantly died.]

*This document certainly concerns the Richard Baines who took his B.A. from
Christ's College and his M.A. from Caius College, Cambridge, in 1576. Presumably
he is the same Richard Baines who went over to the English seminary when it
relocated at Rheims in 1578—either as a sincere Catholic or as a government agent.
His movement from Christ's to Caius for his M.A. would suggest that he had
genuine Catholic leanings. One of Baines's fellow students at Rheims was John
Ballard, who had migrated to Caius College a few years before Baines. Ballard was
ordained at Rheims, and later was implicated in the Babington conspiracy and
executed. Baines was also ordained at Rheims, but he returned to England in 1583
after being imprisoned as a suspected spy and induced to confess. He seems to have
worked for Walsingham or the Privy Council as a newsgatherer before seeking
William Ballard's help in securing a benefice in 1587. This Richard Baines probably
knew the plaintiff William Ballard because both were natives of Southwell,
Nottinghamshire. A Thomas Baines of Southwell, son of John Baines, yeoman,
followed Richard Baines to Cambridge, matriculating at Caius on 1 April 1577. It
seems likely he was Richard's younger kinsman.*

*While we cannot be certain that this is the same Richard Baines who informed
twice on Marlowe, the dates and other facts of his life available at the time of this
writing are consistent with this conclusion. But whether he was or not, what we
have learned about him adds to our understanding of Marlowe's government
service.*

To the Right honorable Sir Christopher Hatton of the most honorable order of
the Garter Knight Lord Chancellor of Englande.

Humbly complayninge sheweth unto your good Lordshipp your daylye orator William Ballard of Southwell in the Com[itatu—i.e. county] of Nottingham
gentleman that whereas one Rychard Banes clarke beinge of acquaintance with
your saied orator & destitute of anie staye of lievinge, did about twoe yeares & a
halffe past earnestly entreate your said orator to be some meanes for him that he
mighte be preferred as a personne to some benefyce in some convenyente place,
faithfully promisinge him your said orator in so doynge that he the said Rychard
Banes would not only paye unto him your sayd orator such sommes of monye as
he should disbursse in that behalffe to the uttermoste but would allso be thanke-
full to him your sayde orator, for his your said orators paynes takynge in that behalffe whereuppon he your saied orator havinge a good opynion in the said
Richard & thinkynge he mighte geve creditt to his word, did att this your saied
oratours own costes and charges travell on the behalffe of the sayd Rychard & in
thend by and througe his your said orators great travell diligent Inquisition &
charges to the valewe of twentye poundes & above, did procure for him the sayd
Rychard the benefyce of the parishe churche of Waltham within the com[itatu]
of Lyncolne whereuppon by and att his your saied orators meanes procurment
& charges as aforesaid he the sayd Richard about twoe yeares laste paste was in

dewe form of lawe presented as parsone to the sayd churche. And to the same in lycke due formes of lawe _____tted [manuscript damaged], _____ituted, & Inducted and att this present dothe and ever sithence hathe Injoyed the sume as parsonne the yearly revenewes thereof to hym comming beinge to the valewe of threscore pound and above./ But nowe so yt is yf yt may please your good Lordship that the sayd Rychard Banes nothinge att all regardynge his faythfull promisse made to your sayd orator (as aforesayd) now the great benefitt to hym receyved by the meanes of your sayd orator as afforesayd dothe denye to paye to your sayd orator the sayd Some of twenty poundes as afforesaid disburssed & laied out for his great benefitt by your sayd orator havinge bene sundrye tymes requested to pay the same./ Albeit he certenlye knoweth your saied Orator hathe disbursed the same without fraud./ And for that also the saied promisse was made in secrett betwene him & your saied Orator & the sayd Richard wythout anye wyttnesse & therefore hath your sayd orator no remedy att the common lawe unlesse the sayd Rychard will confesse the same uppon his othe which by all lycklyhood he will doe in discharge of his consyence./ May it therefore please your good Lordshipp the promisse consydered to graunt unto your sayd orator the Queenes Majesties most gracious writt of Subpoena to be directed to the saied Rychard Baynes comanndinge him _____ att a certen daie & under a certene payne therein to hym to be lymitted & appoynted to be and personallye to appeare before your good Lordshipp in her Majesties hyeghe court of Chauncerye, then and their to answere to his promisse and to receive suche order as to your good Lordhshipp shall seme to stand with equytye and good conscience & your sayd orator as his bounded dutye ys shall dayly praye for your good Lordshippe longe in health to contynewe.

PARDON OF THOMAS WALSINGHAM FOR OUTLAWRY, 27 MAY 1590, PRO C66/356, M. 35

p[er]d[o]n[a]	Regina Omnibus Balliuis & fidelibus suis ad quos &c salutem
utlagar[ia]	Cum Thomas Lounde nuper in Curia nostra coram Justiciariis
[pro] Thomas	nostris de Banco per breve nostram implacitasset Thomam
[W]alsingham	Walsingham nuper de London Generosum alias dictum
	Thomam Walsingham de Chislehurste in Comitatu Kancia
	generosum unus filiorum nuper Thome Walsinham nuper de
	Chiselhurste praedicto militis defuncti de debito ducentarum
	marcarum quod idem Thomas Lounde a praefato Thoma
	Walsingham exigit Ac idem Thomas Walshingham pro eo
	quod non venit coram praefato Justicariis nostris praefato
	Thome Lounde secundum legem & consuetudinem regni
	nostri Anglie inde responsurus in exigendo positus fuissit in
	hustengo nostro London ad utlagandum & ea occasione
	postmodum utlagatus sicut per tenorem recordi & processus

utlagariae praedicte quem coram nobis in Cancellaria nostra
venire fecimus plene liquet Iamque idem Thomas Walsingham
se reddiderit Prisone nostre de Flete occasione praedicta & in
eadem moretus sicut dilectus & fidelis noster Edmundus
Anderson milites Capitalis Justicarius noster de Banco
praedicto nos in Cancellaria nostra praedicta ad mandatum
nostrum certificavit. Nos pietate moti perdonavimus eidem
Thomas Walsingham utlageriam praedictam & firmam pacem
nostram ei inde concedimus Ita tamen quod stet rectum in
Curia nostra si praedictus Thomas Lounde versus eum loqui
voluerit de debito supradicto. In Cuius rei &c Teste Regina
apud westminster xxvii die Maii./

[Pardon of outlawry for Thomas Walsingham

Whereas Thomas Lund recently in our court of the Queen's Bench before our
Justices, by our writ pled against Thomas Walsingham, late of London,
gentleman, alias Thomas Walsingham of Chiselhurst in the County of Kent,
gentlemen, one of the sons of the late Thomas Walsingham, knight, late of the
said Chislehurst, deceased, concerning a debt of two hundred marks, which the
same Thomas Lund had demanded of the said Thomas Walsingham. And
because the same Thomas Walsingham did not come before the said Justices,
the said Thomas Lund, according to the law and custom of our English queen,
therefore filed a writ of exigent of outlawry in our court of Hustings in London,
and when, for this reason, the outlawry described and the said action of
outlawry shortly came before us in our court of Chancery, we found it evident.
Therefore the same Thomas Walsingham was delivered to our Fleet Prison for
the said reason and in the same remained, as our beloved and faithful Edmund
Anderson, knight, Chief Justice of our said Queen's Bench, certified in our said
Chancery according to our mandate. Moved by pity, we have pardoned the
same Thomas Walsingham for the said outlawry and grant our firm peace to
him henceforward. Provided nevertheless that the jurisdiction remain in our
court if the said Thomas Lund should wish to complain of him concerning the
above-mentioned debt.
Witness the Queen at Westminster the 27th day of May.]

MARLOWE IN FLUSHING, 26 JANUARY 1591/92, PRO SP 84/44

*A letter from Sir Robert Sidney, the governor of Flushing, to Lord Treasurer
Burghley. Although his older brother Philip criticized Robert's poor penmanship,
his clear, flowing hand is less ornate and more modern in appearance than
secretary hand. Sidney wrote on the front and part of the back of an unusually thin
sheet of paper. Consequently the ink bled through, making parts of the letter less*

legible. Sidney signed in a bold signature script, quite distinct from the script he used in the rest of the letter.

Right Honorable
Besides the prisoner Evan Flud, I have also given in charge to this bearer my anciant twoe other prisoners, the one named Christofer Marly by his profession a scholer and the other Gifford Gilbert a goldsmith taken heer for coining, and their mony I have sent over unto yowr Lo:[rdship] The matter was revealed unto me the day after it was done, by one Ri: Baines whome also my Anciant shal bring unto yowr Lo:[rdship] He was theyr chamber fellow, and fearing the succes made me acquainted with all. The men being examined apart never denied anything, onely protesting that what was done was onely to se the goldsmith's conning: and truly I ame of opinion that the poore man was onely browght in under that couler, what ever intent the other twoe had at that time. And indeed they do one accuse another to have been the inducers of him, and to have intended to practis yt heerafter: and have as it were justified him unto me. But howsoever it hapned a dutch shilling was uttred and els not any peece: and indeed I do not thinck that they would have uttred many of them: for the mettal is plain peuter and with half an ey to be discovered. Notwithstanding I thowght it fitt to send the[m] over unto yowr Lo:[rdship] to take theyr trial as yow shal thinck best. For I wil not stretch my commission to deale in such matters, and much less to put them at liberty and to deliver them into the towns hands being the Queens subjects and not required neyther of this sayd town I know not how it would have bin liked, especially since part of that which they did counterfet was Her Ma:[jesties] coine. The goldsmith is an eccellent worckman and if I should speake my conscience had no intent heerunto. The scholer sais himself to be very wel known both to the Earle of Northumberland and my Lord Strang. Bains and he do also accuse one another of intent to goe to the Ennemy or to Rome, both as they say of malice one to another. Hereof I thowght fitt to advertis yowr Lo:[rdship] leaving the rest to their own confession and my Anciants report. And so do humbly take my leave at Flushing the 26 of January 1591

> Yowr honors very obedient
> to do yow service
> R. Sydney

MARLOWE'S BOND, 9 MAY 1592, GLRO MIDDLESEX SESSIONS ROLL 309, NO. 13

Evidently Marlowe was brought before the Middlesex justice of the peace on 9 May 1592, and was bound to appear at the next general session of the court, or else pay a penalty of £20. The next session would have begun in the second week of October, but there is no indication that Marlowe appeared. His absence is probably explained by the fact that in late September and early October of 1592, he was defending himself in a civil suit in Canterbury. Such failures to appear in court were far from unusual, because it was easy to flee county jurisdictions, but Marlowe's absence seems to have been involuntary. Standard legal abbreviations have been silently expanded.

Endorsed: Chr[ist]ofer Marle his Recognizance

Middlesex sessionis [?] memorandum quod ix^{no} die Maii 1592 Annoque Regni domine nostre Elizabethe Nunc &c xxxiiii^{to} Venit coram me Owino Hopton Milite uno Justiciariorum dicte domine Regine ad pacem in comitatu predicto conservandam assignatorum Christopherus Marle de London generosus et recognovit se debere dicte domine Regine xx^{li} bone et legalis monete Anglie: Sub condicione quod personaliter comparebit ad proximam generalem Sessionem pacis in et pro comitatu predicto tenendam: et interim geret pacem versus cunctum populam dicte domine Regine et praecipue versus Allenum Nicholls Constabularium de Hollowellstreet in comitatu predicto et Nicholaum Helliott subconstabularium de eadem:/ Quam summam predictam concessit de bonis et Cattallis terris atque tenementis suis ad usum dicte domine Regine per formam Recognicionis levari Si defecerit in praemissis &c.

[Middlesex Sessions memorandum: that on the 9th day of May, 1592, in the 34th year of our lady queen Elizabeth, now etc., there came before me, Owen Hopton, Knight, one of the Justices of the Peace appointed by the said lady the queen in the aforesaid county, Christopher Marlowe of London, gentlemen, and acknowledged himself bound to the said lady the Queen in the amount of 20 pounds of good and lawful English money: on the condition that he personally appear at the next general session of the peace held in and for the aforesaid county: and in the meantime that he keep the peace toward all subjects of the said lady the Queen and especially toward Allen Nicholls, Constable of Holywell Street in the aforesaid county, and Nicholas Helliot, subconstable of the same:/ Which aforesaid sum conceded to be levied from his goods and chattel lands and tenements for use by the said lady the Queen according to his recognizance if he should fail to keep his promise, etc.]

CORKINE'S CHARGES AGAINST MARLOWE, SEPTEMBER 1592, CCA BAC J/B/391, I, F. 13V

This entry in the Plea Roll of the Canterbury Civil Court, initiated on 26 September 1592, records the filing of charges against Marlowe by Corkine, the

amount of bail and who paid it, the dates on which Marlowe was scheduled to answer the charges (apparently he asked for a brief postponement), and the outcome of the case.

Manucapcio iiii d.	Willelmus Corkyn (ponit loco Egidium Winston) queritur versus Christopherum Marlowe (ponit loco Johannem Smith) in placito transgressionis plegii de presequendo Johhanes Doo Et Richarum Roo/defendens captus est et manucaptus per Johannem Marlowe iiii^d iiii^d secundo Octobris querens narravit defendens habet licenciam loquendi/quinto Octobris defendens habet licenciam loquendi/ix° Octobris non pros'/ex assensu /
[Bail 4^d	William Corkyn (represented by Giles Winston) sues Christopher Marlowe (represented by John Smith) on a plea of transgression and pledges to prosecute viz. John Doo and Richard Roo. The defendant was arrested and bailed by John Marlowe 4d 4d the second of October the suit narrated the defendant has license to speak/the fifth of October the defendant has license to speak/9 October not prosecuted/by agreement/]

CORKINE'S COMPLAINT AND MARLOWE'S COUNTERCHARGES, SEPTEMBER 1592, CCA BAC J/B/S/391

Corkine's attorney submitted the following narrative of his plaint on 25 September 1592 in the Canterbury Civil Court.

Civitas Cantuar'
Willelmus Corkyn queritur de Christophero Marlowe generoso in placito transgressionis Et sunt plegii de prosequendo scilicet Johannes Doo et Ricardus Roo Et unde idem querens per Egidium Wynston attornatum suum queritur quod predictus defendens quinto decimo die Septembris anno regni domine nostre Elizabeth Dei gracia Anglie Francie et Hibernie regine fidei defendoris etc. tricesimo quarto hic apud civitatem Cantuar' predictam in parochia sancti Andree et in warda de Westgate eiusdem civitatis vi et armis videlicet baculis et pugionibus in ipsum querentem insultum fecit et ipsum querentem adtunc et ibidem verberavit vulnerabit et maletractavit Et alia enormia dicto querenti adtunc et ibidem intulit ad grave dampnum ipsius querentis et contra pacem dicte domine regine nunc unde idem querens dicit quod deterioratus est et dampnum habet ad valenciam quinque librarum et inde producit sectam.

[City of Canterbury
William Corkine sues Christopher Marlowe, gentlemen, on a plea of transgression. And pledges to prosecute viz. John Doo and Richard Roo. And hence the same plaintiff, by Giles Winston his attorney, makes plaint that the foresaid defendant on the fifteenth day of September in the thirty-fourth year of our lady Queen Elizabeth, by the grace of God Queen of England, France, and Ireland, Defender of the Faith, etc., in the city of Canterbury aforesaid, in the parish of Saint Andrew and in the ward of Westgate of this same city, by force of arms, that is to say with staff and dagger, assaulted this same plaintiff and then and there struck, wounded, and maltreated this same plaintiff. And then and there inflicted other outrages on the said plaintiff to the grave damage of the same plaintiff and against the peace of the said lady the queen, wherefore the same plaintiff says that he has suffered loss and incurred damages to the value of five pounds and hence brings this suit.]

The following Grand Jury indictment was sought by Marlowe at the Canterbury Quarter Sessions held 26 September 1592. The jury threw out the indictment.

Endorsed: Ignoramus ["We disregard." Three diagonal slashes further invalidate it.]

Civitatis Cantuar'
Jur' present' pro domina regina quod Willelmus Corkyn de civitate Cant' predicta tayler decimo die septembris anno regni domine Elizabethe dei gracia Anglie Francie et Hibernie regine fidei defensoris etc. tricesimo quarto hic apud civitatem Cant' predictam in parochia sancti Andree et in warda de Westgate eiusdem civitatis in quendam Christopherum Marlowe generosum insultum fecit ac ipsum Christopherum Marlowe adtunc et ibidem verberavit *et* vulneravit et male tractavit et alia enormia dicto Christophero Marlowe adtunc et ibidem intulit ad grave dampnum ipsius Christopheri et contra pacem dicte domine regine nunc etc.

[City of Canterbury
The Grand Jury present for our lady the queen that William Corkine of the city of Canterbury aforesaid tailor on the tenth [evidently an error for quinto decimo—fifteenth] day of September in the thirty-fourth year of our lady Queen Elizabeth, by the grace of God Queen of England, France, and Ireland, defender of the faith, etc., in this same city of Canterbury aforesaid, in the parish of Saint Andrew and in the ward of Westgate of this same city, assaulted a certain Christopher Marlowe, gentleman, and then and there struck, wounded, and maltreated the same Christopher Marlowe and then and there inflicted other

outrages on the said Christopher Marlowe, to the grave damage of the same Christopher and against the peace of the said lady the queen, etc.]

AGENT'S REPORT ON RICHARD CHOLMELEY, DATE UNKNOWN, PROBABLY MARCH 1593, PRECEDING A WARRANT FOR CHOLMELEY'S ARREST ON 19 MARCH 1593, BL HARLEIAN MSS 6848, F. 190, R. AND V.

The manuscript is a fair copy of an unknown agent's report. It is in the same hand as Harleian MS 6848, fol. 191, a fair copy of a letter concerning Cholmeley. Both this document and the letter presumably represent the work of the same informant.

The document is endorsed in a different hand. The "Yong" mentioned in the endorsement is no doubt the Henry Young referred to in the manuscript, "borage" is Jasper Borage, also identified in the manuscript as one of Cholmeley's followers, while "hariet" presumably refers to the mathematician and scientist Thomas Harriot, an associate of the Earl of Northumberland and Sir Walter Raleigh and an acquaintance of Marlowe. However, there is no evidence that Harriot was arrested or questioned as a result of this report. The Tipping brothers, James and John, were implicated in Catholic plots and counterplots. James, like Robert Poley, was involved in the Babington plot.

Endorsed: The atheisme of Cholmeley & others
    yong taken & made an instrument to take the rest
    hariet./
    borage dangerous
    tippinges ii.
        Remembrannces of wordes & matter againste Ric Cholmeley

That hee speaketh in generall all evill of the Counsell; sayenge that they are all Atheistes & Machiavillians, especially my Lord Admirall/
That hee made certen libellious verses in commendacon of papistes & seminary priestes very greately inveighenge against the State, amonge which lynes this was one, Nor may the Prince deny the Papall crowne/
That hee had a certen booke (as hee saieth) delivered him by Sir Robert Cecill of whom he geveth very scandalous reportes. That he should incite him to consider thereof & to frame verses & libells in the commendacon of constant Priestes & vertuous Recusantes, this booke is in custodie & is called an Epistle of Comforte & is printed at Paris
That he rails at Mr. Topcliffe & hath written another libell jointlye against Sir Francis Drake & Justice Younge whom hee saith hee will couple up together because hee hateth them alike
That when the muteny happened after the Portingale voyage in the Strand hee

said that hee repented him of nothinge more then that hee had not killed my
Lord Threasorer with his owne handes sayenge that hee could not have done
god better service, this was spoken in the hearinge of Francis Clarke & many
other Souldiours

That he saieth hee doeth entierly hate the Lord Chamberleyn & hath good
cause so to doe/

That he saieth & verely beleveth that one Marlowe is able to shewe more sounde
reasons for Atheisme then any devine in Englande is able to geve to prove
devinitie & that Marloe tolde him that hee hath read the Atheist lecture to
Sir Walter Raliegh & others.

That he saieth that hee hath certen men corrupted by his persuasions who
wilbee ready at all tymes & for all causes to sweare whatsoever seemeth good
to him. Amonge whom is one Henry Younge & Jasper Borage & others.

That he so highly esteemeth his owne witt & judgement that hee saieth that
noman are sooner deceyved & abused then the Counsell themselves. & that
hee can goe beyonde & cossen them as he liste & that if hee make any com-
plainte in behalfe of the Queene hee shall not onely bee privately heard &
enterteyned, but hee will so urge the counsell for money that without he
have what he liste hee will doe nothinge/

That beinge imployed by some of her Majesties prevy Counsaile for the appre-
henson of Papistes & other daungerous men hee used as he saieth to take
money of them & would lett them passe in spighte of the Counsell/

That hee saieth that William Parry was hanged drawen & quartered but in jeste,
that he was a grosse asse overreached by conninge, & that in trueth hee never
meante to kill the Queene more then himselfe had/

A SECOND REPORT ON CHOLMELEY, MARCH 1593, BL HARLEIAN
MSS 6848, F. 191

Righte worshipfull whereas I promised to sende you worde when Cholmeley
was with mee; these are to lett you understande that hee hath not yet bene with
mee for hee doeth partely suspecte that I willl bewray his villanye & his compa-
nye. But yesterday hee sente two of his companions to mee to knowe if I woulde
joyne with him in familiaritie & bee one of their dampnable crue. I sothed the
villaynes with faire wordes in their follies because I would thereby dive into the
secretes of their develishe hartes that I mighte the better bewray their purposes
to drawe her Majesties subjectes to bee Athiests, their practise is after her
Majesties decease to make a kinge amonge them selves & live accordinge to
their owne lawes, & this saieth Cholmeley wilbee done easely, because they bee
& shortely willbe by his & his felowes persuasions as many of their opynion as
of any other religion Mr Cholmeley his manner of proceedinge in seducinge
the Queenes subjectes is firste to make slannderous reportes of most noble

peeres & honorable Counsailors, as the Lord Threasorer the Lord Chamberleyn
the Lord Admirall, Sir Robert Cecill. Those saieth hee have profounde wittes,
bee sounde Athiestes & their lives & deedes showe that they thinke their soules
doe ende vanishe & perishe with their bodies

his second course is to make a jeste of the Scripture with these fearefull horrible
& damnable speeches, that Jhesus Christe was a bastarde St Mary a whore & the
Anngell Gabriell a Bawde to the holy ghoste & that Christe was justly perse-
cuted by the Jewes for his owne foolishnes. That Moyses was a Jugler & Aaron a
Cosoner the one for his miracles to Pharao to prove there was a god, & the
other for taking the Eareringes of the children of Israell to make a golden calfe
with many other blasphemous speeches of the devine essence of god which I
feare to rehearse This Cursed Cholmeley hath Lx of his company & hee is sel-
dome from his felowes & therefore I beeseech your worship have a speciall care
of your selfe in apprehendinge him for they bee resolute murderinge myndes

Your worshippes

SIDNEY TO BURGHLEY CONCERNING WALTER MARSH, 22 MARCH
1592/93, PRO SP 84/44, F. 145

*Another letter of Robert Sidney to Burghley, which indicates that it was not
unusual for English students at Rheims to have second thoughts, as Richard Baines
may well have done. In these cases, turning informer was the safest and surest
means of effecting repatriation. The letter also reveals Flushing's importance as a
center of intelligence activity on the continent. Sidney's comments about the
duration of Marsh's stay in Flushing are probably meant as assurances of Marsh's
good faith. The last sentence seems to be inspired by the serious illness Burghley
suffered in the early months of 1593.*

Right Honorable.
This bearer Walter Marsh having bin a certen time in the seminary at Reims (as
he tels me) and finding at the last his error came hether from Cales voluntarily
to yeald himself unto me and tels me that he wil discover matters which do
greatly concearn her Ma:[jesty] and the State of England: Hath therefore desired me to direct him unto yowr Lo:[rdship] which I would not fayle to do,
withall signifying unto yow that his abode hath not bin longer heer then he
hath bin forced to stay for wind. And this being to no other effect. I humbly
end yt praying God to graunt your Lo:[ordship] long and happy lyfe at Flushing the 22 of March. 1592.

Yowr Honors very humble to do yow service.
R: Sydney.

This manuscript was probably copied from John Proctour's The Fall of the Late
Arian, *an attack on anti-trinitarianism. However, it consists of one of the
heretical arguments that Proctour quotes at length rather than Proctour's own
views. John Bakeless suggests in* The Tragicall History of Christopher Marlowe
*(Cambridge, Mass., 1942), 1:115–16, that the "Arian" (whom Proctour never
names) was probably John Assheton, a priest arrested for heresy in 1549.
According to Proctour, copies of the Arian's attempt to explain and justify his
views were circulated in manuscript, and one of these copies came into Proctour's
possession, inspiring him to write an answer. Bakeless concludes that the
manuscript found among Kyd's papers was one of these copies, but Proctour's
book was more widely available and is therefore a more likely source. Since
Proctour's book is extant, I have transcribed only a brief portion of the
manuscript that illustrates its use of biblical references. The endorsement is
arguably more important, since it indicates what the investigator thought he had
found when he read the manuscript. Kyd seemingly had no idea where the
manuscript originated, because if he had known about Proctour's book, he could
have claimed that the manuscript derived from a perfectly orthodox source. All
Kyd knew was that he was in serious trouble and that the manuscript was
considered incriminating. He therefore denied his knowledge and ownership of it
and declared that it must belong to Marlowe. This was plausible, not only
because Kyd and Marlowe had once shared a workroom, but also because
Marlowe had already acquired a reputation for heterodoxy.*

*Perhaps this manuscript actually belonged to Marlowe. Marlowe's schoolmaster
in Canterbury, Mr. Gresshop, owned a copy of Proctour's book, but since Marlowe
was only sixteen or younger when he studied with Mr. Gresshop, it is unlikely that
he acquired a copy of portions of the book then. All Mr. Gresshop's ownership of the
book indicates certainly is that it was not rare. We do not know if Marlowe was the
only writer with whom Kyd shared a workroom, or the only person whose papers
might accidentally have been shuffled in with Kyd's, but if Kyd still did some
copying work or collaborated with other playwrights, he almost certainly was not
alone in these regards. Tucker Brooke felt that the manuscript might be in Kyd's
hand, since it is written in a neat italic script. However, the hand is not similar to
the italic in Kyd's letter to Sir John Puckering, and if Kyd had copied passages from
Proctour's book, he would certainly have known their origin. The manuscript does
cite "contrarities out of the scripture," which Richard Baines accused Marlowe of
doing. Later Vaughan claimed that Marlowe "wrote a book against the Trinity"
(Bakeless,* Tragical History, *1:147), and since Vaughan obviously had inside
information about Marlowe (Charles Nicholl,* The Reckoning *[London, 1992],
78–80), his source may have believed that Marlowe was the author of this
manuscript. Indeed, the Arian's arguments might have appealed to the skeptical*

Marlowe, and he might have kept a copy of them for reference, but this is only a possibility.

One page of the manuscript and the endorsement are reproduced in Wraight, In Search of Christopher Marlowe, *239.*

Endorsed: 12 May 1593
                      Vile hereticall conceiptes denyinge the
                      deity of Jhesus Christ our Saviour fownd
                      amongest the papers of Thos Kydd prisoner
                      Which he affirmeth that he had ffrom Marlowe

What the Scriptures do witness of God it is clere & manifest enough for first Paul to the Romains declareth that he is everlasting. And to Timothi immortall & invisible to the Thessalonians living & true. James teacheth also that he is incommutable which thing in the old law & prophecy likewise are thought infixed inculcate so often that they cannot escape the Reader. . . . We therefor call God which onlie is worthie this name & appellation Everlasting, Invisible, Incommutable Incomprehensible Imortall &c. . . .

And if Jhesus Christ even he which was borne of Marie was God so shall he be a visible God comprehensible & mortall which is not compted God with me quoth great Athanasius of Allexandria &c.

For yf we be not able to comprehend nor the Angels nor owr own sowles which ar things creat so wrongfully then & absurdly we mak the creator of them comprehensible especiallie contrary to so manifest testimonies of the Scriptures &c.

WARRANT FOR MARLOWE'S ARREST AND HIS APPEARANCE, 18 AND
20 MAY 1593, PRO ACTS OF THE PRIVY COUNCIL

As C. F. Tucker Brooke pointed out long ago in his Life of Marlowe *(New York, 1966), 58–60; 69 n. 2, there is nothing extraordinary about this document. The Privy Council required numerous individuals to appear before them using similar formulaic language. Individuals were summoned either to answer charges or to serve as witnesses, often regarding rather trivial matters, and the council's summons and instructions were occasionally ignored or even flouted. Failure to comply usually resulted in no more than a reprimand and an emphatic repetition of the order to appear. The warrant for Marlowe contains no indication that he was being brought before the council to answer charges, since such warrants normally contained a variation of the phrase "to answer such matters as should be objected against him before their Lordships."*

When Marlowe appeared promptly in response to the council's warrant, his treatment continued to be routine. He was not imprisoned, but instead was required to give his daily attendance (that is, remain conveniently available) until their lordships dismissed him. He was then ignored for over a week, so it hardly seems that the council had urgent business with him. Perhaps they merely wanted information regarding his association with Kyd, or wanted to know more about the "vile hereticall Conceiptes" Kyd had claimed belonged to Marlowe. Kyd, who was imprisoned and apparently tortured in connection with the recent anti-alien libels, appears to have been in far more trouble than Marlowe.

The reference to Marlowe's probable whereabouts in the warrant indicate that his association with his patron Thomas Walsingham and his frequent presence at Scadbury, Walsingham's estate, were well known to the council.

In the entry recording Marlowe's appearance, the spelling of his name shifts to the form he used himself. Perhaps, as he probably did at Cambridge, Marlowe insisted that his name be properly recorded.

Legible plates of these documents can be found in Wraight, In Search of Christopher Marlowe, 284.

18: May: 1593	A warrant to Henry Maunder one of the Messengers of her Majesties chamber to repaire to the house of Mr. Tho. Walsingham in Kent, or to anie other place where he shall understand xpofer Marlow to be remayning, and by vertue hereof to apprehend and bring him to the court in his companie. And in case of need to require ayd.
20: May:	This day xpofer Marley of London gent, being sent for by warrant from their lordships hath entered his apparance accordinglie for his indemnity herein; and is commanded to give his daily attendance on their lordships, untill he shalbe lycensed to the contrary./

BAINES'S NOTE ON MARLOWE, CA. 26 MAY 1593, BL HARLEIAN MSS 6848, FF. 185—86

The Baines Note is one of the most puzzling of the Marlowe documents. The manuscript, which was preserved among the papers of Sir John Puckering, seems to have been hastily prepared, because it contains a number of corrections and revisions and, particularly toward the end, lacks the cogency of a carefully composed statement. The list of allegations proceeds roughly by association or random recollection. This spontaneity is evident in the first entries, where several items about Moses are followed by several items about Christ. The format of beginning each item with "that" (implying "he affirmeth that" or "he saieth that") was widely used in state papers to record testimony, to make note of answers given during an interrogation, or to report what someone said. The same pattern is followed in Harleian MS 6848, f. 190, a copy of an informer's report on Richard

Cholmeley's conversation. However, in the latter document the person whose statements are being recorded is clearly the informant, whereas initially the Baines note seems to be reporting Marlowe's opinions directly. But in the last two paragraphs of the note the writer vacillates confusingly between direct statements by Baines and alleged statements by Marlowe. Whether the note is in Baines's autograph, or was taken down by someone else and signed by Baines, is uncertain. For that matter, the note may be entirely a copy, since the edited copy sent to the queen also includes a simulated signature which differs from that on the supposed original text, or it may have been compiled by more than one person, though Richard Baines signed it. The document falls into two sections. After the heading, which provides a context for what follows, it begins abruptly with a list of alleged statements by Marlowe, not all of which are consistent with the heading's emphasis on religion. It then shifts to a sweeping first-person denunciation of Marlowe's conduct, apparently by Baines, and a promise to produce more witnesses.

The main body of the note is written in a pedestrian but legible secretary hand, while the signature, like those on many documents of the period, is executed in a different, bolder style. The signature is not, however, particularly ornate. Marlowe's name is spelled three different ways in the manuscript. The two spellings used toward the end are common sixteenth-century variants of the name as we know it today. But the spelling used in the heading, Marly, suggests a different pronunciation, the one used by Marlowe himself, raising the possibility that the heading and the note were not composed by the same person.

We cannot be absolutely certain which of several men named Richard Baines was the informant—if indeed any of the candidates who have been suggested are this man—but he must have been the same Richard Baines who informed on Marlowe at Flushing in January 1592.

The manuscript is undated. However, the heading of the edited copy of it intended for the queen seems to indicate that it was delivered on Saturday evening a few days before Marlowe's death. It was probably submitted on 26 May in response to Marlowe's summons by the Privy Council on 18 May.

Portions of the manuscript which were deleted during revision are enclosed in angle brackets.

A tightly cropped and not quite complete plate of the Baines note, along with a fairly accurate transcript, is supplied by Wraight, In Search of Christopher Marlowe, 308–9.

Endorsed: Bayns Marlow of his blasphemyes

A hand with index finger pointing to "Marlow" has been drawn beside the endorsement.

A note containing the opinion of on Christopher Marly concerning his damnable <opini> Judgment of Re <g>ligion, and scorn of Godes word. That the Indians and many Authors of antiquity have assuredly writen of above

16 thousand/ yeares agone wher as <Moyses> Adam is <said> proved to have lived within 6 thowsand yeares.

The handwriting of these two inserted corrections is neater than the handwriting of the rest of the note.

He affirmeth that Moyses was but a Jugler, & that one Heriotes being Sir W Raleighs man can do more then he.

That Moyses made the Jewes to travell xl yeares in the wildernes (which jorney might have bin done in lesse then one yeare) ere they came to the promised land to thintent that those who were privy to most of his subtilties might perish and so an everlasting superstition remain in the hartes of the people.

That the first beginning of Religioun was only to keep men in awe.

That it was an easy matter for Moyses being brought up in all the artes of the Egiptians to abuse the Jewes being a rude & grosse people.

That Christ was a bastard and his mother dishonest.

That he was the sonne of a carpenter, and that if the Jewes among whome he was borne did crucify him theie best knew him and whence he came.

That Crist deserved better to dy then Barrabas and that the Jewes made a good choise, though Barrabas were both a theif and a murtherer.

That if there be any god or any good Religion, then it is in the papistes because the service of god is performed with more ceremonies, as Elevation of the mass, organs, singing men, Shaven Crownes, &cta. That all protestantes are Hypocriticall asses.

That if he were put to write a new religion, he would undertake both a more Exellent and Admirable methode and that all the new testament is filthily written.

That the woman of Samaria and her sister were whores & that Christ knew them dishonestly.

That St John the Evangelist was bedfellow to Christ and leaned alwaies in his bosome, the he used him as the sinners of Sodoma.

That all they that love not Tobacco & Boies were fooles.

That all the apostles were fishermen and base fellowes neyther of wit nor worth, that Paull only had wit but he was a timerous fellow in bidding men to be subject to magistrates against his conscience.

That he had as good right to coine as the Queen of England and that he was aquainted with one Poole a prisoner in Newgate who hath greate skill in mixture of mettals and having learned some thinges of him he ment through help of a cuning stamp maker to coin French crownes, pistoletes and English shillinges.

That if Christ would have instituted the sacrament with more ceremoniall reverence it would have bin had in more admiration, that it would have bin much better being administred in a Tobacco pipe.

That the Angell Gabriell was baud to the holy ghost, because he brought the
salutation to Mary.

*The next two lines are cramped and might have been inserted later. Unlike the
preceding statements, they do not seem to be a report of what Marlowe said.*

<That {illegible}> That on Ric Cholmley<hath Cholmley> hath confesst that
he was perswaded by Marloes reasons to become an Atheist.

These thinges with many other shall by good & honest witnes be aproved to be
his opinions and comen speeches and that this Marlow doth not only hould
them himself but almost into every company he cometh he perswades men to
Atheism willing them not to be afeard of bugbeares and hobgoblins and utterly
scorning both god and his ministers as I Richard Baines will Justify & approve
both by mine oth and the testimony of many honest men, and almost al men
with whome he hath conversed any time will testify the same, and as I think all
men in Christianity ought to indevor that the mouth of so dangerous a
member may be stopped, he saieth likewise that he hath quoted a number of
contraieties oute of the Scripture which he hath given to some great men who
in convenient time shalbe named. When these thinges shalbe called in question
the witnes shalbe produced.

Richard Baines

The signature is in a large quasi-italic script.

CORONER'S INQUEST ON MARLOWE, 1 JUNE 1593,
PRO C260/174, NO. 127

*Two documents accompany the inquest: a writ of certiorari dated 15 June
requesting the results of the coroner's inquest, in order to determine whether or not
Marlowe's slayer acted in self-defense, and a pardon issued to Frizer on 28 June
1593. The writ is catalogued with a copy of the inquest. The pardon is in the Patent
Rolls, PRO C66/1506, mm. 17, 18. Since the writ solicits information rather than
containing any, only the inquest and the pardon are transcribed here.*

*Many of the speculative theories about what happened in Deptford implicitly or
explicitly question the competence or integrity of the presiding coroner William
Danby, who had jurisdiction because the incident occurred within the verge—a
twenty-mile radius of the body of the queen. However, Danby was appointed
coroner of the queen's household for good reason. A number of his inquests survive
in the Middlesex records, and all those I examined were models of efficiency.
Danby was a shrewd, experienced professional.*

*Conspiracy theories about Marlowe's death generally assume that only
Marlowe, Frizer, Skeres, and Poley knew what happened in the room where they*

dined. However, the verb "publicaverant" used in the inquest suggests that Marlowe and Frizer quarreled loudly enough to be heard in other parts of the house, and information about the men's quiet behavior earlier in the day must have come from other witnesses as well.

The inquest is reproduced in Frederick S. Boas, Christopher Marlowe (Oxford, 1940), between pages 270 and 271.

Kanc./ Inquisicio indentata capta apud Detford Strand in praedicto comitatu Kancia infra virgam primo die Junii anno regni Elizabethe dei gratia Anglie Francie &Hibernie Regine fidei defensoris &c tricesimo quinto coram Willelmo Danby Generoso Coronatore hospicii dicte domine Regine super visum corporis Christoferi Morley ibidem iacentis mortui & interfecti per sacramentum Nicholai Draper Generosi Wolstani Randall generosi Willelmi Curry Adriani Walker Johannis Barber Roberti Baldwyn Egidii Feld Georgii Halfepenny Henrici Awger Jacobi Batt Henrici Bendyn Thome Batt senioris Johannis Baldwyn Alexandri Burrage Edmundi Goodcheepe & Henrici Dabyns Qui dicunt sacramentum suum quod cum quidam Ingramus Frysar nuper de Londonia Generosus ac praedictus Cristoferus Morley Ac quidam Nicholaus Skeres nuper de Londonia Generosus ac Robertus Poley de Londonia praedicta Generosus tricesimo die Maii anno tricesimo quinto supradicto apud Detford Strand praedictam in praedicto Comitatu Kancia infra virgam circa horam decimam ante meridiem eiusdem diei insimul convenerunt in Camera infra domum cuiusdam Elionore Bull vidue & ibidem pariter moram gesserunt & prandebant & post prandium ibidem quiete [sic] modo insimul fuerunt & ambulaverunt in gardinum pertinentem domui praedicto usque horam sextam post meridiem eiusdem diei & tunc recesserunt a gardino praedicto in Cameram praedictam & ibidem insimul & pariter cenabant & post cenam praedicti Ingramus & Christoferus Morley locuti fuerunt & publicaverunt unus eorum alteri diversa maliciosa verba pro eo quod concordare & agreare non potuerunt circa solucionem denariorum summe vocatum le recknynge ibidem & praedictus Cristoferus Morley adtunc iacens super lectum in Camera ubi cenaverunt & ira motus versus praefatum Ingramum Frysar super verbis ut praefertur inter eos praelocutis Et praedictus Ingramus adtunc & ibidem sedens in Camera praedicta cum tergo suo versus lectum ubi praedictus Cristoferus Morley tunc iacebat prope lectum vocatum nere the bed sedens & cum anteriori parte corporis sui versus mensam & praedicti Nicholaus Skeres & Robertus Poley ex utraque parte ipsius Ingrami sedentes tali modo ut idem Ingramus Frysar nullo modo fugam facere potuit Ita accidit quod praedictus Cristoferus Morley ex subito & ex malicia sua erga praefatum Ingramum praecogitata pugionem praedicti Ingrami super tergum suum existentem maliciose adtunc & ibidem evaginabat & cum eodem pugione praedictus Cristoferus Morley adtunc & ibidem maliciose dedit praefato Ingramo duo vulnera super caput suum longitudinis duorum policium & profunditatis quartii unius policis Super quo praedictus Ingramus metuens occidi & sedens in forma praedicta inter praefatos Nicholaum Skeres & Robertum Poley Ita quod ulterius aliquo modo recedere non potuit in sua defensione & salvacione vite sue adtunc & ibidem contendebat cum praefato Cristofero Morley recipere ab eo pugionem suum praedictum in qua quidem affraia idem Ingramus a praefato Cristofero Morley ulterius recedere not potuit Et sic in affraia illa Ita accidit quod praedictus Ingramus in defensione vite sue cum pugione praedicta precii xii^d dedit praefato Cristofero adtunc & ibidem unam plagam mortalem super dexterum oculum suum profunditatis duorum policium & latitudinis unius policis de qua quidem plaga mortali praedictus Cristoferus Morley adtunc & ibidem instanter obiit Et sic Iuratores praedicti dicunt super sacramentum suum quod praedictus Ingramus praefatum Cristoferum Morley praedicto tricesimo die Maii anno tricesimo quinto supradicto apud Detford Strand praedictam in praedicto Comitatu Kancia infra virgam in Camera praedicta infra virgam modo & forma praedictis in defensione ac salvacione vite sue interfecit & occidit contra pacem dicte domine Regine nunc coronam & dignitatem suas Et ulterius Juratores praedicti dicunt super sacramentum suum quod praedictus Ingramus post occisionem praedictam per se modo & forma praedictis perpetratam & factam non fugit neque se retraxit Sed que bona aut catalla terras aut tenementa praedictus Ingramus tempore occisionis praedicte per se modo & forma praedictus facte & perpetrate habuit Iuratores praedicti penitus ignorant In cuius rei testimonium tam praedictus Coronator quam Iuratores praedicti huic Inquisicioni sigilla sua alteratim affixerunt

Datum die & anno supradictis &c

Per Willelmum Danby
Coronatorem

[Kent./ Inquisition in duplicate taken at Detford Strand in the aforesaid county of Kent within the verge on the first day of June in the thirty-fifth year of the reign of Elizabeth, by the grace of God Queen of England, France & Ireland, defender of the faith, etc., in the presence of William Danby, gentleman, coroner of the household of our said lady the Queen, in view of the body of Christopher Morley, there lying dead & slain, upon the oath of Nicholas Draper, gentleman, Wolstan Randall, gentleman, William Curry, Adrian Walker, John Barber, Robert Baldwin, Giles Feld, George Halfepenny, Henry Awger, James Batt, Henry Bendyn, Thomas Batt senior, John Baldwyn, Alexander Burrage, Edmund Goodcheape & Henry Dabyns, who say upon their oath that when one Ingram Frysar, late of London, gentleman, and the aforesaid Christopher Morley and one Nicholas Skeres, late of London, gentleman, and Robert Poley of London aforesaid, gentleman, on the thirtieth day of May in the thirty-fifth year above mentioned, at Detford Strand aforesaid in the aforesaid County of Kent within the verge around the tenth hour before noon of the same day met together in a room at the house of one Eleanor Bull, widow and there passed the time together and lunched, and after lunch kept company quietly and walked in the garden belonging to the aforesaid house until the sixth hour after noon of the same day, and then returned from the aforesaid garden to the room aforesaid and there together and in company dined, and after dinner the aforesaid Ingram and the said Christopher Morley were in speech and publicly exchanged divers malicious words because they could not concur nor agree on the payment of the sum of pence, that is to say, *le recknynge*, there; and the aforesaid Christopher Morley then lying on a bed in the room where they dined and moved by ire towards the aforesaid Ingram Frysar because of the aforesaid words that had passed between them, and the aforesaid Ingram then and there sitting in the aforesaid room with his back towards the bed where the aforesaid Christopher Morley then lay, near the bed, that is sitting *nere the bed* and with the front part of his body towards the table and the aforesaid Nicholas Skeres and Robert Poley sitting on either side of the same Ingram so that the same Ingram Frysar could in no way flee, thus it befell that the aforesaid Christopher Morley suddenly and of malice aforethought towards the aforesaid Ingram then and there maliciously unsheathed the dagger of the aforesaid Ingram which was visible at his back and with the same aforesaid dagger then and there maliciously gave the aforesaid Ingram two wounds on his head of the length of two inches and of the depth of a quarter of an inch; whereupon the aforesaid Ingram, in fear of being slain and sitting on the aforesaid bench between the aforesaid Nicholas Skeres and Robert Poley, so that he was not able to withdraw in any way, in his own defense and to save his life then and there struggled with the aforesaid Christopher Morley to take back from him his aforesaid dagger, in which same affray the same Ingram could not withdraw further from the aforesaid Christopher Morley. And thus it befell in that affray that the said Ingram, in defense of his life and with the aforesaid dagger of the value of 12 pence, gave the aforesaid Christopher then and there a mortal wound above his right eye of the depth of two inches and of the breadth of one inch, of which same mortal wound the aforesaid Christopher Morley then and there instantly died. And thus the aforesaid jurors say upon their oath that the aforesaid Ingram killed the aforesaid Christopher Morley the aforesaid thirtieth day of May in the thirty fifth year abovementioned in the aforesaid Detford Strand in the aforesaid county of Kent within the verge in the room aforesaid within the verge in the manner and form aforesaid in defense and for the salvation of his life, against the peace of the said lady the Queen, her present crown and dignity. And further the said jurors say upon their oath that the said Ingram after the slaying aforesaid perpetrated & done by him in the manner & form aforesaid neither fled nor withdrew himself. But concerning what goods or chattels, lands or tenements the said Ingram had at the time of the aforesaid slaying done & perpetrated by him in the manner and form aforesaid, the said jurors are totally uninformed. In witness whereof the aforesaid Coroner as well as the jurors aforesaid to this inquisition have in turn set their seals.

Dated the day and year abovementioned, etc.
by William Danby
Coroner

MARLOWE'S BURIAL ENTRY, 1 JUNE 1593, PARISH REGISTER, CHURCH OF ST. NICHOLAS, DEPTFORD, GREATER LONDON AUTHORITY RECORD OFFICE, WESTMINSTER BRIDGE

The original vicar's error in recording Ingram Frizer's given name as "Francis," and a nineteenth-century vicar's misreading of "Frezer" as "Archer," caused a long delay in the discovery of documents such as the coroner's inquest on the death of Marlowe. J. Leslie Hotson finally ferreted out Frizer's actual name, a process he describes in detail in The Death of Christopher Marlowe *(New York, 1965).*

Plates of this document can be found in Hotson, facing page 21; Bakeless, Tragicall History, *vol. 1, facing page 152; Boas,* Christopher Marlowe, *facing page 277; and Wraight,* In Search of Christopher Marlowe, *305.*

Anno Domini 1593

Christopher Marlow slaine by Francis Frezer; the ·1· of June

COPY OF THE BAINES NOTE, JUNE 1593 OR LATER, BL HARLEIAN MSS 6853, FF. 307–8

Not long after Marlowe's death, someone copied the Baines note, revised or shortened several items, and deleted allegations not directly bearing on Marlowe's alleged religious opinions. The deleted portions are included here, enclosed in angle brackets. The manuscript is, as indicated by the endorsement on the back, a rough draft of a copy sent to the queen. Among the items shortened was the reference to Harriot, in which the phrase "being Sir W Raleigh's man" was omitted. The omission appears to be deliberate, and it is hard to reconcile this with the theory that Raleigh was the target of the attacks on Marlowe.

Why should the opinions of a man who was already dead, as the heading clearly indicates, be of any interest to the queen? Apparently someone was trying to convince Elizabeth that an atheist threat existed, and that vigilance and timely action on the part of the government were necessary to contain it.

This manuscript is in a different hand from the Baines note, and exhibits very different spelling characteristics. The endorsement and the notation that Cholmeley is "layd for" are not in the same hand as the rest of the manuscript.

Endorsed: Copye of Marloes blasphemes
As sent to her H. [ighness]

Original heading: A note contayninge the opinon of one Christofer Marlye concernynge his damnable opinion and Judgment of Relygion and scorne of Gods worde. who since Whitsundy dyed a soden & vyolent deathe.

Revised heading: A note delived on Whitsun eve last of the most horrible blasphemes and damnable opinions uttered by Xpofer Marly who wthin iii dyes after came to a soden & fearfull end of his life.

That the Indians and many Authors of Antiquitei <have> have assuredly written of above 16 thowsande yeeres agone, wher Adam is proved to have lyved within 6 thowsande yeeres.

<He affirmeth> That Moyses was but a Juggler and that one Heriotes can do more then hee.

That Moyses made the Jewes to travell fortie yeeres in the wildernes (which jorny might have ben don in lesse then one year) er they came to the promised lande, to the intente that those whoe wer privei to most of his subtileteis myght perish, and so an everlastinge supersticion remayne in the harts of the people.

That the firste beginnynge of Religion was only to keep men in awe.

That it was an easye matter for Moyses beinge brought up in all the artes of the Egiptians, to abuse the Jewes beinge a rude and grosse people.

That Christ was a Bastard and his mother dishonest.

That he was the sone of a carpenter and that yf the Jewes among whome he was borne did crucifye him, thei best knew him and whence he came.

That Christ deserved better to dye then Barrabas, and that the Iewes made a good choyce, though Barrabas were both a theife and a murtherer.

That if ther be any God or good Religion, then it is in the Papists because the service of God is performed with more ceremonyes, as elevation of the masse, organs, singinge men <shaven crownes >, &c. That all protestantes ar hipocriticall asses.

That, if he were put to write a new religion, he wolde undertake both a more excellent, and more admirable methode and that all the new testament is filthily written.

That the woman of Samaria were whores and that Christ knew them dishonestlye.

That St John the Evangelist was bedfellow to Christe, that he leaned alwayes in his bosum, that he used him as the synners of Sodoma.

<That all thei that love not tobacco and boyes ar fooles.>

That all the Appostles were fishermen and base fellowes, nether of witt nor worth, that Pawle only had witt, that he was a timerous fellow in biddinge men to be subject to magistrates against his conscience.

<That he had as good right to coyne as the Queen of England, and that he was acquainted with one Poole a prisoner in Newgate whoe hath great skill in

mixture of mettalls, and havinge learned some things of him he ment through help of a connynge stampe maker to coyne french crownes, pystolettes and englishe shillinges.>

That if Christ had instituted the Sacraments with more ceremonyall reverence, it wold have been had in more admiration, that it wolde have been much better beinge administered in a Tobacco pype.

That the Angell Gabriell was bawde to the holy Ghoste because he brought the salutation to Marie.

That one Richard Cholmelei hath confessed that he was perswaded by Marloes reason to become an Atheiste.

There is a marginal note in an italic hand on the above entry: "he is layd for." The remainder of the note, including the name of Baines, is deleted.

<Theis things with many other shall by good and honest men be proved to be his opinions and comen speeches, and that this Marloe doth not only holde them himself, but almost in every company he cometh, perswadeth men to Atheisme, willinge them not to be afrayed of bugbeares and hobgoblins, and utterly scorning both God and his ministers as I Richard Bome will Justify both by my othe and the testimony of many honest men, and almost all men with whome he hath conversed any tyme will testefy the same. And as I thinke all men in christianitei ought to endevor that the mouth of so dangerous a member may be stopped.

he sayeth moreover that he hath coated a number of contrarieties out of the scriptures, which he hath geeven to some great men whoe in convenient tyme shalbe named. When theis things shalbe called in question, the witnesses shalbe produced.

Richard Baines>

KYD'S LETTER TO PUCKERING, CA. JUNE 1593, BL HARLEIAN MSS 6848, F. 154

Kyd, after his release from prison, sought Sir John Puckering's aid in his attempts to regain the favor of his patron, Lord Strange. This letter is a further attempt, after a personal meeting, to persuade Puckering of his innocence in all matters of which he was suspected, especially, it appears, of atheism. The fact that Kyd emphasizes this issue suggests that he knew it was a matter of special interest to Puckering. The letter is written in an elegant secretary hand, with a highly ornate signature appended far below the text of the letter.

Excellent plates of Kyd's letter and note are included in Frederick S. Boas, Marlowe and His Circle *(Oxford, 1931), frontispiece, and facing page 73. They are also reproduced in Wraight,* In Search of Christopher Marlowe, *314, 316.*

Addressed: To the R.[ight] honorable Sir John Puckering Knight Lord Keeper of
   the great seale of England.
Notation: Kidde

At my last being with your L[ordshi]p. to entreate some speaches from yow in
my favor to my Lorde, whoe (though I thinke he rest not doubtfull of myne
inocence) hath yet in his discreeter judgment feared to offende in his reteyning
me, without your honors former pryvitie. So is it nowe R.[ight] ho:[norable]
that the denyall of that favor (to my thought reasonable) hath movde me to
conjecture some suspicion, that your L[ordshi]p holdes me in, concerning
Atheisme, a deadly thing which I was undeserved chargd withall, & therefore
have I thought it requisite, aswell in duetie to your L[ordshi]p, & the Lawes, as
also in the feare of god, & freedom of my conscience, therein to satisfie the world
and yow:
The first and most (thoughe insufficient surmize) that ever..as..[? ms damaged]
therein might be raisde of me, grewe thus. When I was first suspected for that
Libell that concern'd the state, amongst those waste and idle papers (which I
carde not for) & which unaskt I did deliver up, were founde some fragmentes of
a disputation toching that opinion, affirmed by Marlowe to be his, and shufled
with some of myne (unknown to me) by some occasion of our wrytinge in one
chamber twoe yeares synce.
My first acquaintance with this Marlowe, rose upon his bearing name to serve
my Lo:[rd] although his L[ordshi]p never knewe his service, but in writing for
his plaiers, for never cold my L.[ord] endure his name, or sight, when he had
heard of his conditions, nor would in deed the forme of devyne praier used du-
elie in his l[ordshi]ps house, have quadred with such reprobates.
That I should love or be familiar frend, with one so irreligious, were verie rare.
When *Tullie* saith *Digni sunt amicitia quibus in ipsis inest causa cur diligantur*
[They are worthy of friendship in whom there is cause for esteem.] which neither
was in him, for person, quallities, nor honestie, besides he was intemperate & of a
cruel hart, the verie contraries to which, my greatest enemies will saie by me.
It is not to be nombred amongst the best conditions of men, to taxe or to op-
braide the deade *Quia mortui non mordent* [because the dead do not bite], But
thus muche have I (with your L[ordshi]ps favor) dared in the greatest cause,
which is to cleere my self of being thought an *Atheist*, which some will sweare
he was.
For more assurance that I was not of that vile opinion, Lett it but please your
L[ordshi]p to enquire of such as he conversd withall; that is (as I am geven to
understand) with *Harriot, Warner, Royden* and some stationers in Paules
chruchyard, whom I in no sort can accuse nor will excuse by reson of his com-
panie, of whose consent if I had been, no question but I also shold have been of
their consort, for *ex minimo vestigio artifex agnoscit artificem* [from the least
trace the craftsman recognizes the craft].

Of my religion and life I have alreadie geven some instance to the late comissioners & of my reverend meaning to the state, although perhaps my paines and undeserved tortures felt by some, wold have ingendred more impatience when lesse by farre hath dryven so manye *imo extra caulas* [even out of the fold] which it shall never do with me.

But whatsoever I have felt R.[ight] ho:[norable] this is my request not for reward but in regard of my trewe inocence that it wold please your l[ordshi]ps so to use [? ms damaged] the same & me, as I maie still reteyne the favors of my Lord, whom I have servd almost theis vi yeres nowe, in credit untill nowe, & nowe am utterlie undon without herein be somewhat donn for my recoverie. For I do know his L[ordshi]p holdes your honors & the state in that dewe reverence, as he wold no waie move the leste suspicion of his loves and cares both towards hir sacred Majestie your L[ordshi]ps and the lawes whereof when tyme shall serve I shall geve greater instance which I have observd.

As for the libel laide unto my chardg I am resolved with receyving of the sacrament to satisfie your l[ordshi]ps & the world that I was neither agent nor consenting therunto. Howbeit if some outcast *Ismael* for want or of his own dispose to lewdnes, have with pretext of duetie or religion, or to reduce himself to that he was not borne unto by enie waie incensd your l[ordshi]ps to suspect me, I shall besech in all humillitie & in the feare of god that it will please your l[ordshi]ps but to censure me as I shall prove my self, and to repute them as they ar in deed. *Cum totius iniustitia nulla capitalior sit quam eorum, qui tum cum maxime fallunt id agunt ut viri boni esse videantur.* [Since no injustice can be worse than that of those who act deceptively while seeming to be good men.] For doubtles even then your l[ordshi]ps shalbe sure to breake open [? ms damaged] their lewde designes and see into the truthe, when but their lyves that herein have accused me shalbe examined & rypped up effectually, soe maie I chaunce with Paul to live & shake the vyper of[f] my hand into the fier for which the ignorant suspect me guiltie of the former shipwrack. And thus (for nowe I feare me I growe teadious) assuring your good L[ordshi]p that if I knewe eny whom I cold justlie accuse of that damnable offence to the awefull majestie of god or of that other mutinous sedition towrd the state I wold as willinglie reveale them as I wold request your L[ordshi]ps better thoughtes of me that never have offended yow.

Your L[ordshi]ps most humble in all duties
Th Kydde

KYD'S NOTE TO PUCKERING, CA. JUNE 1593,
BL HARLEIAN 6849, F. 218

Puckering evidently pressed Kyd to reveal more of what he knew about Marlowe's opinons and associates. Kyd responded with this note, which shows little enthusiasm for the task, provides minimal information, and does not bother with formalities, including a signature.

Tucker Brooke thought someone other than Kyd added the numbers in the margins, and indeed they enumerate the religious opinions Kyd reports, while the political remark is ignored. The numbers are also slightly out of alignment with the lines they precede.

Pleaseth it your honorable L[ordshi]p touching Marlowes monstruous opinions as I cannot but with an agreved conscience think on him or them so can I but particulariz fewe in the respect of them that kept him greater company, howbeit in discharg of dutie both towrdes god your L[ordshi]ps & the world thus much have I thought good brieflie to discover in all humblenes
First it was his custom when I knew him first & as I heare saye he contynewd it in table talk or otherwise to jest at the devine scriptures gybe at praiers, & stryve in argument to frustrate & confute what hath byn spoke or wrytt by prophets & such holie men/

1   He wold report St John to be our Savior Christes *Alexis* I cover it with rever-
    ence and trembling that is that Christ did love him with an extraordinary love/
2   That for me to wryte a poem of St *Paules* conversion as I was determined he
    said wold be as if I shold go wryte a book of fast & loose, esteming *Paul* a
    Jugler.
3   That the prodigall childes portion was but fower nobles, he held his purse so
    neere the bottom in all pictures and that it either was a jest or els fower no-
    bles then was thought a great patrimony not thinking it a parable.
4   That things esteemed to be donn by devine power might have aswell been
    don by observation of men all which he wold so sodenlie take slight occa-
    sion to slyp out as I & many others in regard of his other rashnes in attempt-
    ing soden pryvie injuries to men did overslypp though often reprehend him
    for it & for which god is my witnes aswell by my lords comaundment as in
    hatred of his life & thoughts I left & did refraine his companie/
    He wold perswade with men of quallitie to goe unto the K[ing] of *Scotts*
    whether I heare *Royden* is gon and where if he had livd he told me when I
    sawe him last he meant to be.

INGRAM FRIZER'S PARDON, 28 JUNE 1593, PRO C66/1401, MM. 33–34

Frizer's pardon closely follows the wording of the coroner's inquest. A few minor changes were necessary to accommodate the text to the formula for pardons. The detail that Frizer did not flee, which was necessary for the jury to find that he acted in self defense, and the reference to the jury's lack of knowledge regarding his possessions, are omitted. The ending is purely conventional. Only the final section is translated here.

Regina perdona se defendendo pro Ingramo Frisar

Regina Omnibus Ballivis & fidelibus suis ad quos &c salutem Cum per quandam Inquisiocionem indentatam captam apud Detford Strand in praedicto comitatu nostro Kancia infra virgam primo die Junii ultimo praeterito coram Willelmo Danby Generoso Coronatore hospicii nostri super visum corporis Christoferi Morley ibidem iacentis mortui & interfecti per sacramentum Nicholai Draper Generosi Wolstani Randall generosi Willelmi Curry Adriani Walker Johannis Barber Roberti Baldwine Egidii Feld Georgii Halfepenny Henrici Awger Jacobi Batte Henrici Bendin Thome Batte senioris Johannis Baldwyn Alexandri Burrage Edmundi Goodcheape & Henrici Dabyns compertum existit Quod quidam Ingramus Frisar nuper de Londonia Generosus ac praedictus Cristoferus Morley Ac quidam Nicholaus Skeres nuper de Londonia Generosus ac Robertus Poley de Londonia praedicta Generosus tricesimo die Maii ultimo praeterito apud Detford Strand praedictam in praedicto Comitatu nostro Kancia infra virgam circa horam decimam ante meridiem eiusdem diei insimul convenerunt in Camera infra domum cuiusdam Elionore Bull vidue & ibidem pariter moram gesserunt & prandebant & post prandium ibidem in quieto modo insimul fuerunt & ambulaverunt in Gardinum pertinentem domui praedicto usque horam sextam post meridiem eiusdem diei & tunc recesserunt a gardino praedicto in Cameram praedictam & ibidem insimul & pariter cenabant & post cenam praedicti Ingramus & Christoferus Morley locuti fuerunt & publicaverunt unus eorum alteri diversa maliciosa verba pro eo quod concordare & agreare non potuerunt circa solucionem denariorum summe vocatum le Reckoninge ibidem & praedictus Xpoferus Morley adtunc iacens super lectum in Camera ubi cenaverunt & ira motus versus praefatum Ingramum Frisar super verbis ut praefertur inter eos praelocutis Et praedictus Ingramus adtunc & ibidem sedens in Camera praedicta cum tergo suo versus lectum ubi praedictus Cristoferus Morley tunc iacebat prope lectum vocatum nere the Bedd sedens & cum anteriori parte corporis sui versus mensam & praedicti Nicholaus Skeres & Robertus Poley ex utraque parte ipsius Ingrami sedentes tali modo ut idem Indramus Frysar nullo modo fugam facere potuit Ita accidit quod praedictus Cristoferus Morley ex subito & ex malicia sua erga praefatum Ingramum praecogitata pugionem prae-

dicti Ingrami super tergum suum existentem maliciose adtunc & ibidem evaginabat & cum eodem pugione praedictus
Cristoferus Morley adtunc & ibidem maliciose dedit praefato
Ingramo duo vulnera super Caput suum longitudinis duorum policium & profunditatis quartii unius policis Super quo
praedictus Ingramus metuens occidi & sedens in forma praedicta inter praefatos Nicholaum Skeres & Robertum Poley Ita
quod ulterius aliquo modo recedere non potuit in sua defensione & salvacione vite sue adtunc & ibidem contendebat
cum praefato Xpofero Morley recipere ab eo pugionem suum
praedictum In qua quidem affraia idem Ingramus a praefato
Xpofero Morley ulterius recedere not potuit Et sic in affraia
illa ita accidit quod praedictus Ingramus in defensione vite
sue cum pugione praedicta precii duodecem denariourm
dedit praefato Cristofero adtunc & ibidem unam plagam
mortalem super dexterum oculum suum profunditatis duorum policium & latitudinis unius policis de qua quidem
plaga mortali praedictus Xpoferus Morley adtunc & ibidem
instanter obiit Et sic quod praedictus Ingramus praefatum
Cristoferum Morley praedicto tricesimo die Maii ultimo
praeterito apud Detford Strande praedictam in praedicto
Comitatu nostro Kancia infra virgam in Camera praedicta
infra virgam modo & forma praedictis in defensione ac salvacione vite sue interfecit & occidit contra pacem nostram,
coronam & dignitatem nostras Sicut per tenorem Recordi Inquisicionis praedicte quem coram nobis in Cancellaria nostra
virtute brevis nostri venire fecimus plenius liquet Nos igitur
pietate moti perdonavimus eidem Ingramo Frisar sectam
pacis nostre que ad nos versus praedictum Ingramus pertinet
pro morte supradicta & firmam pacem nostram ei inde concedimus Ita tamen quod stet rectum in Curia nostra siquis
versus eum loqui voluerit de morte supradicta In cuius rei &c
Teste Regina apud Kewe xxviii die Junii

[And thus because the aforesaid Ingram killed & slew the aforesaid Christopher
Morley on the aforesaid thirtieth of May last at Detford Strand aforesaid in our
aforesaid County of Kent within the verge in the aforesaid room within the
verge in the manner and form aforesaid in defense and salvation of his life
against our peace, crown, and dignity, according to the tenor of the Record of
Inquisition aforesaid which we caused to come before us in our Chancery by
virtue of our writ. We therefore, moved by pity, pardon the same Ingram Frisar
the breach of our peace which pertains to us against the said Ingram for the
death above mentioned & grant him our firm peace, provided nevertheless that

the jurisdiction remain in our court if anyone should wish to speak against him concerning the above mentioned death, in which case etc. Witness the Queen at Kew the 28th day of June]

WILL OF JOHN MARLOWE, 23 JANUARY 1605, CKS PRC 16/125/M (REGISTERED COPY: PRC 17/52, FF. 373V-374R)

Marlowe's parents both outlived him. Their wills, and the inventory of John Marlowe's possessions, reflect the family's modest means and social standing, especially when their wills are compared to the far more elaborate will of Katherine Benchkin that Marlowe, his father, his uncle, and his brother-in-law witnessed in 1585.

In the name of God, Amen, 1604 [1605]. the xxiiith day of January, I John Marlowe beeing sicke of body, but thankes be to Almightie God of good & perfect remembraunce, doe make constitute & ordeyne this my last Will & Testament in maner and forme following. First I give & commend my soule into the handes of Almightie God my maker & Redeemer, & my body to be buried in the churcheyeard of the parish of St George within Canterbury. As touching my temporall goods my debts & funeralls dischardged & paid I give and bequeath wholy to my wyfe, Katherine whome I make my sole executrix. In witnesse whereof I John Marlowe have to this my last Will & Testament set to my hand & seale the day and yeere above written.

The marke of John Marlowe. [mark]

In the presence of us whose names are heere underwritten.

James Bissell the writer hereof./
Vyncent Huffam
Thomas Plesyngton

INVENTORY OF JOHN MARLOWE'S GOODS, 21 FEBRUARY 1605, CKS PRC 10/34, F. 80

This inventory was taken not quite a month after John Marlowe's death. In contrast to the inventory of James Benchkin's goods, which contains a superfluity of items, it indicates that Marlowe's aging parents lived comfortably, but simply. Many of the items in this inventory appear in Katherine Marlowe's will in the same numbers, although the pillowcoates seem to have multiplied. The inventory indicates seven pairs, but ten pairs and an odd one are mentioned in Katherine's will.

Given the appraised value of the sheets and silver spoons in the inventory, one can understand why Katherine was particularly anxious to divide these items equally among her daughters and grandchildren.

An inventorye of the goodes of John Marlowe taken uppon the 21 daye of Feb-
ruarye Anno Domini 1604 [1605]. Prized by Mr Cripse Thomas Pleasington and
Robert Lyon.

Inprimis his girdle and his purse—iiii^s

In the litle parlour nexte the streete
A litle table with a frame and 3 joyne stooles—v^s
Item a court cubborde with a carpet, a greate cushion, and 5 other—v^s

In the halle
Item a litle table with a frame—iii^s
Item one chest 3 chayres, and a glasse cage—iii^s iii^d
Item one payre of brandirons, a payre of tonges, and a fire shovell, a payre of
    bellowes, a fire rake, and a payre of pothangers—iiii^s
Item the paynted clothe—xii^d

In the kitchen
Item a litle table with a cubbord in it, an olde joyne stoole and an olde form and
    one cushion a dressinge borde and an old coupe—ii^s
Item one olde plate cubborde and brine tubbe—iiii^s
Item one brandiron, one creeper, one spitte, one gridgiron, one drippinge
    panne and a choppinge knife—iiii^s
Item 6 ketles 2 brasse pots, 2 stupnets, 2 iron pots, one chafinge dishe, 6 brasse
    candlestickes, and a morter with a pestle, one chafer of brasse a skimmer and
    a bastinge ladle, and a warminge panne—xx^s
Item a payre of reckes, a fryinge panne, a trivet, and a tostinge iron—ii^s
Item 3 basons x great platters, two chamberpots, 3 small dishes, 5 porrengers, 7
    spoones, x saucers, 2 pewter cuppes, 2 salt sellers, <3>4 pewter pots—xx^s

In the seller
Item 3 stellinges, and a litle table—v^s
Item for pots and glasses—xii^d

In the greate chamber
Item a playne bedstedle, matte and rope, and a flocke bed and a fether bed, one
    blanket and a rugge, two boulsters, 5 curtaines and roddes—xxxx^s
Item one presse, and 3 chests—xx^s
Item one wicker chayre—viii^d
Item one truckle bed, and a boulster, and a bagge of feathers—ii^s
Item eighteene payre of sheetes—iiii^{li}
Item 4 fine tablecloathes, and 4 course ones, and 2 dosen of napkins and a
    doson of course ones—xxvi^s iiii^d

Item 4 payre of fine pillowcoates, and 3 payre of course—xii^s
Item halfe a dosen of course hand towells—ii^s

In the litle chamber

A litle standinge bed without a testerne. And a truckle bed with two flocke beds, 2 boulsters, 2 blankets and a coverlet—xvi^s
Item 3 blankets more and 2 kiveringes and a rugge—xv^s
Item 4 pillowes—v^s
Item 6 cushions—vi^s
Item his wearinge apparell—xxxx^s
Item an olde cheste, and olde presse, a buntinge hutche and a meale tubbe—ii^s
Item 4 payre of bootes—xx^s
Item a bible—vi^s
Item for X silver spoones—xxxx^s
Item 3 loade of woode—xv^s
Item for olde lumber about the howse—ii^s vi^d

The whole summe xxi^l xiiii^s ii^d
Thomas Crispe
Thomas Plesyinton
Robart Lyon

WILL OF KATHERINE MARLOWE, 17 MARCH 1605, CKS PRC 16/127/M
(REGISTERED COPY 17/54)

The dating of Katherine Marlowe's will has misled many Marlowe biographers about the time of her death. The will is dated 1605 and was probated on 22 July 1605, but if the will was probated in July 1605, the day and month of the will, 17 March, would have fallen in 1604 under the system of dating then in use in Elizabethan England, according to which the new year began on Lady Day, 25 March. Katherine's burial in All Saints churchyard (not in St. George's, as she wished) is recorded on 18 March 1604/5, so the writer of the will, Thomas Hudson, evidently dated it incorrectly. Katherine survived her husband by less than two months, not by over a year, as William Urry was the first to point out.

In her will, Katherine seems anxious to distribute her property as equitably as possible among her three surviving children—all daughters. In deference to the principle of primogeniture, she gives somewhat more to her eldest daughter, Margaret Jordan, and also entrusts Margaret with the family christening linen. She treats all her grandchildren equally within gender, but the males get larger silver spoons than the females. Interestingly, she leaves John Moore, the husband of her third daughter, Joan, who died at fourteen, a sizable legacy. Apparently she was fond of him.

Katherine certainly had more property than she mentions in her will. She had shoes and other items of clothing, kitchen utensils, a bed, and coverlets in addition to the sheets she parcels out so meticulously, and probably all of the furniture noted in the inventory of her husband's possessions. All this she gives to John Cranford, the husband of her second oldest daughter Ann, whom she appoints her executor, in lieu of the legacies of forty and twenty shillings she gives to the eldest and youngest daughters. Since John Cranford was, according to Urry, "literate and able," he was a logical choice for this task.

Perhaps the most touching detail of Katherine's will is her concern that the odd tablecloth replace "the sheete which is taken awaye"—that is, her winding sheet— so that none of her daughters need feel deprived by the humble requirements of her burial.

Endorsed (in Latin): Will of Katherine Marlowe widow, late of All Saints Canter-
    bury, deceased.
Probated: 22 July 1605

In the name of god amen. I Katherine Marlowe widdowe of John Marlowe of Canterbury late deceased though sicke in bodye yet in perfect memorye I give god thankes, do ordayne this my last will and testament written one the 17 of Marche, in the yeare of our Lorde god 1605 in manner & forme as followethe.

ffirst I doe bequeathe my soule to god my saviour, and redeemer, and my bodye
    to be buryed in the Churcheyarde of St Georges in Canterburye neare where
    as my husbande John Marlowe was buryed.
I doe bequeathe unto my daughter Margaret Jurden the greatest golde ringe.
I doe beequeathe unto my daughter An Cranford a golde ringe which my
    daughter Cradwell hath which I would have her to surrender up unto her
    sister An. and an other silver ringe.
I doe bequeathe unto my daughter Doritye Cradwell, the ringe with the double
    posye, <she>
I doe bequeathe unto my daughter Jurden my <cloathe> stufe gowne <which I
    weare everye daye> and my kirtle.
I doe bequeathe unto my daughter Cranforde my best cloathe gowne and the
    cloathe that is lefte of the same.
I doe beequeathe unto my daughter Cradwell my cloathe gowne which I did
    weare everye daye.
I doe bequeathe unto my daughter Jurden <two> one silver spoone<s> and
    unto her eldest sonne John Jurden one greate silver spoone and unto her
    <yongest> sonne William one of the greatest silver spoones of the six, and
    to Elsabethe Jurden, one spoone.

I doe bequeathe unto my daughter An Cranforde one silver spoone and to her sonne Anthonye one of the greatest spoones, and to John an other of the greatest silver spoones, and unto Elisabeth Cranforde one spoone.

I doe beequeathe unto my daughter Dorytye Cradwell one silver spoone and to her sonne John Cradwell on of the greatest silver spoones.

I doe beequeathe unto my daughter Jurden two cushions and unto my daughter Cranforde 2 cushions of taffate, and to my daughter Cradwell two cushions./

I doe beequeathe my Christeninge linnen as the kercher, the <drinkinge> dammaske napkin, a face cloathe, and a bearinge blanket to bee used equal-lye betweene them, and to serve to everie of theire needs but if my daugher Jurden doe goe out of the towne, my daughter An Cranforde to have the keepinge of the same Christeninge linnen.

I doe beequeathe to everye one of them one tablecloathe, and the fourthe, to goe for an odde sheete that he which hath the odde sheete may have the tablecloathe.

I doe bequeathe unto everye one of my daughters six paire of sheetes, to be <chossen> divided equallye. And in steade of the sheete which is taken awaye, there is one <sheete> tablecloathe added.

I doe bequeathe to every one of my daughters a dosen of napkins to be divided equallye beecause some are better then other.

I doe beequeathe unto my daughter Jurden three payre of pillowecoates, and to my daughter Cranforde three payer of pilleocoates, unto my daughter Crad-well three paire of pilloecoates/ one payre of pilloecoates I doe bequeathe unto Katherine Reve. and unto Goodwife Morrice one pilloecoate./

I doe beequeathe unto John Moore fortye shillinges, and the joyne presse that standeth in the greate chamber where I lye.

I beequeathe unto Mary May my mayde my red petticoate, and a smocke.

I beequeathe unto goodwife Morrice my petticoate that I doe weare daylye and a smocke and a wastcoate.

I doe beequeathe unto Goodwife Jurden fortye Shillinges.

I doe beequeathe unto my daughter Cradwell twentye shillinges.

I <doe> would have All these porcions <are> to bee paied within one yeare after my decease.

I doe beequeathe unto my sonne Cranforde all the rest of my goodes <so> payinge my debts and legacyes and excharginge my funeralls, whoome I doe make my whole executor of this my laste will and testamente.

In witnesse whereof I have heereunto set my hande and seale.

Wittneses <I> those names that are heere under written, and I Thomas Hudson. the writer heereof.

The marke of Katherine Marlowe
[mark and seal]
The marke of [mark] Sarai Morrice
The marke of [mark] Mary Maye

*The dating of these notes suggests that Oxinden frequently recorded memorable
bits of his conversations with his neighbor Simon Aldrich. The duplication of much
of their content in the Folger Commonplace Book probably represents a later
recollection of their conversations.*

*Some of the lore Oxinden repeats, such as the story about the book against the
scripture, and the claim that Marlowe was stabbed in the head with a dagger and
died swearing, seems to be based on Thomas Beard's* Theater of Gods Judgments.
*At one time, an edition of this book existed with handwritten notes in it that
closely resemble some of the entries in Oxinden's commonplace books, so it is likely
that Oxinden had a copy of Beard in his large library. Aldrich may also have
owned or read a copy of Beard, of course.*

Feb. 10, 1640 He [Simon Aldrich] said that Marlo who wrot Hero, & Leander
was an Atheist, & had wrote a book ag[ain]st. the Scripture, how that it was all
one mans making, & would have printed it but would not be suffered. He was
the son of a shoemaker in Cant: he [Aldrich] said hee was an excellent scholler
& made excellent verses in Latin. Died aged about 30. He was stabd in the head
with a dagger, & dyed swearing.

Feb. 12 He said that one Finei of Dover was an Atheist, & that he would goe out
at midnight into a wood, & fall down uppon his knees & pray heartily that the
Devill would come & he would see him: for he did not beleive there was a Devill: Mr Alderich said he was a very good scholer but would never have above one
book at a time, & when he was perfect in it he would sell it away, & by another.
He learned all Marlo by heart & divers other bookes. Marlo made him an Atheist. This Finei was faine to make a speech uppon the foole hath said in his heart
there is no god, to gett his degree. Finey would say as Galen said that man was
of a more excellent composition than a beast, & thereby could speake: but affirmed his soul dyed with his body & as we can remember nothing before we
were borne: soe we shall remember nothing after.

Mr Ald. sayd that Mr Fin[eau]x of Dover was an Atheist & that hee would go
out at midnight into a wood, & fall downe uppon his knees & pray heartily that
the devil would come, that he might see him (for hee did not beleive that there
was a devil) Mr Ald: sayd that hee was a verie good scholler, but would never

have above one booke at a time, & when hee was perfect in it, hee would sell it away & buy another: he learned all *Marlo* by heart & divers other bookes: *Marlo* made him an *Atheist*. This Fineaux was faine to make a speech uppon *The foole hath said in his heart there is no God*, to get his degree. Fineaux would say as Galen sayd that man was of a more excellent composition than a beast, & thereby could speake: but affirmed that his soule dyed with his body, & as we remember nothing before wee were borne, so we shall remember nothing after wee are dead. (page 54)

he [Aldrich] said that Marlo who wrot Hero & Leander was an Atheist: & had wrot a booke against the Scriptur, how that it was al of one mans making, & would have prooved it but wold not be suffered,: he said that the sayd Marlo was an excellent scoller, & made excellent verses in latin hee was stabd with a dagger & dyed swearing. (page 56)

References

MANUSCRIPT SOURCES

Since some of the manuscript locations specified in Bakeless's *Tragicall History of Christopher Marlowe*, such as Middlesex Guildhall and Christ Church Gate, are outdated, as are some of his document references, I have listed the Marlowe documents by current archival location. Within locations, items are arranged in chronological order as they pertain to events in Marlowe's life, insofar as that is possible. Documents concerning Marlowe's birth and family background are located at Canterbury; therefore the Canterbury and Kent archives are listed first, followed by the Cambridge archives, the London archives, and the Folger Shakespeare Library, whose biographically significant documents date after Marlowe's death. Archives containing the most material are listed first, followed in descending order by those containing less material. I have of course relied on Bakeless and Urry for some information on John Marlowe and other members of Marlowe's family; those particularly interested in Marlowe's relatives should consult Bakeless's and Urry's documentation for further references.

I have recently been advised by the cathedral archivist at Canterbury that the BAC (city collection) and DAC (diocesian collection) references for CCA documents are now being replaced, respectively, by CC and DCb. However, the references in effect during my research, which are those supplied in this book, should present no difficulty in accessing the Canterbury documents.

CANTERBURY CATHEDRAL ARCHIVES (CCA)

Parish registers of All Saints, St. Andrew's, St. George the Martyr, St. Mary Bredman, and St. Mildred's, Canterbury.

Archdeacon's transcripts of parish records.

Treasurer's accounts, King's School, New Foundation, #9, 20–21 Elizabeth, 1578–79.

John Benchkin identified as student of Cambridge, 29 June 1592, BAC J/B/391 iv.

Corkine vs. Marlowe, 15 September–9 October 1592, BAC J/B/391 i, f. 13v.

Deposition of John Benchkin re. Harflete will, 2 December 1617, DAC X.11.15, ff. 245–47.

CENTRE FOR KENTISH STUDIES, MAIDSTONE (CKS)

[Copies of the records held at Maidstone are available at CCA on microfilm.]

Deposition of John Marlowe et al.: *Hurte vs. Applegate*, 19 February 1565, PRC 39/5, ff. 55+.

John Gresshop inventory, 23 February 1580, PRC 21/4, ff. 169–75.

James Benchkin inventory, 30 November 1582, PRC 10/10, ff. 740–50.

Will of Katherine Benchkin, 19 August 1585, PRC 16/36.

Deposition of John Moore re. Benchkin will, 30 September 1586, PRC 39/11, f. 234.

Deposition of John Marlowe re. Benchkin will, 5 October 1586, PRC 39/11, f. 237.

Nuncupative will of Dorothy Arthur, 21 August 1597, PRC 17/50, f. 161.

Will of John Marlowe, 23 January 1605, PRC 17/52, ff. 373–74.

John Marlowe inventory, 21 February 1605, PRC 10/34, f. 80.

Will of Katherine Marlowe, 18 March 1605, PRC 16/127.

ARCHIVES OF CORPUS CHRISTI COLLEGE, CAMBRIDGE

Buttery Books, 1580–86 (1586–87 missing).

Chapter Book, which includes the Registrum Parvum (1581).

Audit Books, 1580–85, 1586–87 (1585–86 missing).

UNIVERSITY ARCHIVES, CAMBRIDGE UNIVERSITY LIBRARY

Matriculation Book (1581).

Supplicats for degrees, 1584 and 1587.

Cambridge University Grace Book Delta, 1542–1588.

PUBLIC RECORD OFFICE (PRO), LONDON

Clitherowe to Baines, 21 September 1586, S. P. 53/19.

Acts of the Privy Council, 29 June 1587; 18 and 19 May, 1593.

Petition of William Bradley re. Watson et al., 15 March 1589, K. B. 29/226.

Coroner's inquest on William Bradley 19 September 1589, C 260/174, no. 5.

Gaol Delivery Roll (killing of Bradley), 3 December 1589, C 268/12, no. 362.

Ballard vs. Baines, 1590, C 2 Eliz I, Bundle B 7/8.

Watson's pardon, 10 February 1590, C 66/1340.

Thomas Walsingham's pardon for outlawry (debt), 27 May 1590, C 66/1356, m. 35.

Letter from Robert Sidney to Burghley, 26 January 1592, S. P. 84/44, f. 60.

Letter from Robert Sidney to Burghley, 22 March 1593, S. P. 84/44, f. 145.

Coroner's inquest on Marlowe, 1 June 1593, C 260/174, no. 27.

Pardon of Ingram Frizer, 28 June 1593, C 66/1401, mm. 33–34.

Inquisition post mortem, Robert Woodleff, 15 March 1593, C 142 234/34.

Pardon of alienation for Anne and Drew Woodleff, 2 April 1596, C 66/1443, m. 2.

Pardon of alienation for Anne and Drew Woodleff, 2 September 1596, C66/1445, m. 24.

BRITISH LIBRARY (BL)

Names of auditors of lectures, Cambridge, 1581, Lansdowne 33, ff. 84–85.

Evil dealings of Thomas Parish, May 1581, Lansdowne 33, ff. 67–68, and 33, f. 56.

Words and matter against Ric Cholmeley, ca. March 1593, Harleian 6848, f. 190, r. and v.

Another report on Cholmeley, ca. March 1593, Harleian 6848, f. 191.

Heretical papers found in Kyd's possession, May 1593, Harleian 6848, ff. 187–89.

Baines note, 26 [?] May 1593, Harleian 6848, ff. 185–86.

Copy of Baines note, June 1593, Harleian 6853, ff. 307–8.

Kyd's letter to Sir John Puckering, June 1593, Harleian 6848, f. 154.

Kyd's note to Sir John Puckering, June 1593, Harleian 6849, f. 218.

Commonplace book of Henry Oxinden, February 1640, Addit. 28012, ff. 492, 495, 496, 514–15.

GREATER LONDON RECORD OFFICE (GLRO)

Marlowe and Watson committed to Newgate, 18 September 1589, MJ/SR 284, no. 12.

Marlowe bailed, 1 October 1589, MJ/SR 284, no. 1.

Marlowe bound to keep the peace, 9 May 1592, MJ/SR 309, no. 13.

LAMBETH PALACE LIBRARY (LP)

Thomas Drury, letter to Anthony Bacon, 1 August 1593, LP MS 649, f. 246.

FOLGER SHAKESPEARE LIBRARY

Thomas Walsingham conveys Rose Acre, 3 May 1630, MSS Z.c.24 (18).

Henry Oxinden's commonplace book, "Miscellanea," 1640s, MS 750.1.

Oxinden Amici (ca. 1640s).

Letter of Andrew Blair to John Wilson, 29 April 1819, Y.c.165 (1).

PRINTED SOURCES

Allen, William. *The First and Second Diaries of the English College, Douay.* Edited by Thomas Francis Knox. London: David Nutt, 1878. Reprint, Westmead, Hants., Eng.: Gregg International Publishers Limited, 1969.

Alumni Cantabrigienses. Part 1. Compiled by John Venn and J. A. Venn. 4 vols. Cambridge: Cambridge University Press, 1922–27.

Archer, John Michael. *Sovereignty and Intelligence: Spying and Court Culture in the English Renaissance.* Stanford: Stanford University Press, 1993.

The A to Z of Elizabethan London. Compiled by Adrian Prockter and Robert Taylor. London: London Topographical Society, 1979.

Bakeless, John. *Christopher Marlowe: The Man in His Time.* New York: William Morrow and Company, 1937.

——. *The Tragicall History of Christopher Marlowe.* 2 vols. Cambridge: Harvard University Press, 1942.

Baldwin, T. W. *William Shakspeare's Small Latine and Lesse Greeke*. 2 vols. Urbana: University of Illinois Press, 1944.

Bevington, David, and Eric Rasmussen, eds. *Doctor Faustus: A-and B-texts (1604–1616)*. Manchester: Manchester University Press, 1993.

Boas, Frederick S. *Christopher Marlowe: A Biographical and Critical Study*. Oxford: Clarendon Press, 1940.

——. "Informer against Marlowe." *Times Literary Supplement*, 16 September 1949, 608.

——. *Marlowe and His Circle*. Oxford: Oxford University Press, 1931.

Bowers, Fredson, ed. *The Complete Works of Christopher Marlowe*. 2 vols. London: Cambridge University Press, 1973.

Briggs, Julia. "Marlowe's *Massacre at Paris*: A Reconsideration." *Review of English Studies* 34 (1983): 257–78.

Brooke, C. F. Tucker. *The Life of Marlowe and The Tragedy of Dido, Queen of Carthage*. In *The Works and Life of Christopher Marlowe*, general editor R. H. Case. London: Methuen and Co., 1930. Reprint, New York: Gordian Press, 1966.

——. *The Reputation of Christopher Marlowe*. Transactions of the Connecticut Academy of Arts and Sciences 25. New Haven: Connecticut Academy of Arts and Sciences, 1922.

Butcher, Andrew, ed. *Christopher Marlowe and Canterbury*. London: Faber and Faber, 1988.

Calendar of State Papers, Foreign Series, Elizabeth I 14, 1579–80.

Carroll, D. Allen, ed. *Greene's Groatsworth of Wit: Bought with a Million of Repentance*. Attributed to Henry Chettle and Robert Greene. Medieval & Renaissance Texts & Studies 114. Binghamton, N.Y.: Center for Medieval and Early Renaissance Studies, 1994.

Cellini, Benvenuto. *The Life of Benvenuto Cellini: Written by Himself*. Translated by John Addington Symonds. New York: Tudor Publishing Company, 1906.

Chalfant, Fran C. *Ben Jonson's London: A Jacobean Placename Dictionary*. Athens: University of Georgia Press, 1978.

Chambers, E. K. *The Elizabethan Stage*. 4 vols. Oxford: Clarendon Press, 1923.

Charlton, Kenneth. *Education in Renaissance England*. London: Routledge & Kegan Paul, 1965.

Chaudhuri, Sakanta. "Marlowe, Madrigals, and a New Elizabethan Poet." *Review of English Studies*, N.S. 39 (1988): 199–216.

Chettle, Henry. *Kind-Hartes Dreame*. Elizabethan and Jacobean Quartos. Edited by G. B. Harrison. New York: Barnes & Noble, 1966.

Collier, John Payne. "On the English Dramatic Writers Who Preceded Shakespeare." *Edinburgh Review* 6 (June 1820): 517–522; 7 (August 1820): 148–52.

——. *The Poetical Decameron: Or Ten Conversations on English Poets and Poetry, Particularly of the Reigns of Elizabeth and James I*. 2 vols. Edinburgh: Archibald Constable and Co., 1820.

Cowper, Joseph Meadows. *Canterbury Marriage Licenses, First Series.* Canterbury: Cross and Jackman, 1892.

——. *The Register Booke of the Parish of St. George the Martyr, within the Citie of Canterburie, of Christenings, Mariages and Burials, 1538–1800.* Canterbury: Cross and Jackman, 1891.

Cressy, David. *Birth, Marriage, and Death: Ritual, Religion and the Life Cycle in Tudor and Stuart England.* Oxford: Oxford University Press, 1997.

Curtis, Mark H. *Oxford and Cambridge in Transition, 1558–1642: An Essay on Changing Relations between the English Universities and English Society.* Oxford: Clarendon Press, 1959.

Dabbs, Thomas. *Reforming Marlowe: The Nineteenth-Century Canonization of a Renaissance Dramatist.* Lewisburg, Pa.: Bucknell University Press, 1991.

de Kalb, Eugenie. "Robert Poley's Movements as a Messenger of the Court, 1588–1601." *Review of English Studies* 9 (1933): 13–18.

The Dictionary of National Biography. 24 vols. Edited by Sir Leslie Stephen and Sir Sidney Lee. London: Oxford University Press, 1921–27.

Disher, M. Willson. *Clowns and Pantomimes.* New York: Houghton Mifflin, 1925.

Du Maurier, Daphne. *Golden Lads: A Study of Anthony Bacon, Francis and Their Friends.* London: Victor Gollancz Ltd., 1975.

"The Early English Drama, Art. X." *Retrospective Review, and Historical and Antiquarian Magazine* 4 (1821): 142–81.

Eccles, Mark. "Brief Lives: Tudor and Stuart Authors." *Studies in Philology* 79.4 (1982): 1–135.

——. *Christopher Marlowe in London.* Cambridge: Harvard University Press, 1934.

——. "Marlowe in Kentish Tradition." *Notes and Queries* 139 (1935): 20–23, 39–41, 58–61, 134–35.

Edwards, D. L. *A History of the King's School, Canterbury.* London: Faber and Faber, 1957.

The First and Second Diaries of the English College, Douay. Edited by Fathers of the Congregation of the London Oratory. Introduction by Thomas Francis Knox. London: David Nutt, 1878. Reprint, Westmead, Hants., Eng.: Gregg International Publishers Limited, 1969.

Freeman, Arthur. "The Deptford Killer." *Times Literary Supplement*, 28 May 1993, 30.

——. "Marlowe, Kyd, and the Dutch Church Libel." *English Literary Renaissance* 3 (1973): 44–52.

Friedenreich, Kenneth. "Marlowe's Endings." In *"A Poet and a filthy Play-Maker": New Essays on Christopher Marlowe*, edited by Kenneth Friedenreich, Roma Gill, and Constance Kuriyama, 361–69. New York: AMS Press, 1988.

Gostling, William. *A Walk in and about the City of Canterbury.* Canterbury: Simmons and Kirkby, 1777.

Gray, Austin K. "Some Observations on Christopher Marlowe, Government Agent." *PMLA* 43 (1928): 682–89.

Greenblatt, Stephen J. *Renaissance Self-Fashioning: More to Shakespeare*. Chicago: University of Chicago Press, 1980.

———. *Sir Walter Ralegh: The Renaissance Man and His Roles*. New Haven: Yale University Press, 1973.

Greene's Groatsworth of Wit: Bought with a Million of Repentance. Attributed to Henry Chettle and Robert Greene. Edited, with an introduction, by D. Allen Carroll. Medieval & Renaissance Texts & Studies 114. Binghamton, N.Y.: Center for Medieval and Early Renaissance Studies, 1994.

Hammer, Paul E. J. *The Polarisation of Elizabethan Politics: The Political Career of Robert Devereux, 2ⁿᵈ Earl of Essex*. Cambridge: Cambridge University Press, 1999.

———. "A Reckoning Reframed: The 'Murder' of Christopher Marlowe Revisited." *English Literary Renaissance* 26 (1996): 225–42.

Hardin, Richard. "Marlowe and the Fruits of Scholarism." *Philological Quarterly* 63 (1984): 387–400.

Hotson, J. Leslie. *The Death of Christopher Marlowe*. 1925. Reprint, New York: Haskell House, 1965.

The Household Papers of Henry Percy Ninth Earl of Northumberland (1564–1632). Edited by G. R. Batho. London: The Royal Historical Society, 1962.

Howell, Wilbur Samuel. *Logic and Rhetoric in England, 1500–1700*. Princeton: Princeton University Press, 1956.

Ingram, John H. *Christopher Marlowe and His Associates*. London: Grant Richards, 1904.

Jardine, Lisa, and Alan Stewart. *Hostage to Fortune: The Troubled Life of Francis Bacon*. New York: Hill and Wang, 1999.

Johnson, Richard. *The Pleasant Walkes of Moore-Fields* (1607). Reprinted in *Illustrations of Early English Popular Literature*, edited by John Payne Collier, i–ii, 5–9. London: n.p., 1864.

Jones, John Henry, ed. *The English Faust Book*. Translated by P. F. Cambridge: Cambridge University Press, 1994.

Kendall, Roy. "Richard Baines and Christopher Marlowe's Milieu." *English Literary Renaissance* 24 (1994): 507–52.

Kohut, Heinz. *The Analysis of the Self: A Systematic Approach to the Psychoanalytic Treatment of Narcissistic Personality Disorders*. New York: International Universities Press, 1971.

———. *The Restoration of the Self*. New York: International Universities Press, 1977.

Kuriyama, Constance Brown. "Marlowe, Shakespeare, and the Nature of Biographical Evidence." *University of Hartford Studies in Literature* 20 (1988): 1–12.

———. "Marlowe's Nemesis: The Identity of Richard Baines." In *"A Poet and a filthy Play-Maker": New Essays on Christopher Marlowe*, edited by Kenneth

Friedenreich, Roma Gill, and Constance Kuriyama, 343–60. New York: AMS Press, 1988.

———. "Second Selves: Marlowe's Cambridge and London Friendships." *Medieval & Renaissance Drama in England* 14 (2001): 86–104.

Lambarde, William. *Perambulation of Kent.* 1570. Reprint, Bath: Adams & Dart, 1970.

Lasch, Christopher. *The Culture of Narcissism: American Life in an Age of Diminishing Expectations.* New York: Norton, 1978.

Loades, David. *Power in Tudor England.* New York: St. Martin's Press, 1997.

———. *Tudor Government.* Oxford: Blackwell, 1997.

Marlowe, Christopher. *Christopher Marlowe: The Complete Plays.* Edited by Mark Thornton Burnett. London: J. M. Dent, 1999.

———. *Christopher Marlowe: The Complete Poems.* Edited by Mark Thornton Burnett. London: J. M. Dent, 2000.

McMullan, John L. *The Canting Crew: London's Criminal Underworld: 1550–1700.* New Brunswick, N.J.: Rutgers University Press, 1984.

Middlesex County Records. Vol. 2. Edited by John Cordy Jeaffreson. London: Middlesex County Records Society, 1887.

Montaigne, Michel de. *The Complete Works of Montaigne: Essays, Travel Journal, Letters.* Translated by Donald M. Frame. Stanford: Standford University Press, 1967.

Morgan, Victor. "Cambridge University and 'The Country' 1560–1640." In *The University and Society,* Vol. 1, *Oxford and Cambridge from the 14th to the Early 19th Century,* edited by Lawrence Stone, 183–245. Princeton: Princeton University Press, 1974.

Nashe, Thomas. *Works.* Edited by R. B. McKerrow and F. P. Wilson. 5 vols. Oxford: Blackwell, 1958.

Nicholl, Charles. *The Reckoning: The Murder of Christopher Marlowe.* London: Jonathan Cape, 1992.

Patten, John. *English Towns, 1500–1700.* Studies in Historical Geography. Edited by Alan R. H. Baker and J. B. Harley. Folkestone, Kent: William Dawson & Sons Ltd., 1978.

Pinciss, Gerald M. *Christopher Marlowe.* New York: Unger, 1975.

———. *Forbidden Matters: Religion in the Drama of Shakespeare and His Contemporaries.* Newark: University of Delaware Press, 2000.

Plowden, Alison. *The Elizabethan Secret Service.* New York: St. Martin's Press, 1991.

Porter, H. C. *Reformation and Reaction in Tudor Cambridge.* Cambridge: Cambridge University Press, 1958.

Read, Conyers. *Mr Secretary Walsingham and the Policy of Queen Elizabeth.* 3 vols. Oxford: Oxford University Press, 1925.

Registrum Matthei Parker, Diocesis Cantuariensis. 3 vols. Edited by W. H. Frere. Oxford: Oxford University Press, 1928.

Rowse, A. L. *Christopher Marlowe, His Life and Work*. New York: Harper & Row, 1964.

Salgado, Gamini. *The Elizabethan Underworld*. London: J. M. Dent & Sons Ltd., 1977.

Seaton, Ethel. "Marlowe, Robert Poley, and the Tippings." *Review of English Studies* 5 (1929): 273–87.

———. "Robert Poley's Ciphers." *Review of English Studies* 7 (1931): 137–50.

Shakespeare, William. *The Riverside Shakespeare*. 2nd ed. Edited by G. Blakemore Evans et al. Boston: Houghton Mifflin, 1997.

Shirley, John W. *Thomas Harriot: Renaissance Scientist*. Oxford: Clarendon Press, 1974.

Simon, Joan. *Education and Society in Tudor England*. Cambridge: Cambridge University Press, 1966.

Slater, Miriam. *Family Life in the Seventeenth Century: The Verneys of Claydon House*. London: Routledge & Kegan Paul, 1984.

Sprott, S. E. "Drury and Marlowe." *Times Literary Supplement*, 2 August 1974, 840.

The State of the Church in the Reigns of Elizabeth and James I, as Illustrated by Documents Relating to the Diocese of Lincoln. Edited by C. B. Foster. Lincoln: The Lincoln Record Society, 1926.

Stone, Lawrence. *The Crisis of the Aristocracy, 1558–1641*. Oxford: Clarendon Press, 1965.

———. "The Educational Revolution in England." *Past and Present* 28 (July 1964): 41–80.

———. *The Family, Sex, and Marriage in England: 1500–1800*. London: Weidenfeld and Nicolson, 1977.

Stone, Lawrence, and Jeanne C. Fawter Stone. *An Open Elite? England 1540–1880*. Oxford: Clarendon Press, 1984.

———. "Size and Composition of the Oxford Student Body, 1580–1909." In *The University and Society*, Vol. 1, *Oxford and Cambridge from the 14th to the Early 19th Century*, edited by Lawrence Stone, 3–110. Princeton: Princeton University Press, 1974.

Strauss, Gerald. "The State of Pedagogical Theory c. 1530: What Protestant Reformers Knew about Education." In *Schooling and Society: Studies in the History of Education*, edited by Lawrence Stone, 69–94. Baltimore: Johns Hopkins University Press, 1976.

Strong, Roy. *Artists of the Tudor Court: The Portrait Miniature Rediscovered, 1520–1620*. London: The Victoria & Albert Museum, 1983.

Tannenbaum, Samuel A. *The Assassination of Christopher Marlowe*. Hamden, Conn.: The Shoe String Press, 1928.

Townsend, William. *British Cities: Canterbury*. London: B. T. Batsford, 1950.

Urry, William. *Christopher Marlowe and Canterbury*. Edited by Andrew Butcher. London: Faber and Faber, 1988.

———. "Christopher Marlowe and Canterbury." Unpublished book manuscript.

——. *Christopher Marlowe Quatercentenary, 1564–1964: Souvenir Book.* N.p., 1964.

——. City Archivist's Reports. Unpublished manuscripts, 1951–58. Canterbury City Library.

——. *The House of Jacob the Jew of Canterbury: Notes on the History of the County Hotel, Canterbury.* Canterbury: J. J. Jennings Ltd., 1953.

——. "Marlowe and Canterbury." *Times Literary Supplement*, 13 February 1964, 136.

Wernham, R. B. *After the Armada: Elizabethan England and the Struggle for Western Europe, 1588–1595.* Oxford: Clarendon Press, 1984.

——. "Christopher Marlowe at Flushing in 1592." *English Historical Review* 91 (1976): 344–45.

——. *The Making of Elizabethan Foreign Policy, 1558–1603.* Berkeley: University of California Press, 1980.

Weston, William. *An Autobiography from the Jesuit Underground.* Translated by Philip Caraman. New York: Farrar, Straus and Cudahy, 1955.

Williams, David. Introduction to *John Penry: Three Treatises Concerning Wales.* Cardiff: University of Wales Press, 1960.

Wraight, A. D. *In Search of Christopher Marlowe; A Pictorial Biography.* Photography by Virginia F. Stern. New York: The Vanguard Press, 1965.

Yungblut, Laura Hunt. *Strangers Settled Here Amongst Us: Policies, Perceptions and the Presence of Aliens in Elizabethan England.* New York: Routledge, 1996.

Index

Blunt, Edward, 157–58
Boleyn, Anne, 100
Bonham, Julyan, 196
Borage, Jasper, 126, 214–15
Bostock, Thomas, 102
Bosworth, William, 157
Bradley, William, 3, 81–85, 88, 112, 118, 175, 203–6
Bradley, William, Sr., 82
Browne, Mrs. Francis, 78
Browne, William, 179, 182
Buckhurst, Lord, 146
Bull, Eleanor, 135, 137, 223–24, 232
Bull, Richard, 137
Burbage, Cuthbert, 77
Burbage, James, 75, 77–78, 96
Burbage, Richard, 77
Burghley, Lord. *See* Cecil, William
Burnell, Mrs., 90
Burrage. *See* Borage, Jasper
Burrage, Alexander, 223–24, 232
Byrd, William, 88–89

Caesar, Dr. Julius, 123
Caius, Dr. John, 64
Cecil, Sir Robert, 101, 128–30, 136, 148, 151, 214, 216
Cecil, William, Lord Burghley, 70, 78, 89, 101, 128–30, 137, 147, 151, 202
    letter from Sir Robert Sidney to, 66, 90, 107–8, 111–12, 176, 209–10, 215–16
Cellini, Benvenuto, 16n. 18, 93
Chaderton, Laurence, 55–56
Chamberlain, Andrew, 105
Chapman, George, 92, 101, 156–57
Chapman, Goodwife, 12, 178
Chapman, Godelif, 12, 178
Chapman, Robert, 101
Chaucer, Geoffrey, 104
Chettle, Henry, 113–15, 134, 153
Cholmeley, Sir Hugh, 126
Cholmeley, Richard, 90, 126–32, 134, 146–49, 151, 214–16, 222
Clarke, Francis, 215
Clarke, Mark, 191
Clarke, Samuel, 154
Clitherowe, Margaret, 66
Clitherowe, William, 66–68, 86, 199–201
Cobham, George, 126
Collier, John Payne, 167, 169
Corkine, William, 3, 115–16, 135, 212–13
Cornwallis, William, 88–89
Cornwallis, William, Jr., 88, 90
Coward, Noël, 162
Coxeter, Thomas, 87
Cranmer, Archbishop Thomas, 35
Cranford, Ann Marlowe, 17, 20, 39, 142, 177, 236–38
Cranford, Anthony, 238
Cranford, Elizabeth, 238

Cranford, John, 142, 177, 237, 238
Cranford, John, Jr., 238
Crispe, Thomas, 235, 236
Crowder, 196
Curry, William, 223–24, 232

Dabyns, Henry, 223–24, 232
Danby, William, 105, 222, 223–24, 226
Daniel, Samuel, 156
Deane, Sir James, 105
Dekker, Thomas, 28
Devereux, Lady Dorothy, 92
Devereux, Robert, Earl of Essex, 88–89, 92, 125, 128–31, 136, 139, 147
Dixon, Alice, 105
Dormer, Robert, 104
Drable, widow, 196
Drake, Sir Francis, 130–31, 136, 214
Draper, Nicholas, 223–24, 232
Drawnam, Margery, 196
Drayton, Michael, 156–57
Drury, Drew, 103
Drury, Sir Robert, 103
Drury, Thomas, 126, 131, 133, 146–151, 176
Dyce, Alexander, 169–70
Dyne, Tomsyn, 15

Edward I, 76
Edward the Confessor, Saint, 76
Elizabeth I, 37, 84, 100, 129–31, 142, 145, 215, 221, 226–28
Elliot, Nicholas, 112, 211
Essex, Earl of. *See* Devereux, Robert
Evance, 48, 93

Faunt, John, 72
Faunt, Nicholas, 72, 85–86, 90, 95, 98
Faunt, singing man, 179
Faust, Dr. Johan, 26
Feld, Giles, 223–24, 232
Fineaux, Christopher, 178
Fineaux, John, 160
Fineaux, Mr., 159–60, 178, 239–40
Fineaux, Thomas, 160, 178
Fines, Katherine, 76
Fines, Mary, 76
Fines, Sir William, 76
Fleetwood, William, 78, 204
Fletcher, John, 28, 163
Flud, Evan, 210
Flushing (Vlissingen), 66, 68, 107–12, 128, 133, 209–10, 216
Ford, John, 28
Ford, widow, 196
Francisci, Iacomo, 200
Frizer, Ingram, 102–6, 142
    fight with Marlowe, 3, 131, 135–40, 146, 155, 222–26, 231–34